D0312578

WHAT MATTERS

A Novel

By

Cam Thornton & Rod Zeeb

First Printing December 2011
ISBN 1-933694-20-3

Mitchell Thornton, *Editor*

This book is a work of fiction. Any resemblances to actual persons, living or dead, are purely coincidental.

HERITAGE
Institute Press

Brad Haga, *Senior Editor*

5 Centerpointe Drive, Suite 400
Lake Oswego, OR 97035
info@heritageinstitutepress.com

WHAT MATTERS

CONTENTS

LEADERSHIP

THE FIRST TIME I BEAT MY DAD AT ANYTHING, I was fourteen. It was Independence Day, 1939. My best friend Patrick and I spent the day with our families and most of the citizens of Salem, Oregon in a grassy field along the Willamette River. We encamped among the cottonwoods lining the riverbank, and when the whistle rang out to announce the first games of the day, Patrick and I grabbed a gunnysack and prepared to face off against our fathers in the three-legged sack race.

Our dads had the confidence of age on their side, but Patrick and I had an edge: every day for the past week we'd taken a burlap bag out into the alley behind the hardware store, tied our adjoining legs together, pulled the bag up around our waists and practiced until we perfected a hop, skip and jump technique that was half-bullfrog, half Olympic sprinter.

When Mr. Tilden fired his starter pistol, Patrick and I took the lead. Our dads quickly figured out that they were in a race they just might lose, and began to pour it on. My dad flashed me a victory grin as they matched our stride and started to pass us. Then, just ten yards from the finish line their gunnysack snagged on a rock, and our fathers tumbled to the ground. Patrick and I flew across the line to the cheer of the crowd—and the sputtering and colorful mumbling of our chagrined dads.

In the heat of the afternoon we feasted on platters of buttermilk fried chicken, sweet watermelon and red, white and blue potato salad, washed down with ice-cold root beer. Later we spread blankets on the cool grass beneath a great white oak and lazed until the breeze off the river brought the temperature down a few degrees. Then we played a final game of touch football in the gathering twilight and sat down to my mother's fresh marionberry cobbler with vanilla ice cream. All around us, families waited for the night sky to darken enough for the Fourth of July fireworks to begin.

My Scout troop had been tapped to help set the fireworks launch tubes on the riverbank. Patrick and I placed dozens of pre-loaded tubes in launchers that had been dug into the sandy bank, and attached fuse cord to each one. Once the show was underway our job was to keep the firemen supplied with freshly lit sawdust punks to light their fuses. As the show neared its finale, the chief let me light off a few of the smaller pyrotechnics. One of my shots fired prematurely when the aluminum tube came loose in the sand. The tube canted to its side, launching the red and green projectile horizontally instead of straight into the night sky. It shot directly toward the west bank of the river, rocketing just a few feet above the water's surface.

It was a pretty sight, though the folks enjoying the fireworks from the deck of the barge anchored in the middle of the river didn't seem too tickled when the fireball screamed low across their bow and plowed into the rocky riverbank behind them in a shower of sparks. The crowd on my side of the river roared with delight, though, as the partygoers on the barge dropped to their knees and covered their heads. The fire chief was none too pleased, but Patrick and I chalked it up as a grand success, and conspired to do it again the next year.

By the time the last ribbons of colored light floated down and disappeared into the dark green water, I was smoky, sweaty, tired, and hungry.

So I was a little beat when I lugged my bags over to Patrick's house just after sunup the next morning to join my Scout troop for a week long hike into the Cascade Mountains. Patrick was waiting for me on his porch, haversack and fishing pole at his side. His father was nursing a cup of black coffee, and warming up his '37 Chevrolet pickup.

"You boys toss your bags in the back," he said. "We're late."

We rolled our heavy bags over the side of the pickup, and hopped into the front seat for the five-minute drive into downtown Salem.

•••

PATRICK'S FAMILY OWNED O'Hagan's Hardware Store on High Street, across from the Elsinore Theatre. It had sixteen-foot ceilings, creaky wooden floors, and a cantankerous wood stove whose care and feeding was our daily responsibility from fall through spring. In the summer we hauled seasoned oak, maple and Douglas fir from my dad's wood lot, and split and stacked eight or nine cords in the woodshed behind the store. We kept the crib beside the stove fully stocked, and cleaned out the ashes on Saturdays.

In 1939 the hardware store was about the most important business in town. It was also my idea of paradise. When you stepped off the sidewalk and through the double oak doors, the smell of varnish and sawdust hit you like perfume. Rows of wooden display shelves were packed solid with plumbing fixtures, kerosene lamps, and hand tools of every shape, size and design. You could buy a fifty-gallon iron kettle, one hundred yards of barbed wire, bear traps, rifles and ammunition, or a can of ether to kick-start your tractor when the ice hung thick on the viney maple.

In the display windows facing the street, Patrick's mother laid out tools and gifts according to the season. I liked Christmas best. An electric train wound through a landscape of snow-covered mountains and gumdrop forests in the display window. In one corner of the window were two giant glass jars filled with candy canes. The sign above them read: "Guess how many and win a prize." Six years running I had guessed, and six years running I had lost.

•••

PATRICK'S FATHER'S TRUCK ground to a halt at the bus stop. We unloaded our gear and went through it one last time on the sidewalk, making sure we hadn't missed anything—first aid kits, flashlights, compass, pocketknives and mess kits. We thought we were as ready as a couple of Second Class Scouts could be.

While we waited, Patrick talked of rank advancement. "I just need to get my fourteen-mile hike done, and make one meal from scratch for all of you in camp. That done, I make First Class. What's left on your list?"

"Hiking, just like you," I answered. "Plus, I have to demonstrate at least one practical first aid technique. Suppose I might get a chance to do that after we've tried your food."

Patrick tossed a pebble in my direction.

"You wouldn't mind falling down a rock ledge or something, would you?" I asked. "Break a couple bones, let me really get some first aid practice?"

"Well, sure," said Patrick as a bus pulled up to the curb. "Consider it done. In fact, I tell you what: I'll do my best to make sure everybody contributes at least one broken bone to the effort."

We tossed our gear through the rear hatch door, and climbed aboard the big, navy blue bus. The bus was built for thirty passengers, but today it would carry just eight Boy Scouts and one Scoutmaster over the Cascades and down into central Oregon.

We waved to Patrick's dad as the bus pulled away, and settled in for the five-hour drive. Hal Stannard and Gary Hartzell stretched out across two front seats next to our Scoutmaster, Nate Holden. At sixteen, Hal and Gary were the only First Class Scouts in the troop. At the back of the bus sat the two Tenderfoots. Scattered everywhere else were the fourteen- and fifteen-year-olds, including Patrick Michael O'Hagan, and yours truly, Martin Jacob Forrestal.

We had waited all year for the adventures ahead; seven days of hiking, fishing, stargazing, rock climbing, and swimming. Maybe we'd even discover some lost Indian village, or a fur trapper's cache of gold and silver. The boys of Troop 11 dreamed big.

High up on the slopes of the Cascade Range, meadow grasses were breaking through the melting snow, and black bears scoured brushy thickets in search of sweet, plump berries. Bobcat cubs wrestled on carpets of alpine wildflowers, and small mouth bass darted through the clear, icy streams that tumbled out of the mountain vastness. The July sky shone brilliant blue from horizon to horizon, unblemished by so much as a wisp of cloud, as our bus ambled toward the wild.

My Grandfather Jake used to say that in life we seldom end up where we want to go, but we almost always end up where we need to be. Thinking back on that summer day from near seventy years on, I have no doubt that if we'd known about the cold, dark and danger that lay ahead we would have turned that bus around and high-tailed it home. Had we done that, though, each of us boys would have missed out on one of the greatest adventures of all: the opportunity to learn who you are, and what you are made of, under the duress of danger.

•••

"MR. FORRESTAL. Excuse me—are we awake?"

Now, of all the indignities one faces while hospitalized—and they are legion, I assure you—it is the tiny ones that can most readily blossom like the barnacles on a ship's hull. One of the most irritating barnacles in my present circumstance was the way that nurses and lab technicians spoke to me in the royal third person, as if we were conjoined twins.

"*I*" was, for the record, perfectly alert. Just the same, it is a wise prisoner who does not upset his jailer.

"Oh, I'm awake," I said. "How about you?"

"Wide awake," Nurse Marsden said. She held an empty specimen bottle up to eye level, and gave it a little shake. "I wouldn't be carrying one of these if I were dreaming, not unless they could be used as currency on some tropical island."

Judging from her pallid complexion and puffy eyes, I guessed that dreams were the only place my chief day nurse was getting much rest.

"Your temperature is a little high, and your last white count says it's time for you to make another donation to the cause," she said. " Shall we say a half-pint, in fifteen minutes?"

She handed me the container and whisked out of the room, closing the door behind her. I contemplated the deadline and the plastic bottle for a moment, then tossed the bottle to the foot of my bed. Fifteen minutes? A half-pint?

She might just as well asked for me to do a handspring off the foot of my bed. I switched the digital recorder back on. The bottle could wait. My story couldn't.

•••

"HEY, OVER HERE," yelled Eddy Teachout.

Wade Gonzalez tossed the wide brim hat he had just snatched from Perry Young's head across the aisle. Eddy caught it between two fingers, snapped his wrist in a fluid motion, and sent the hat gliding through the air toward the front of the bus, where it landed next to Mr. Holden's foot. Holden didn't turn, or even say a word. He leaned down, grabbed the hat, and threw it back in Perry's general direction. The greenhorn put it on, and secured it with the chinstrap. Meanwhile, Toby St. Clair and Gary were arguing over whether Seabiscuit would heal from his injuries and race again.

Just one hour into the trip battle lines were being drawn, alliances were being forged, and a week's worth of general mayhem was being happily mapped out.

As the bus rolled past the fir and cedar forest bordering Lost Lake, I thought about our Scoutmaster. Nate Holden was still a mystery to me, even though I had been in his troop for over a year. We fished and hiked and helped with WPA projects around Salem, and I had spent hundreds of hours with the man, but I still didn't feel like I knew him very well.

Holden was in his mid-forties. He owned a hops farm along the river at Independence, where Patrick and I had worked the previous fall. He was tall, and whipcord lean. You'd say he was handsome were it not for the ragged scar that ran from his left ear, across his jaw and down his neck. He never explained it, and we didn't ask. My mother heard that he had been wounded in France in the Great War, and we left it at that.

Some said that Mr. Holden didn't like to talk; I say he was simply tight-fisted with his words. He doled them out sparingly, as if there were a finite, irreplaceable inventory of sentences in his personal storehouse. Adjectives and adverbs didn't play much of a role in his vocabulary. When he spoke, it was pure Oklahoma prairie; firm and measured, never hesitant. A thing was what it was, no more, no less. And never once, even when we were in the thick of it, did he raise his voice in anger.

He wasn't given to ladling out praise, that's for sure. When one of his Scouts did well, he acknowledged it with a simple nod, or a slight, half bemused smile. Boys new to the troop learned his core philosophy on day one: anything that is worth doing is worth doing well.

I know it is popular these days to congratulate children for everything they do—even when they fail to hit the mark, even when they lose at something in the most miserable fashion—but the logic of rewarding a person for failure ran contrary to everything he believed. Learn it, remember it, and be able to demonstrate it on short notice—that was Mr. Holden's way.

It was commonplace for him to be hiking along in silence, and then, without preamble, to turn to the nearest Scout and begin rattling off questions. "What are the sixteen principal points of the Mariner's Compass," or, "How do you bake bread on a stick?" A correct answer earned at best a muffled *"hmph."* Answer incorrectly, though, and you could find yourself lugging the cast-iron Dutch oven for the next mile.

Holden turned his head, caught my stare, and raised an eyebrow. Then, before I could think of anything to say, he shifted in his seat and gazed out the window. Maybe he could read minds, too.

A few minutes later the driver pulled into the gravel turnout at the crest of the mountain pass to check the radiator. He untied the canvas water sack tied to the front grill of the bus to top the radiator off, and we fanned out along the low granite retaining wall to take in the scenery.

The air was crisp and unseasonably cool. Eight thousand foot Mt. Washington, just to the south, was almost close enough to touch. Its upper slopes and granite crags were covered with snow year round. Hidden behind its silver and white mass lay our destination, the emerald lakes and alpine meadows around South Sister, the southernmost of the dormant volcanoes known as the Three Sisters Mountains. Tonight we were going to bunk at the ranch of a Scout leader outside the small town of Sisters, and begin our hike at first light.

•••

WE SLEPT IN A BARN near Sisters that night—or at least we tried to. Hal and Gary hung storm lanterns along the tack wall, and we spread our sleeping bags out on beds of sweet alfalfa hay. The fact that the barn had a loft that was perched directly above a huge pile of loose hay wasn't much of an invitation to rest, though.

One by one, we climbed the ladder to the loft, and then dove, cannon-balled, flipped or just plain dropped the ten feet down into the hay pile. Mr. Holden finally had to come down from the main house around midnight to quiet us down.

In the morning, after a pre-dawn breakfast of sausage and pancakes, we climbed onto the bus for the drive to the trail head. The bus did poorly with the twists and turns of the back country road, and it took a few hours to drive just twelve miles to the downed tree that marked the literal end of the line. We unloaded our gear and waved as the bus disappeared back toward town in a cloud of dust.

Mr. Holden lined us up, and then walked from boy to boy, checking the weight of each haversack, adjusting loads where needed, and shaking canteens to make sure they were full. The still, cloudless sky promised a scorching day ahead, and made the prospect of camping by a creek sound better by the minute.

The ground at the trail head was flat and rocky. There were a few lodgepole pines, and plenty of scrub brush, but not much else. We could see the snowfields and glaciers on North Sister, but low hills and trees blocked the view of her sisters and the neighboring peaks. We had a short hike planned for this morning—just three miles to Soap Creek, where we would spend the day setting up our first camp. Short day or not, Mr. Holden wanted to make sure everyone understood their responsibilities along the way.

"Boys," he said, "it's going to be a hot one, and you're each carrying at least 25 pounds. Your packs are that *light* because we're going to pick up the rest of our food at the cache the local council left for us at Camp Lake. Today we get acclimated, and focus on the basics. I want you to drink when you're thirsty, and I especially want you to pay attention to your feet. One blister can ruin an entire trip. If you feel one starting to chafe, let the Scout on point know, and we'll stop to patch it up. You ignore the pain, and push on like a tough guy, and before long one of us will have to carry you." He let that sink in for a moment, and then we were off.

I swung into line behind Hal. There were no signs for us to follow, but the trail incline was gentle, and we had plenty of visual markers to keep to a true path. After an hour of slow, steady climbing, we came to the crest of a hill dominated by the first Ponderosa pine of the day. Mr. Holden stopped us for a boot and haversack check.

He put another boy on point, pulled Gary and Hal to the rear to keep the line moving at a good clip, and pointed us westward. The trail narrowed, and grew a little steeper, and the landscape underwent a dramatic change. The scruffy lodgepole forest faded away, replaced by stands of Mountain Hemlock. It even cooled a few degrees.

As we climbed, we began to see patches of meadow grass, and occasional bunches of summer wildflowers. Eddy spooked a doe out of a fern patch beside the trail. She flipped her tail, scrambled up a hillside, and was gone in a heartbeat.

I heard the water before I could see it. Hal lit out first, and in a few seconds the entire troop was boiling over the rise toward the sound of rushing water. It was a pretty creek—forty or fifty feet across, no more than two or three feet deep, and cold as polar ice. The water was so clear you could count the speckles on the smooth rocks that covered the creek bed. Wade and Patrick had their boots off first, and by the time Mr. Holden caught up with us, we had our trousers rolled up to our knees and were splashing around.

Mr. Holden dropped his pack, sat on a rock beside a patch of red monkey-flower, and pulled out his pipe. That was our signal to cut loose. Shirts and pants flew to the mossy bank, and we yipped and hollered and splashed and skipped rocks downstream. The hot sun beat down on our backs even as the frigid water chilled us through. It was flat out glorious.

By the time we made camp at mid afternoon, the sun was directly overhead. We set our pup tents in a straight line, with the creek in front and a cluster of hemlock and brush behind us.

Patrick's debut as chef wasn't scheduled for a few days yet, so Gary and the tenderfoots had the job. An hour later our mess kits were filled with canned chicken and noodle goulash, boiled potatoes and peaches. And after KP duty, it was time to stoke the fire and get on with the really important business for the evening—scaring the willies out of the greenies with our most finely tuned and drawn out ghost stories.

•••

THERE IS SOMETHING ABOUT a blazing fire, a star-strewn sky and the gentle swaying of tall trees in the soft night breeze that makes listening to a story you would yawn at in school seem as real as rain. Gary Hartzell told the first story. At sixteen, he'd been on enough campouts to appreciate that the darkness was his best prop. It helped to make his garden-variety tale of a half-man, half-beast who roamed the mountains and forests of central Oregon in search of children to eat all the more sinister.

As Gary wove his story in a quiet, urgent voice, Toby and Perry scooted closer to the fire. The payoff came when Patrick and Hal jumped out of the darkness and clapped their cold hands over the boys' faces while letting out a Comanche war cry. Toby and Perry flew a couple feet in the air. The rest of us laughed and hooted and slapped one another on the back, as much in relief, I think, that we didn't have to go through that initiation again ourselves as it was the sheer entertainment of watching the young guys get the scare of their lives.

When the laughter faded, Gary helped to salvage some of the boys' dignity. "Gentlemen," he said, "welcome to the troop. There might still be a black bear out there with your smiling faces painted on his menu, but I promise you this: from now on, it will take more than a ghost story to make you jump out of your socks."

Each of us took a storytelling turn beside the fire that night. We even humored the greenhorns by letting them make up a story of their own. By the time Patrick acted out his tale of blood-soaked Irish banshees, the yellow moon rested just above the snowy peaks, and the fire had burned down to a bed of scarlet coals.

That's when I noticed that Mr. Holden had disappeared. I stepped away from the fire, and let my eyes adjust to the dark. A minute later I saw the red glow of his pipe, down at the creek's edge. He was always leading his troop—even when he stepped aside to let us lead ourselves.

•••

I RELUCTANTLY SWITCHED OFF THE RECORDER. Some memories are hard to leave. But Nurse Marsden and the plastic container awaited.

A few minutes later the door to my room flew open. I reached for the specimen bottle, which, pride compels me to note, was full enough to satisfy the most demanding lab tech. But it was my wife, not my nurse, who appeared through the opening. My sweet Constance.

"A gift for me?" she smiled, reaching for the bottle.

We both laughed. She brushed her hand across my forehead, pushed my hair from my eyes, and kissed me. Then she settled into the chair beside my bed, and laid her hand close to the IV tube in my forearm.

"Did you sleep last night?"

"Yes, pretty well, in fact."

"But you haven't eaten breakfast," Connie said. She pointed at the tray of plastic-wrapped eggs, dry toast and oatmeal on the stand beside my bed.

"Hard to figure how a fellow could turn down a meal like that, now isn't it?" I said.

"Eat. And then we'll visit."

Connie unpacked the book, notepad and magazine that would occupy her for the day. She would leave my side only when the duty nurse or physician needed to poke or prod me, or change out the sentinel IV pump next to my bed.

When Dr. McGuire gave me the long face last week, and told me that I wouldn't be going home this time, Connie essentially moved into the hospital with me. Before I checked in, though, she piled me into the car and drove us to Neskowin Beach. Fifty-six years earlier, on our first trip to the Oregon seaside village, I was the one doing the driving, and when we got there, I wasted no time in asking her to marry me.

When she said, "Yes!" I tossed her across my shoulders and raced into the surf in a whirlwind of laughter and shouting and splashing and kissing. We sat by a driftwood fire later that night and made promises that only the young are foolish enough to speak, and only the old are wise enough to keep. Connie wasn't forgetting the "till death do you part" one.

That was in 1953. A half-century later, I was an old man, and I was dying. It took some doing for me to muster the strength to pull off my shoes and walk from the car to the beach. The sand felt gritty and warm beneath my eighty-two-year-old toes, just as it did when I was a boy chasing my dog along the surf-line over seventy years ago. The towering offshore rock—now known as Proposal Rock—with its wind-sculpted trees and water-etched caves had weathered the decades with little visible change. That realization made me smile.

•••

CONNIE UNPACKED A SIMPLE PICNIC of cold chicken, fruit and iced tea, but I had an appetite only for conversation. How was it possible, after living with someone for nearly sixty years, that there could still be so much to talk about?

I finished my beach reverie, and my scrambled eggs, just as Nurse Marsden returned to collect her golden prize in the specimen bottle.

She and Connie had sized one another up, and established their own
ground rules relative to the care of one Martin Forrestal on the first day
of my hospitalization. Now, several days into this odyssey, the two most
important women in my life were settled comfortably into their respective
routines and responsibilities.

Connie kept her head in a magazine as the nurse gathered my breakfast
dishes and made chart notes. She wore a long-sleeved white blouse with
a Chinese collar under a pale green cashmere sweater. Even at rest, she sat
with extraordinary grace. She was born with a dancer's posture, her mother
said.

In fact, many people mistook Connie for a member of that distinctive
class of elegant blue-blood patricians who populate fashionable country
club soirees and glittering charity galas. Those folks would sputter in their
champagne cocktails, however, if they could see my dear wife string up,
dress out and neatly butcher a six-point buck, or chum for King salmon in
a fishing boat in the rough waters off Depoe Bay, or split a chunk of alder
with an axe as handily as the best man at the wood lot. This elegant dame
once drove a fully-loaded logging truck over fifty miles of hard rock and
dirt road from Sweet Home to Salem with me laid out beside her with
a busted leg. The logs had to be delivered to the mill before 8 AM, or we
wouldn't get paid—that meant we would miss payroll for our small crew,
and a payment to the bank. The fact that I'd been smacked by a flying
choker cable and needed to have my leg set and plastered came second to
the need to get those logs delivered. And Connie always delivered.

She caught me looking. "How did your recording go this morning?"

"I'm getting the hang of it. In fact, I'm starting to enjoy it. Did you bring
more batteries?"

"Right here. And at the end of each day Rachel or I will make sure that
whatever you've recorded is loaded onto the computer. We'll back it all up,
and get it transcribed."

"Thank you for helping me do this. I'm still not sure if it's the right
thing to do, or the best thing to do."

"But you're sure you have to do it."

"I am. It's a big job, and it gets bigger every time I push the record
button."

She reached over to my nightstand, and lifted the yellow legal pad on
which I had scribbled my list of fifteen values. "You don't have to do all of

them," she said.

"Leave it to someone else to tell my story? How will I look like a hero if I do that?"

Constance handed me back the recorder, and put a hand on my shoulder. "I'm going for coffee," she said. "Try not to do anything heroic until I get back."

•••

"BREAK OUT YOUR FISHING POLES, boys. Today you catch your dinner!"

Mr. Holden's order sent us scrambling for prime positions along the creek. We'd seen plenty of bluegill and white crappies whisking past as we hiked along the creek, but it was bass we were after for dinner. Their brown and yellow-green shapes were hard to spot against the speckled rocks, but we were sure the creek was filled with them.

Patrick and I picked a deep, still pool a hundred yards upstream from the camp. In an hour we were rewarded with three, large, fat fish to add to the skillet. It was our finest meal yet: we had fresh bass rolled in cornmeal and fried in hot oil, served with buttermilk biscuits and honey, baked beans and Dutch-oven apple crisp.

That night we banked the fire down to just a few coals so that we could scan the sky in near-pitch darkness. The stars stretched out on a black velvet curtain above our heads, like thick clusters of luminous grapes.

Eddy used a stick to trace the outline of the constellation Ursa Major's arms and legs, low in the northwest sky. As the immense inverted bowl of the night sky made its slow turn around the earth, we spotted Cassiopea, Andromeda, and Hercules. Tenderfoot Toby got a round of applause when he identified the North Star.

It was late when Patrick and I crawled into our tent. The camp was still. Through the tent flap I saw Mr. Holden dampen the fire for the night so we would have coals to start the breakfast fire. A minute later all human sounds ceased. There was only the rushing of the creek over the rocks, the stir of a breeze in the treetops, and the mournful howl of a coyote from the slopes of South Sister Mountain.

•••

WE HIT THE TRAIL early the next morning. It was four and a half miles, mostly uphill going to Camp Lake, where we planned to pitch our tents by early afternoon. I walked point for the first two-mile leg to the north fork of Squaw Creek. Thick brush blocked much of the view ahead, until I rounded a narrow switchback and Middle Sister Mountain appeared right in front of me. We stopped for lunch beside a cascading waterfall, and then Patrick took the lead for the final mile to our new campsite.

From the trail along the alpine ridge the horizon seemed endless. We could finally see the snowfields and glaciers of all three Sisters mountains, shimmering white under the cloudless July sky. Patches of wildflowers dotted meadows that were thick with elderberry, alpine fir and black huckleberry. Wade and Perry spotted bear signs—tracks and scat—and Mr. Holden told us to keep our conversations loud as we hiked along to make sure that we did not come face-to-face with the berry-loving beasts without the benefit of a proper introduction.

We followed the ridge to a break in the trees, and were rewarded with our first view of Camp Lake. Its frost-blue waters were still partially rimmed with snow, and the small icebergs floating across the surface reminded us that winter lasted a long time at this elevation. Rock-strewn hills ringed the shore, rising steadily until they folded into the basalt slopes of South Sister, towering 10,000 feet above the lake.

There wasn't much in the way of natural wind shelter around the lake, which is why we would only be camping here for one night. When Alaskan weather moved inland off the Pacific Ocean and down the eastern Cascades, freezing winds could blast down the valley without warning, even in summer.

Mr. Holden settled on a patch of trees and boulders about fifty yards from the lake. We pitched our tents in a semicircle on the leeward side of the boulders, and the Scoutmaster showed us how to build our fire between two giant rocks so that one rock would shield the fire from the wind and reflect the smoke upwards, and not into our eyes, while the other rock would absorb heat from the fire and warm our backs.

We broke into teams once camp was set. Our move to the next campsite at Demaris Lake the next morning would only take a few hours, so Gary and Hal were charged with finding some interesting trails for us to meander along on the way. The rest of us were sent to collect firewood, prepare dinner, or to work on the tasks we needed to complete in order to move up to the next rank.

•••

THE TENDERFOOTS SPOTTED the trouble first. Toby and Perry raced into camp late that afternoon. They tossed their kindling on the ground, and shouted for Mr. Holden.

"There's snow coming," said Perry.

"Don't be a wise-guy, greenie," said Eddy. "It's July. It never snows up here after June. You can bank on that." All of us had come into camp by now. We leaned on rocks, and shot one another knowing glances. *Tenderfoots.*

Mr. Holden set down the boot he had been patching for Wade. "That's usually true, Eddy. But, 'usually' is not a good rule of thumb when you're out in the open at four thousand feet above sea level, surrounded by volcanic mountains and glaciers."

"What makes you think there's snow on the way, Perry?" asked Mr. Holden. "Sky's clear. Temperature's holding, too."

Thirteen-year-old Perry held his ground. He scraped the toe of one boot in the gravel, and then looked at Mr. Holden. "I was born in Idaho. On a farm. I know a snow sky when I see one."

"All right, Perry," said Mr. Holden. "I expect you would. Let's have a look at your evidence." We followed Perry through a stand of spruce trees, and up the rise of a hill where we could see for miles in all directions.

Perry pointed to the northwest. "There," he said. The sky was pearl blue and cloudless from the western to the eastern horizons, and as far south as we could see. But to the north a thin, dark band of color was settling upon the crest of the Cascades.

"That's haze," said Hal Stannard.

"Haze or a forest fire," added Gary. "There's no way that's snow."

"Perry, has that cloud line moved since you first spotted it?" asked Mr. Holden.

"Yes, sir, it has. A lot," said Perry.

"It really has," agreed Toby St. Clair.

"When did you first notice it," asked Mr. Holden.

"About ten minutes ago."

Mr. Holden sent Patrick back to camp for his field glasses, and scanned the northern horizon for several minutes with the binoculars.

"I want every boy to take a look," he said.

When it was my turn I saw what looked like dark grey cotton balls spreading across the sky, rolling fast over the mountain peaks and down into the valley. You did not need to be a weather expert to see that they were headed our way, and fast. I thought I was imagining that it was turning cold, but when I looked at Patrick I saw that he was starting to shiver. It *was* getting colder.

"Let's get back to the camp, boys," said Mr. Holden. "We have work to do."

It was 5 PM. Sunset was at 9:15 the night before, but the approaching clouds made it feel like dusk, and the temperature continued to fall.

Mr. Holden sat us down in the shadow of a massive granite outcropping. He was more intense than I had ever seen him. Not fearful—I didn't see that. It was more the attitude of a military commander who is preparing his troops on the eve of a great battle.

"Men," he said, "first things first: Perry was right. We've got weather moving in, fast, and it just might be snow. This is not the spot I would have picked to make a snow camp. We're too exposed. But, I'm guessing that whatever is on its way is going to hit us pretty quick, and we don't have enough time to scout out and move to a better camp. We're going to hunker down right here and ride this storm out."

Patrick and I exchanged glances. He shrugged, and pulled his cap tight on his head.

"We've got some cover between the trees and the rocks," Mr. Holden continued. "We're going to reinforce our tents, and tie them down with more stakes. And we're going to gather more wood—a lot more."

"Hal, you and Gary take Wade and Eddy. Get the biggest logs you can carry. Don't waste time chopping them with axes; smash the ends over a rock to break off chunks. Pile them under those rock overhangs, as close to the fire as you can. We need them close, and we need them dry."

"Forrestal, you and Patrick will help me with the tents. Perry, Toby, off you go for more kindling. Try to find as much dry moss as you can, too. We're going to need plenty of tinder."

"Mr. Holden, what about food?" asked Hal.

"We'll have pemmican and fruit in a while. No time to cook tonight."

"No, that's not what I mean," said Hal. "What about the food that the council cached for us up here? If we get snowed in, won't we need it?"

Mr. Holden hesitated for a second. "You're right about that Hal, but we don't have time. We'll have to go after it later. Now, everybody move out."

As we turned to our tasks, Mr. Holden called to Perry. He put his hand on the boy's shoulder. "You did good, son," he said. "And you just might have saved our bacon. You're going to make a fine Scout."

I swear Perry was two inches taller when he hustled off to gather kindling. As he passed Hal, the First Class Scout said, "Anybody calls you greenie again, Perry, and they'll have to answer to me." Perry didn't say a word, but his grin was bright enough to light the darkening path for a hundred yards.

• • •

MR. HOLDEN CUT LENGTHS of rope while Patrick and I pulled down two of the troop's five pup tents. We would sleep three to a tent tonight, instead of the usual two. It would reduce the number of potential tent collapses to deal with, and the body heat from three people in a small space would help to keep us warm.

I used my knife to cut the downed tents into square sheets, and punched grommet holes along the edges. Then we draped the material over the top of the three standing tents, threaded rope through the grommet holes, and tied figure-eight knots to attach the material to a separate line of aluminum tent stakes. We would weather the snow under two layers of water repellent cotton-duck, each layer with its own set of tie-downs.

"We've got the boulders behind us to shield us from the worst of the north wind," said Mr. Holden, "and if it snows, the trees will keep some of it off of us. But the open rock fields around the lake and the mountain are going to create a wind bowl, and if she starts to blow hard, the wind is going to whip around in circles and tear down anything that isn't nailed to the ground." As the Scoutmaster spoke, the sky continued to darken, and the clouds thickened and dropped lower, until the mountain was lost in a roiling gray shroud.

"Those sure are snow clouds," said Patrick, "and at this elevation that means we're going to get it, summertime or not."

"Some guys will do anything to get out of cooking for the troop," I said.

"Yeah, well, don't get your hopes too high. When this little blow is over,

I'll be putting the apron on, and making the best cherry crisp you've ever smacked your lips on, laddie."

Toby and Perry appeared out of the gloom, their arms piled high with kindling and moss, and the other boys came in with firewood. Hal supervised the stacking of the wood under a rock ledge, where it would stay dry and easy to get at.

Mr. Holden had us gather a pile of fallen hemlock branches and lash them together into a six by six foot wind barrier, which we secured between the end of a boulder and a spruce tree. That blocked the wind path from the north. Then, we started a fire. In a few minutes it was blazing, sheltered from the wind by the trees, the rocks and our windscreen. The warmth from the flames cheered us all, and we started to feel a little better about the storm sweeping our way.

Mr. Holden didn't let us rest, though. As the temperature continued to drop, and the wind from the leading edge of the storm began to whistle overhead, he told us all to pull on an extra pair of socks, trousers, and a second shirt and undershirt before we put on our ponchos.

We filled our canteens, and laid cedar branches on the floor of our tents to keep our sleeping bags off of the ground. Mr. Holden made tent assignments, and told everybody to make a final latrine visit. We hung stormproof candle lanterns inside each tent, and assembled by the fire. Gary distributed pemmican and beef jerky, and we ate in silence.

It was almost 7:30. The sky, which should have been softening from bright blue to summer dusk, was a dull, pewter gray, and looked as if it was dropping straight down on top of us. It was cold enough to see our breath. I held my hands close to the fire as Mr. Holden began to speak.

"This is not the trip any of us expected," he said. "It hasn't snowed up here in July since I was a pup. But, this is the hand we've been dealt, and we're Scouts, so we'll get through it. You boys all understand that?" Eight heads nodded in the firelight. It was clear from looking at my friend's faces that they were worried. But they weren't scared—not yet. If the storm got bad, we would head straight back down to the trailhead after it lifted. "We'll stay out here by the fire for as long as we can. If the snow hits hard, we'll stay in the tents. I'll take over the fire duty for now, and keep it lit for as long as possible. With three of you in a tent, it will be a little cozy—"

"I've gotta be cozy with Gonzalez, and not with Olivia DeHaviland?" said Patrick.

His wisecrack about the beautiful star of the new Robin Hood movie broke the tension.

"I'm sure Miss DeHaviland would love to have joined us, O'Hagan," said Mr. Holden. "What movie star could resist sitting out a blizzard with a fine bunch of lunkheads like you?"

I felt the first snowflakes. They were big and spongy, and at first I thought it might still be too warm for any serious snow. We sat quietly as the snow drifted around us, hoping that this was the worst the storm was going to throw our way. But the temperature kept falling, and the flakes became smaller and harder. In just a few minutes there was an inch on the ground. We bunched close to the fire as snow streamed down in a widening curtain. Suddenly, the wind evaporated. But the snow kept falling, heavier and thicker and colder and faster.

"What's that?" said Eddy. "Listen. What's that sound?"

I strained to hear through the snowfall and the darkness. There was something. A low rumbling, like a steam locomotive struggling up a steep canyon. The sound grew louder, deeper and closer. An avalanche? Rockslide?

Then the rumbling was joined by a whistling sound, weaving high and low and then high again. Years later, Hal would say that it reminded him of something he heard in 1944, in Belgium's Ardennes Forest during the Battle of The Bulge. Only then it was hundreds of German Panzer tanks rumbling through the frozen forests, firing their turret guns in waves at the scattering American troops.

"It's time," Mr. Holden finally said. "Let's get into the tents. Secure the flaps as tight as you can. I'll be checking in on you. Don't come out of your tent until I tell you to. Everybody got that?"

I took one last look around our camp as my friends began crawling into their tents. The sky was nearly black, and the snow was starting to blow in thick, eddying swirls around the boulders and the trees, then out onto the lake where waves were forming and rolling to the shore. Mr. Holden and I were the last to get into our tents. I looked at the ground. It had been snowing for less than ten minutes, but already it was piled midway up my ankle.

"You joining your troop, Forrestal?" he asked.

"Yes, sir," I said.

As I ducked into my tent, he said, "I hear you like poetry, Martin."

I straightened up, only to be slammed by a blast of wind and snow.

"Yes, I do," I yelled over the wind. "Why?"

He shouted back: "You ever read Robert Service, the poet of the Alaska Yukon?"

I cupped my hands around my mouth. "No, I can't say that I have." I could barely hear his reply.

"After tonight you'll want to look him up, Forrestal. Batten it down now."

He disappeared into his tent. I brushed the snow from my poncho, and crawled in between Gary and Toby St. Clair.

I laced the front flap tight, and then hell descended upon us.

•••

ACCORDING TO THE NEWSPAPERS, the storm that careened out of Alaska and down the Cascade Mountains that night was the biggest summer blow ever recorded. To an eagle circling high above, our three little tents would have looked kind of pitiful compared to the massive line of churning black clouds and wind that were about to smash into the boulders and trees around us.

Our tent was four feet wide at the base, and four feet high at the center pole. The reflecting candle-lantern spread a soft golden glow, and the smell of the cedar branches under our sleeping bags was sweet and strong.

I snapped my sleeping bag tight.

"You okay?" asked Gary.

"Wouldn't mind being out at Ayre's pond fishing instead of here in this hotel," I said, "but I'm alright."

"How long will it last?" asked Toby.

"That depends on how fast the front is moving, and how much punch is behind it," said Gary. "A few hours—maybe even the whole night. Hard to see it lasting much longer than—" a burst of wind slammed into my side of the tent, and the tent pole and lantern crashed over. Gary quickly righted the pole, but the candle in the lantern was blown out, and we were plunged into darkness. I got to my knees and fumbled in my poncho for my waterproof matchbox. As I lit the first match, something heavy fell on the tent and pushed the canvas roof down on top of our heads.

"Must be a tree branch," said Gary. "Get that lantern lit!"

The weight of the branch and the collapsed roof were stifling; I struck another match, and lit the candle. Toby and Gary were both on their knees, holding the tent roof above their heads.

"Let the tent rest on your head, and hold the lantern," I told Toby. "I've got to get whatever is on top of us off."

I untied the flap, and stuck my head and shoulders outside the tent. The wind was ferocious. Snow hit my face like stinging needles, and I could barely make out the shape of the other tents just a few feet away. I fought my way to a standing position in the darkness, and reached out. Sure enough, a five-foot spruce limb had fallen on our tent. I shook the snow off of the branch and lifted it up, only to be caught by a gust of wind and blown back several feet. I let go of the limb and tripped, falling face first onto the frozen ground.

I got to my knees, and brushed the snow and ice crystals from my face. My right cheek felt hot and wet, and when I pulled my hand back, it was bloodied. I bent down in the blasting wind, and felt around on the ground until I found the tent flap. Gary and Toby were getting the tent pole secured as I lurched back inside, and collapsed on my sleeping bag.

"Good job," Gary said. "We've got it back up." Then he saw my face. "Martin, you lay still. Toby, get my first aid kit over there in the corner."

"Had to kiss a boulder, didn't you?" Gary asked. He pressed gauze against the three-inch cut on my cheek. "Keep pressure on this while I cut some tape. It looks pretty clean, but we'll want to wash it out in the morning."

I held the gauze against my face. It was starting to throb. "I'm supposed to be doing the first aid," I said. "That's on my list for my First Class rank."

"I guess we can get you credited for this one, Martin. Now lie back."

We huddled in our sleeping bags as the wind howled off the mountain and swept around the lake. The trees behind us swayed and creaked through the night, and we heard branches crack and crash nearby several times, but no more fell on us. I slept fitfully; the cold and the wind and the pain from my cheek did not subside. Once, I woke to the sound of Toby sobbing quietly under his cover. I rolled onto my side, and put my hand on his shoulder.

"Pancakes in the morning," I said. "Don't let a little snowstorm spoil your appetite." He quieted, and a few minutes later his breathing slowed into rhythmic sleep.

Twice during the night our tent flap opened, and Mr. Holden's head popped through.

"This tent doing okay?" he asked.

"We're good," Gary replied, and I hoped he was right.

I came to at dawn. I was cold, and my cheek hurt badly. But it was quiet outside, and I could see light through the tent flap.

"Gary, you awake?"

"Yes. You hear that—no wind!"

"Yeah, and there's a little light, too."

Toby stirred. "Is it over?" he asked.

"Looks like it, kid," said Gary. "Let's see."

"Boys, are you with us?" called Mr. Holden. "Don't try to open your flap—the snow's halfway up the door. We'll shovel you out."

A few minutes later Hal undid our flap from the outside, and popped his head in. "You fellas need an invitation to breakfast…geez, Forrestal, who smacked your face?"

I crawled out of the tent and into an unfamiliar landscape. The boulders around the camp looked like huge marshmallows, and the trees behind our tents were coated with snow. Hal's tent had lost its outer shell in the windstorm, but, other than that, we had all weathered the blizzard pretty well.

Mr. Holden washed out the cut on my face with hot water and mercurochrome, and closed it with butterfly sutures. "You'll need some real stitches when we get home," he said. "A little bigger rock and you would have looked just like me."

As we dug into bowls of oatmeal with dried fruit, Mr. Holden gave us his assessment.

"This may not be the end of the storm. In any event, even if it is, we can't hike out today, and no one from town can hike in. We're going to have to find a better place with more shelter to spend tonight."

"Gary, Hal—I want you to head up the mountain slope, due west, no more than half a mile. Look for a cliff overhang, a cave, anything that provides a barrier from the wind and snow. Take a compass bearing right here, and plant sticks along the trail to mark your path. We'll break camp, and be ready to go as soon as you return."

Hal and Gary set off, and in a minute they disappeared beyond the tree line.

We policed the campsite, packed our gear, and stood close by the fire to await their return. To pass the time, Mr. Holden quizzed us on Indian sign language and Morse code. The sky was still gray, and the clouds were thickening. Even though we had the trench fire to keep us warm, we all could feel the temperature starting to fall again.

Anytime the conversation died, the stillness wrapped around us like a blanket. For the most part, we were holding up well, but when an hour passed without Gary and Hal returning, we began to worry.

•••

IT BEGAN TO SNOW AGAIN. Softly at first, and then steadily. We backed under the boulder overhangs we'd dug out that morning, but that would only do for a short while. We were going to have to reset our tents right here, or go in search of Hal and Gary and take our luck up the mountain slope. Neither choice sounded very good.

Then we heard Gary's voice, far off. "Hello to the camp! We found a cave, a really big cave!"

"Okay, fellas," Mr. Holden said. "Let's saddle up and get ready to move out of here."

A minute later Gary appeared through a curtain of snow.

"Where's Hal?" asked Mr. Holden. Gary came close to the fire. His face was red with cold, and the bottom of his poncho was crusted with icicles.

"He's just up the slope," said Gary. "The cave is about a quarter mile up, it's fantastic. You guys are going to love it. The entrance is tiny, so you have to crawl in, but then it opens up into a huge room that's tall enough to stand up in."

"Hear that Toby," I said. "We're going to have a warm, dry place to stay in just a few minutes." Toby gave me a weak smile. He was shivering even though he was closest to the fire.

"So, why did Hal stay behind?" asked Mr. Holden.

"Oh, right," said Gary. "When it started to snow we came down the slope as fast as we could. It was kind of hard to follow our own trail, so we decided to tie our rope off a tree to give us something to follow on the way back up. Hal is waiting where the rope ran out."

"How long a rope?" said Mr. Holden.

"About two hundred feet."

"And the cave is a quarter mile away?"

"Yes, but here's what we figured," said Gary. "We'll follow the rope single file, with Hal and I out front. When we get to the uphill end of the rope, everybody will wait while one of us runs it up the next two hundred feet to one of our markers. That way, no matter how hard the snow is coming down, you can just hold onto the rope. We'll just keep laying it out in a line toward the cave until we all get there."

"I don't get it," said Eddy. "Why don't we just all get into line and let you guys lead us straight to the cave? Why do we need a rope?"

The snow was thickening, and coming down fast. Mr. Holden said, "Because if Gary or Hal can't find one of the sticks they planted in the snow and have to look around to find the next marker, we'd all be running around in circles. This way, we only move when we're headed in the right direction. That the way you see it, Gary?"

"That's it, Mr. Holden."

"And what if they can't find one of their markers," Patrick whispered to me as we got ready to move out. "What then? We just trot around on this mountain for days looking for shelter?"

Mr. Holden had us move out in single file, close, with our right hand on the shoulder of the boy in front of us. Gary took the lead, Mr. Holden dropped to the back of the line. It was just after 8 AM. I was sixth in the line, and the snow was heavy enough that I could not see Patrick or Gary at the front. Toby was in front of me. He was shivering, and his teeth were chattering. Like the rest of us, he had a full pack, plus a bundle of kindling on his back. Tough kid, I thought. He and Perry both. One thing for sure: there wouldn't be any rookies coming back down this mountain.

It took five or six minutes to ascend the short distance to where Hal was waiting for us. There were no trees or rocks to shelter him. He was hunched on the ground, with one of the sections of tent we had cut the night before pulled over him. He looked like a Polar bear.

As we neared, Gary shouted out, and Hal stood and shook the snow off his covering.

"Glad to see you boys," he said. "How about we all get out of this weather?"

We stayed in our positions in line and held onto the rope with our left hands as we moved forward. None of us had snow gloves, so the drill was for us to walk the first two hundred feet using our left hand on the rope, while warming our right hand in our poncho pocket, and then to move to the other side of the rope for the next two hundred feet and hold on with our right hand.

The wind picked up as we moved out, and the snow began to blow horizontally against us. Perry stumbled once and fell to the ground, and Eddy slipped off a rock and slid about twenty feet back down the slope before he was able to dig in his boots and stop. It took ten minutes to make it the two hundred feet to where Hal had tied the rope off to a tree branch. He immediately untied the rope, and Gary lit out up the slope in search of the next marker. I could see no more than ten feet through the driving snow, and I didn't see how he was going to be able to find the little wooden stake.

"Hal, you said this cave is about a quarter mile from the camp," said Wade.

"Yes."

"So, that's about thirteen hundred feet. The rope is two hundred feet long. So, we're going to have to do this six or seven times?"

I hadn't done the math. I don't think any of us had, except probably Mr. Holden. For the first time, I started to shiver. The first two hundred feet up the slope wore me out, and I was in great shape. I knew that Toby and Perry were already exhausted. And we had to do this five or six more times? In this beating wind and snow, with the temperature still dropping?

"This is an elephant we're going to eat one bite at a time," said Mr. Holden. "We'll move fast, and within the hour we'll be inside that cave, building a fire and making lunch. You guys alright with that?"

Before we could answer, Gary stepped out of a wall of falling snow. His face was red, and his eyelashes were tipped with frost. But, he was grinning. "I found the stake, no problem," he said. "Let's go!" We didn't need more urging.

Traversing the next two hundred feet was more difficult than ever. We had to navigate a field of barrel-sized boulders, many of them hidden just far enough under the snow that you couldn't tell one was there until your ankle or shinbone collided with the rock.

Mr. Holden moved me to the back of the line. He walked back and forth, from Gary at the lead to Perry just ahead of me. He talked to each boy as he strode past in the thigh-high snow. "Wade, pick it up, you want a hot lunch, we've got to get a fire going in that cave. Eddy, wipe your face, before the snot freezes on it—ladies don't care for that look, believe me.

Perry, pull your poncho hood tighter, keep the wind out, son."

When we got through the rock field, Hal took the point from Gary, and went off in search of the next marker while we huddled by the largest rock. Wade was rubbing his right hand hard, and Patrick was holding his sleeve against his face to slow the bleeding from his nose.

"How'd that happen?" I asked.

"Don't know. I fell back there, but I don't remember hitting anything. I can't feel anything on my face, though. My lips feel funny, like they're asleep."

Mr. Holden passed out pemmican bars, and made us sip from our canteens. He checked our fingers and faces for frostbite, and told Wade to put his hand under his poncho and shirt and into his armpit for warmth.

It took about fifteen minutes for Hal to return. He was too tired to talk. He just nodded and pointed up the trail, and we grabbed hold of the rope and continued up the slope. For the next half-hour, there was no talking. The snow pounded us, and the wind bit through our layers of clothing as though they were made of paper.

It took every fiber of strength I had to simply put one foot ahead of the other. I lost count of how many times we had to stop to wait while Gary or Hal hiked forward with the rope to the next marker stake. I wanted to sit down, to lie down, just to get off my frozen, aching feet. I didn't care if I fell asleep and was buried by the snow. I just wanted to rest, and let it all pass by me.

"….that's what it means. Forrestal, you listening? Martin! Head up!"

I focused on what Mr. Holden was saying. "We're nearly there, boys. And when we crawl into that warm, dry cave you're going to want to just fall down and sleep. But you can't. We have to get a fire going, and make some hot food. I'll need everybody's help to do that. Any of you have a problem with chowing down on a bowl of soup and some hot chocolate?"

No one answered, but I nodded wearily. Hot food. For that, I could make it a little farther. I wasn't sure how long we waited in the unforgiving eye of that blizzard for Gary to return. We wanted to hear him tell us that he had tied the rope off on the last marker, and that the cave entrance was close by. It seemed like an eternity. It might have only been fifteen or twenty minutes.

Finally, Mr. Holden told Hal to go and look for Gary. I heard those words, and my heart sank. Gary couldn't be lost. If he was, we were all lost.

Hal moved out, vanishing into a wall of swirling snow in the blink of an eye. We stayed huddled together, and Mr. Holden prepared us for what our next move might be if we couldn't locate the cave.

"Any of you boys ever dug a snow cave?" he asked. "No? It's really not too hard; in fact, the way this snow has settled, the conditions are perfect. We can even build a fire inside…that's a trick the Eskimos know. If we need to—"

"Mr. Holden!" It was Gary.

"Over here Gary. Follow the sound of my voice! Shout boys—all of you—shout!" We bellowed with everything we had left. A minute later Gary materialized out of the snow.

"I found the cave," he said. "It's only about sixty yards from here. I tied the rope off to a tree right next to the opening."

"What about Hal," said Mr. Holden. "We sent him out after you."

Gary was quiet for a moment. "He must still be looking for the cave."

Patrick shot a worried look my way.

"Let's get into that cave," said Mr. Holden. "Then we'll go and round up Stannard."

A wave of energy ran through the Troop. The cave. A fire. And food! I slapped Toby on the back. "First hot chocolate is yours, kid! Let's get out of this storm." We grabbed hold of the rope for the last time, and in a few minutes we were standing together in front of a brushy thicket at the base of a towering rock cliff. I didn't see a cave entrance, though.

"It's right there," said Gary, "next to that stump." Sure enough, there was a hole at the base of the cliff, about four feet wide and three feet high. Mr. Holden got to his knees and switched on his flashlight. He peered in for a second, and then said, "This is it, boys. Flashlights on. Follow me in and stay right by me until we get our bearings."

With that, he lay down in the snow and disappeared through the opening, pulling his pack beside him. The rest of us hauled out our flashlights and crawled through. We slid on our bellies over the snow and rocks and into the cave. It smelled musty and moldy, but it was mostly dry, and as soon as my shoulders were in I felt the blessed absence of snow and wind.

I only had to crawl six or eight feet before I was able to stand up. Seven flashlights swept around our new home. The cave stretched back to the limit of our beams, at least fifty feet. We were in a vaulted chamber, with a ceiling that rose about fifteen feet at midpoint before dropping away in the darkness. It was wider than Hal and Gary first thought, too, at least twenty feet across at its center point.

I've stayed in some wonderful hotels in my time, but, to this day, I've never had a room as nice as that musty mountain cave.

DETERMINATION

"WAS I SLEEPING?"

"For a half hour or so," Connie said. "I turned your recorder off when I came in with my coffee. Will there be anything in this segment other than snoring?"

"I hope so. With these medications, sometimes I can't tell if I'm dreaming or dictating." I sat up in bed and reached for the recorder. I rewound a few minutes, and hit play.

"…worried about Hal, who was still out in the storm, but we had to get a fire going first, and tend to Toby and Wade who were both suffering the effects of the cold. Mr. Holden said…." I snapped the recorder off.

"It's here," I said.

Connie closed her magazine, and pulled her chair closer to my bed. "The orderly will be here soon to take you down for your treatment," she said.

"I'd like to come with you for this one, if you don't mind."

The infusion treatment I received each day involved more nuisance than any real discomfort. I felt good enough to walk to the elevator and along the hall to the radiology department, but my keepers insisted I be wheeled down.

This was part of the routine that I had hoped to spare Connie. There was, after all, no restorative hope in these treatments. They would not make me better; they would only prolong the inevitable. And that, according to the calendar on my nightstand, was not going to happen for at least a couple more weeks.

"Why don't you go outside instead, and enjoy the weather? The park across the way is lovely—get out in the sunshine for a little while. You know, for April, it's awfully warm. Are the cherry trees blossoming?" I asked.

"Nice try, buster. I walked around the neighborhood before I came this morning, and Rachel and I are going shopping this evening, so I will get plenty of fresh air. I'll take you to the park tomorrow myself, and you can see the trees in bloom. Today, I'm going to the treatment with you. That's it."

I squeezed her hand. After more than half a century of marriage, I knew that some things were open to negotiation, and some things were not. When Connie said, "That's it," it was.

"You're talking about leadership today, aren't you?" she said.

"Yes. And determination, too. It's interesting that when I think of all the times in my life when I've been in the presence of real leaders, that it would be my Scoutmaster who stands out. I've known bosses and professors and rifle platoon leaders and combat officers and corporate types—even a few politicians—who demonstrated great leadership skills, and who were people of enormous determination. I could have chosen any one of them over Nate Holden. He was a simple farmer who spent a few hours a week working with boys like me. He didn't go to college. He didn't have money, he didn't have power. But when I was fourteen, and we were caught in that blizzard, he was the greatest leader you could have had in that situation. He kept his calm, and he kept us calm. He made life or death decisions without vacillating. He kept us focused, motivated, and working together as a team. He was pretty damned heroic. And we wanted to follow him."

"It still seems heroic now, thinking back on it?" Connie asked.

"Yes," I said, "it does. More so than ever."

"It makes sense that you would pick him," Connie said. "His leadership wasn't something abstract, it was real. If he had made a mistake on that mountain, you might all have died. That kind of leadership isn't taught in school—it *can't* be taught in school."

I grinned. "You done yet?"

Connie took her last sip of coffee, and tossed the paper cup in the wastebasket.

"Not by a long shot," she said. "Because if you're serious about this project of yours, if it's how you want to spend your last—this *time*, then make it count. Tell the whole story and especially what you learned. If you don't do that, I don't know what the point is."

She stood and walked over to the door leading into the corridor. For a minute, I thought she was going to leave. Instead, she closed the door, and went into the bathroom. When she came out, I could see that she had been crying. She came back to the chair beside my bed, and took my hand.

"Marty, I'm sorry. I'm so very sorry. This is hard for you. I want to be supportive. I want to do everything I can to help you realize this dream of yours. I just don't know if I'm strong enough, that's all."

I couldn't help but chuckle. "The lightweight champ of the Pacific Northwest not strong enough?" I put my hand on her cheek: "My darling, you have been strong enough for the two of us for longer than I can remember. You'll never fail in that department." I looked in her eyes. "And I guess we haven't really talked about why I'm doing all this recording, have we? I just decided, in my own bull-headed fashion, that this is what I was going to do, and I dropped it on you like a pile of rocks."

"Like you've done since the day I met you."

"Since the day we met. Connie, I don't have to do this. But, I have to do something. I can't just lay here in my bed and feel the life flow out of my body hour after hour. We can watch TV. Or you can read to me. We can even just talk."

"And we'd end up talking about the same things you're recording."

"We probably would. Is that a bad thing? I suppose I'd prefer to talk about what really matters. It's the life I've lived, the life we've shared. It's what I have to give. Oh, there will be a little money and property for Eric and Rachel and the grandkids, and you'll be fine, but I never made a lot of money. There sure won't be any buildings named after me."

"You're bordering on maudlin," she said. "Don't start down that road now."

"Forgive me, beautiful, for thinking about these matters." I nodded toward the IV stand, and around the room. "It would be a bit unrealistic for me not to think about it, don't you think?" She looked down for a moment. When she lifted her gaze back to me there was a tear at the corner of her eye.

"I love you, Marty. I love you so much."

"And I love you. That's why I'm doing this. It's why I must do it."

I picked up the list of fifteen values. "I believe that what I've learned about these, that's something that can make a difference. For our kids, and for theirs. Tell you the truth Connie, I wouldn't mind being remembered for the words on this list. If the kids listen to these stories, they'll know who I was, and what I stood for. I don't know, maybe sometime during their lives something I said here can help pull them through a tough patch. A man could do worse than to have that be his legacy."

Connie leaned over and kissed me. "Martin Forrestal, you are the richest man I know. You always have been, even when I was taking the bus across town to save five cents on a can of peas. I don't want you to stop this project—it's a wonderful idea. Don't be afraid to tell the complete story— and that means *our* story, too."

She walked to the door. "I've got to meet Rachel in the lobby. You get back to work." She stood in the doorway for a moment, her back toward me. Then she turned, and with a sly smile she said, "Martin—about our story? When I said tell all of it, I don't mean every bit of it. What would they think about their Gram if you told it all?"

As I reached for the recorder, I'm sure I saw her blush.

•••

WE BUILT A FIRE against the west cave wall, where the smoke could roll up the rock face and out a small natural chimney. The light from the fire and a half-dozen candle lanterns lit the cave up, and for the first time we could see around our new home.

The walls were damp and mossy, and most of the floor space was covered with stones. But it was fairly flat, and there were enough open spaces that we could spread out our sleeping bags. Toby was verging on hypothermia. We laid him close to the fire. Wade's right hand was still hurting, so Mr. Holden had him keep it under his shirt in his armpit for warmth.

As soon as the fire was going and Patrick and Eddy were getting the soup on, Mr. Holden and Gary went to look for Hal. I was left in charge.

I had Perry gather all of the kindling and wood we had carried up the hill into one pile, and then helped him clear rocks away from around the fire so we'd all have a place to sit.

Gary returned to the cave a half hour later. Without a word he went over and warmed his hands by the fire. It was another ten minutes before Mr. Holden returned—without Hal.

He pulled off his poncho, and accepted a cup of hot soup from Patrick. He took a couple of sips, then put his poncho back on and started for the cave entrance. Gary followed.

"No, Gary," said Mr. Holden. "Your job is here. I'm staying out there until I find Hal. Make sure everybody is fed, and look after Toby. If the storm breaks before I get back, and if you think it's over, get these boys down the mountain. I'll find you." Then he looked at the rest of us. "All of you boys: Gary is in charge. Do what he tells you. I promise, you're all going to be fine."

With that, Mr. Holden was gone. We were quiet for a minute. Then, Wade asked, "What's it like out there?"

"Colder than ever," said Gary. "The wind is something fierce. You can barely see your own feet as you walk. The snow is piling in drifts, and there are even sheets of ice sliding down the mountain. They come out of nowhere, like a freight train. One of those whacks you, and you're going down this mountain fast—and for the last time."

Eddy handed Gary a mug of steaming cocoa.

"What if Mr. Holden doesn't come back?" asked Perry.

"Holden? Listen, bub, and listen well," said Gary. "He'll be back. *With* Hal. And when they get here, we're all getting off this mountain, together. You got that?"

Perry nodded, but there was a voice gnawing inside of me, and probably in all of us, that was asking the same thing.

We finished clearing rocks from around the fire, and we all sat as close as we could. Toby was feeling feverish, but he was able to get some soup down. The fire, the hot soup and cocoa, and just being out of the storm all joined together to brighten my spirits. All we could do now was wait.

•••

EDDY AND PATRICK GATHERED some loose brush and wove it into a small screen. They laid it across the cave opening to stop the moaning noise made by the wind as it whipped past the cave entrance. I sat with Toby and kept a cool, damp cloth on his forehead. Wade tried to sleep, and Gary and Perry inventoried our food and firewood.

"Whatever else happens tonight," Gary said, "we're going to have to make it down the mountain tomorrow and get to that food cache. We have enough for today, if we go easy, but that's it."

He motioned me to follow him to the back of the cave, outside the earshot of the others.

"Martin, it's not looking too good for Hal or Mr. Holden right now. Hal's been out there a few hours—and Mr. Holden almost that long. I hope Hal's hunkered down under a rock ledge or behind a log, protected a little from the weather. Then he'd have a chance..." He trailed off.

I slumped down beside a large rock. I was fourteen—too old to cry. Just the same, I crossed my arms and pressed them tight against my chest to hold back the sob welling up inside me. Gary leaned against the cave wall, staring into space. All around the cave, the other boys sat still or lay quietly beneath their blankets. The only sounds were the crackling of the fire and the muffled moan of the wind outside.

We stayed that way for what seemed like hours.

Then the monotony of that grim wait was broken. I felt a cold draft swirling around the cave. Gary felt it, too. He sent Eddy up to the cave entrance to check to see if the brush screen had fallen down. A minute later, Eddy yelled:

"It's Mr. Holden—and Hal. They're outside! I don't think they can move."

I ran to the cave entrance. Gary beat me, and was the first to crawl outside. I told everybody else to wait inside, and crawled out after him.

The wind and snow slammed into us. It felt like sandpaper bouncing around the rocks and onto our faces. The cold was numbing, and it was so loud I couldn't hear myself think. I was disoriented, and at first I didn't see Mr. Holden, or Hal. Gary was leaning over what looked like two bundles of snow-covered brush. I raced to Gary's side, knelt down, and began brushing snow off of Hal. Gary helped Mr. Holden to sit up.

"Be careful," said Mr. Holden. "Hal's unconscious. His right leg is broken. Pretty badly. We're going to have to immobilize it before we pull him into the cave. And, we can't do that in this snow and wind."

Mr. Holden clutched his left arm against his chest. His face was white with frost, his wool cap was covered with ice, and his left hand was bleeding and swollen. But his voice was strong and firm.

"Forrestal, get Wade and Eddy to bring some blankets out here to make a temporary shelter. And have them bring a cup of something hot."

I stuck my head inside the cave entrance and shouted instructions. A minute later Eddy and Wade were beside us. They handed Mr. Holden a cup of hot soup, and wrapped blankets around he and Hal.

Patrick crawled out with the first aid kit, and Gary and I quickly rigged extra blankets between the cliff wall and a hemlock tree. We tossed a blanket over the top, knowing that it would only hold the snow off for a few minutes. But, at least for a moment, Mr. Holden and Hal were sheltered from the worst of the storm.

Hal lay on his back. His right leg was bent at a forty-five-degree angle. His breathing was fast and shallow. I sat beside him, and lifted his head gently so Patrick could slip a rolled-up sweater under his head.

"Should I give him some soup?" I asked.

"No, not when he's unconscious," said Mr. Holden. He struggled to his knees.

"Look, boys, we're going to have to splint his leg out here, and then haul him into the cave. I can't help much right now—think my shoulder is dislocated. You're going to have to do it, and then help us both get into the cave."

"Just tell us what to do," said Gary.

Mr. Holden gave us instructions, and Patrick and I crawled back into the cave to gather the supplies. I gave Toby the good news, and asked Perry to sit with him until we came back inside.

Hal's fracture was in his upper leg. We could see the broken bone fragment pushing up against his skin through his torn trousers. We'd have to be very careful, or the bone might tear through, and then we'd have to deal with infection as well as the break.

We cut tent poles, laid them along each side of his leg, and tore strips of cloth. We pulled the strips tight around the poles, and tied reef knots on the outside, forming a splint. Hal's breathing seemed to smooth out a bit, but his eyes remained closed. "That's good, fellas," said Mr. Holden as we tied the last knot. "Now, let's engineer a sled to pull him into the cave."

Gary and I helped Mr. Holden up and out of the shelter. I took that moment to have my first look around since we had arrived at the cave that morning. We were about five thousand feet above sea level, sheltered from the worst of the snow and the wind by the rock cliff rising several hundred feet straight up above us. A heavy coat of snow topped the brush and boulders around the cave entrance. The sky was low and dark grey. I couldn't see more than fifty yards downslope. Somewhere down there was a way out. People knew we were out here. Help would be on the way.

I was scared—but determined to do everything I could to help get us through. Help would arrive eventually, but right now we had to take care of ourselves. Mr. Holden and Hal were back—they were in rough shape, alright, but they were back, and there wasn't anyone in the world who I thought could do a better job of getting us off this mountain in one piece than our Scoutmaster—injured or not.

"Here's what we'll do," said Mr. Holden. "We can't carry Hal through the cave opening—it's too low. We're going to have to pull him through. So, let's lay down a bed of hemlock branches to protect him from the rocks, and then lift him onto a doubled-over sheet of canvas tent. One of you will pull from the front, the others will lift and slide from the back."

I got on my knees in front of the makeshift litter, grabbed the edges of the canvas, and began to pull as Patrick and Gary lifted and inched Hal's body forward. At the mouth of the cave, I lay down on my belly and crawled backwards, pulling with every ounce of my strength.

Once inside, we waited for Wade and Mr. Holden to follow. Mr. Holden gingerly slid and wiggled in on his back. When he stood up, his face was ashen with pain.

Where did he find Hal? What had happened to them? And how in the heck did he manage to get Hal back to the cave in the shape they were in?

We carried Hal over by the fire, and put another blanket on him. His skin was cool and clammy, and his eyes were flickering open and closed. Mr. Holden knelt beside him for a minute, and then asked Gary and I to come over to the far side of the cave.

"Boys, I want you to get everybody busy. If they're not keeping the fire going, I want them to be cleaning up, helping with dinner, testing one another's Scoutcraft knowledge, tying knots—anything that keeps them busy. Can you do that?"

"We can do that," I said.

"Good. Head on over and pass the word. Then come back."

When we returned, Mr. Holden asked about our food supply.

"We have enough for a light dinner, and a little beef jerky and dried fruit for tomorrow morning, but that's it," said Gary.

"So, we'll need to get down the hill to the food cache tomorrow. Think you can find it, Gary? If the storm lets up, that is?"

Gary grinned. "I work pretty hard not to miss a meal, Mr. Holden—or so my mom tells me all the time. We'll find it."

"Good. I know you will. And now boys, we've got to take care of this shoulder of mine." He said it so nonchalantly.

Holden motioned us to sit. Eddy had looped a belt around his wrist and behind his neck to take the pressure off his shoulder. The bandage around his left hand was soaked through with blood.

"I'm just about useless with one arm. Either one of you ever set a dislocated shoulder?"

We shook our heads.

"Well, then this is going to be one of those 'first-time-for-everything' events. The important thing is not to let up when I tell you what to do. It's going to hurt like the devil, and I plan on giving out a yelp or two, but, by golly, if you don't set it right the first time, it's going to hurt me a whole lot more. Do you understand?"

We nodded.

"I'm going to lay flat on my back. Patrick, I want you to come around behind me, and put one hand on each side of my head. Keep it from thrashing around. Got that?"

Patrick glanced at me, then back to Mr. Holden. "Okay."

"Martin, take off your right boot, and come over by my bum arm."

I removed my boot, and scooted around to Mr. Holden's side. He stretched out on his back, still clutching his left arm on his chest.

The rest of the troop stopped what they were doing, and gathered silently a few feet away. The light from the fire and the lanterns cast a golden glow around the cave. My friend's faces reminded me of characters I'd seen in a Rembrandt painting at the Portland Museum—shadowy and subdued in the ocher light. A bead of sweat rolled down my brow and into the cut on my cheek. It stung. I steeled myself for what was to come next.

"Alright, Martin," said Mr. Holden. His voice was calm. "Here's what it is. I'm going to straighten my arm out. You put your left hand on my wrist, and your right hand just above my elbow. Got that? Raise my arm up just high enough that you can put your foot right into my armpit. I'll count to three. When I hit three, you push your foot as hard as you can into my armpit, and then yank my arm straight toward you. One pull, Martin. Fast and hard. Understand?"

My throat felt dry. "I understand."

Mr. Holden clenched his teeth, and slowly straightened his arm. His eyes narrowed, and he sucked in his breath. "Now, Martin," he whispered through clenched teeth. "Take my arm like I told you."

I took his wrist gingerly with one hand, and held his arm above the elbow lightly with the other.

"Son, you're not holding a young lady on the dance floor here," said Mr. Holden. "You squeeze my wrist and arm tight—you hear?"

I gulped—and I squeezed.

Mr. Holden gasped in pain, and I started to loosen my grip.

"Don't!" he shouted. "You hang on, got it? Hang on!" And then, "Ready?"

"I'm ready."

"Alright. One…two…"

I squeezed harder on his wrist and arm, and pushed my foot into his armpit with all my might.

"…three!"

I bit into my lower lip, and pulled fast and hard. Mr. Holden's arm slid to the side, and then there was a sensation like a rubber band snapping as his arm popped back into his shoulder socket.

"Lordy!" gasped Mr. Holden. His back arched, and then he lay quiet. No one spoke.

Mr. Holden stared at the cave roof for a minute. Then he said, "Forrestal? You there?"

"I'm right here."

"The last time somebody caused me this much pain I was in a trench somewhere in France. And I'm pretty sure I shot them dead afterwards. But son, you just put me back together."

He sat up, and a grin creased his face. "Now, how about one of you first aid specialists makes me a sling, and then let's do something about some food?"

•••

EVERY HOUR THAT DAY, until nightfall, one of us poked our head out the cave entrance to check on the weather. The news only got worse. More snow, more wind, more cold. But we had plenty of firewood, and that night we chowed down on the last of the salt pork and beans, with one can of peaches to share between all nine of us.

There wasn't any storytelling around the fire that night. We stayed close by the warmth. The cave was dry, but only feet from the fire it was frigid cold. Mr. Holden had us pull our sleeping bags as close as possible to the fire, but nobody could sleep. There were too many questions racing through our heads. How long would the storm last? How many more days would we be stuck on this mountain? What would become of Hal and Toby if we didn't get them to a doctor soon?

And so we sat, our sleeping bags pulled up around us, listening to the wind outside the cave and the crackle of the fire, watching the shadows dance on the cave walls.

Perry broke the silence. "Mr. Holden? What was the war like?"

My head shot up. The question I had wanted to ask—one we had all wanted to ask but never could—had finally been broached—and by a tenderfoot!

Mr. Holden was quiet for a minute. At last he answered. "Do you mean, was being in the war like being on this mountain in the middle of a blizzard?"

"Yeah, I guess so. Is it like that?"

"In some ways, I suppose it is. In a lot of ways, when you think about it. In war you spend a lot of time waiting, doing nothing, just trying to stay ready for when it's your turn to go out into the storm."

"Or waiting to have the storm come to you?" asked Wade.

Mr. Holden chuckled. "That's true, too. In war, most often the storm does come to you—you don't have to chase it."

To my surprise, Hal raised himself up on his elbows.

"Did you worry about dying?" he asked.

"I did, at least at first. But I found out pretty quickly that I had a choice: I could worry all day and accomplish nothing except more worry, or I could focus on my job and make some kind of contribution to my unit. We had a captain in the early days who had a good way of dealing with worry. When he'd see one of us pacing around the trench before a battle, or cleaning our rifle until we wore the bluing off, he'd say, 'You know, there ain't much use putting up that umbrella until it rains...'"

"And when it did rain, what then?" I asked.

"When it finally rained we got those umbrellas up mighty fast—and kept them up," said Mr. Holden.

"Did a lot of people die...people you knew?" asked Perry.

Mr. Holden took a sip from his canteen. "Too many people, Perry, that's for sure. More than twenty million people died in the war, they say. At the Battle of the Somme, nineteen thousand British soldiers were killed and another thirty-five thousand were wounded—and most of that happened in the first hour."

"Were you a general?" asked Eddy.

"Not quite, son. I shipped out of Nebraska as a muleskinner, at the exalted rank of private. My four mules and I were supposed to be attached to a British regiment to pull field artillery, but the mules drowned when the barge they were crossing the English Channel on sunk. I was a muleskinner without a mule, which is why, I guess, the Army went and made me a cook."

"A cook?" said Perry. You could hear the disappointment in his voice. "You mean you didn't get to shoot at people?"

"Well, soldiers have to eat. Tell you the truth, though, I may not have been quite the gourmet chef they were looking for, because after a few weeks of eating my chow, a group of the boys got together and suggested to the CO that a man of my talents shouldn't be wasted on a bunch of Yankee farmers; my cooking skills, they said, were a lot more in line with what the Brits favored. And wouldn't you know it—the company commander agreed. Next thing I knew, I was assigned to a British artillery battery on the front lines. But not as a cook. They shoved a 30-caliber Enfield in my hands and pointed me toward the enemy. Whatever damage I hadn't inflicted on folks as a cook I was going to get to finish as an infantryman."

I leaned over to Patrick. "Let that be a lesson for you when you finally get around to cooking for us," I said.

Mr. Holden got up and went over to check on Toby. He gingerly added another log to the fire, and adjusted the sling on his arm before coming back to sit with us.

"We were part of the big Allied attack on the Hindenburg Line that fall," he continued. "A quarter million of us Americans went over the tops of the trenches in that one. That's where I got this." He traced his finger along the wide scar that ran across his face and down his neck.

"Was that from a bullet?" asked Patrick.

"A bayonet," said Mr. Holden.

All of us sucked in our breath at the same time. As bad as it was to think about getting shot, the idea of a cold-steel bayonet slicing across your face and down your neck was even worse.

"My time in the war was done. I spent two months in an English hospital before being shipped out to New York, where I spent another six months healing up. Long time past, boys. Long time past."

•••

IT WAS QUIET IN THE CAVE. Hal was asleep again, and Toby was curled up under his blanket. Mr. Holden examined the cut on my face, which had caused my right eye to swell nearly shut. He had Gary pour some mercurochrome into a pail with a cup of water and heat it up over the fire. Then he dipped some gauze into the mix and applied it to my face. After about fifteen minutes, he removed the gauze. Gary handed him a pair of tweezers that he had heated in the fire.

"This won't be fun, Martin," said Mr. Holden. "You've got infection in there, and we've got to clean out the wound and drain any pus in there. Lean back now, and grab hold of something."

I put my hands on the ground behind my back, and held tightly to a stick. Mr. Holden peeled the sides of the cut apart, and began to probe inside. I'm pretty sure I screamed. I couldn't remember anything ever hurting like that. I clenched my teeth as tightly as I could, and I held onto that stick with all my might. Tears dripped from my eyes, but I didn't cry out again.

Mr. Holden put a fresh piece of mercurochrome-soaked gauze inside the wound to keep it from closing up and sealing in any of the remaining infection. Then he taped a wide gauze bandage across my cheek.

"Not pretty," said Mr. Holden, "but she'll do until we get you to a proper doctor."

•••

"HELLO, MARTIN."

Dr. McGuire stepped into my room, chart in hand.

"Hello Mac—let me switch this thing off." I clicked the digital recorder off, and set it on the nightstand.

McGuire checked the IV pump, and then placed his stethoscope against my chest. "Connie told me more about your project. Pretty ambitious. Anything I can do to help?"

"Sure. You can keep me alive and alert long enough for me to finish," I said.

My friend pulled a chair close to the bed. "How long have you been my patient, Martin? Twenty-five, thirty years?"

"You want credit for keeping me alive this long, do you?"

"I'll take a little credit, sure. But you've had a run of luck since we discovered your prostate cancer last year. Luck, plus your hardscrabble attitude and the longest-suffering wife on the planet. That's mostly what's kept you with us this long." He removed his stethoscope, and made a few notes.

"Mac, can I ask you something?"

"Would this be a medical question, Martin?"

"It might be. You can be the judge."

"Let's hear it."

"You've attended a lot of people at the end, haven't you?"

"That comes with the job," said my doctor. "I haven't seen quite as many out of this world as I have helped into it, but, the answer is yes, in my thirty-five years as a physician, I have walked as far as I could with patients, right up to the second-to-the-last stepping stone on the path."

"Stepping stone?"

"That's how I've always thought of life, Martin. There's a path we cut by ourselves through the forests in our lives, and there's a path that God makes for us. Our friends and family can walk alongside us most of the way, and even help us to move along now and then when we need a hand. But that last step? The final stepping stone? That's the one we have to stand on all by ourselves." He adjusted his tie. "The last step, Martin, that one's a doozy."

I nodded. "That's a nice way of looking at it—death, I mean."

He shrugged. "Medicine may have become an industry, Martin. Now it's mostly a matter of numbers and technology and bureaucracy. But do you know what hasn't changed, not in all the years I've practiced medicine, not since the first caveman patched a saber-tooth tiger bite on his best friend's behind? Human nature. That hasn't changed."

He looked straight into my eyes.

"And the way we die." He stood up. "Does that answer your question?"

"For now. Thanks, Mac."

Dr. McGuire moved for the door, and then turned to me. "Martin, I can't promise you the three weeks. Truth is, I can't even promise you three days. I do know that right now, your Irish attitude and your focus on your stories is the best thing you can do to stretch time. I'll do my part; I'll keep the drugs to a minimum so you can do your recording. You're going to experience more pain that way, and we'll have to work through that. There's something else you need to consider, though."

"What's that?"

"You might be fine with your decision to forgo all of the pain relief we can provide. Just don't forget that Connie will have to live with your choice too. And buddy, when it gets bad, and you feel like every nerve ending in your body is on fire, she's going to be feeling it with you. Think about what you're about to put her through." He patted my shoulder. "I'll see you tomorrow."

After he left I looked around my room. Until today, I hadn't minded the contrast between the cheery wallpaper and bright prints that were intended to lift my spirits and the utilitarian fixtures and medical equipment that were designed to efficiently manage my transition from life to death.

Through the open door I could see nurses going about their routines. The sounds and the smells of the hospital had become my new normal in the past few days. My bed faced the door—best, I suppose for them to easily check on me. But it made it difficult to see out the windows overlooking the park. If I strained my neck, I could make out the white branches of a flowering cherry tree.

Life and death. Just inches apart.

•••

HAL AND TOBY SLEPT as Mr. Holden lined out his plan. Tomorrow, Patrick and Gary would head down the mountain to the food cache at Camp Lake. When they returned, I would take Perry and look for more firewood and kindling along the rocks and boulders under the cliff, while Patrick and Gary rustled up a meal and looked after Hal and Toby. Mr. Holden, Wade and Eddy would climb to a high-point near the cave and use stones and branches to lay out a large 'X,' the international location and distress symbol. Help would come. We just needed a break in the weather.

I was surprised how quickly we all fell asleep. The cold, the damp, the howl of the wind outside the cave, even the pain of frostbite and cuts and broken bones wasn't enough to keep any of us awake. No sooner had I closed my eyes than I felt Patrick's hand on my shoulder. For a moment, I forgot where I was. But the cold, and my throbbing cheek, brought me quickly back to the present.

"It's stopped snowing," said Patrick. "Sun's out—there's not a cloud in the sky. Come on, come see."

I flew out of my sleeping bag and stepped carefully around the sleeping forms of the rest of the troop. When I crawled through the cave opening and stood up, I was astonished: a warm, bright sun shone in a perfect sky. Not a cloud or a breath of wind.

Outside the cave entrance, Gary and Mr. Holden were scanning the snowy landscape. As far as I could see along the horizon there was only the deep blue of the Oregon sky and the white of the snow and ice. Here and there a tree branch was losing its snowy coverlet, as the warming sun melted the snow and sent it sheeting to the ground. I have never seen so much white, or so much blue, on one single canvas as I saw that morning.

"Good morning, gentlemen," said Mr. Holden. "How do you like our weather?"

"I could get used to this," said Patrick. "Course, a pile of buttermilk pancakes smothered in blueberry syrup wouldn't hurt none, either."

"We'll get to the pancakes soon enough," said Mr. Holden. "Right now, let's talk about getting down to that food cache."

"We figure the snow is three to five feet deep along the slope—deeper in some spots," said Gary. "Too deep to walk in without snowshoes—which we didn't bring. So, we get to practice more Scoutcraft, and make them."

We gathered long, green saplings, and thicker sticks for cross supports. A half hour later we were seated around the fire, bending the saplings back on themselves to form a loop. We lashed twine around the bases, and wove in crosspieces made of sticks. Then we beefed up the center sections with more sticks and twine as a boot hold and support. In a couple of hours we had built two pairs of snowshoes. Gary sat beside Hal for a minute to tell him the plan, and then the rest of us followed he and Patrick outside to see them off.

Mr. Holden talked with Gary and Patrick before they left. "Move fast, watch out for ice slides, and don't take any risks. Get to the cache, and gather only what you can carry in one trip. And lay out an arrow with rocks pointing up the hill this way. Let's make it easy for the folks from Sisters to find us."

"Sorry we couldn't get breakfast for you, boys," said Patrick as he stepped into his snowshoes. "But, I promise we'll have beans and bacon this afternoon."

He and Gary moved swiftly down the hill. We watched them for a few minutes before Mr. Holden turned us to our next tasks. He, Wade and Eddy moved out to construct the 'X' marker on the slopes to the east of the cliff. If the weather stayed clear, the sign could be seen from miles away.

Perry and I returned to the cave to check on Hal and Toby. Toby's fever had raged on and off for two days now. He was shivering when I sat beside him.

"I want to go home, Martin. I want to get warm, and I want something to eat."

"We're about to take care of the food part, Toby. Gary and Patrick are headed down the mountain to the food stores that were packed in for us. Things will look better when you have a full belly."

"Yeah, but you'll still look the same, Forrestal," joked Hal. "What's it looking like outside?"

I told Hal everything I knew. "Wish I could help," he said. "It was dumb of me to get myself busted up like this."

"What happened out there? Holden hasn't told us."

Hal shifted in his sleeping bag. "Put another blanket under my head, would you?" he asked. "When I went off to look for Gary—what, has it been two days now? The blizzard made it impossible to see beyond your own nose, and I lost sight of the marker sticks we had placed earlier. I think I was wandering around in circles for the first couple of hours. At least, the rocks I kept banging into felt like the same ones over and over. I finally figured I'd be better off making a shelter and sitting it out, or I was going to freeze. So, I crawled up next to a boulder, and wrapped my blanket around myself, thinking I'd wait for a break in the storm.

But it was just too cold. I headed back out into it. I knew I couldn't be very far from this cliff. I went for where I thought it was, but the wind was hitting me so hard I couldn't tell if I was taking a step straight ahead or to the side. Then, just like that, I banged into Mr. Holden. Wham! Didn't even see him coming—we just walked into each other."

"Is that how you got hurt?"

"Oh, no. Not then. He gave me a big bear hug and told me we had to move fast. I knew what he meant. I was about done. Never been colder or more tired in my life."

"What'd he do?"

"He tied a rope around my waist, and the other end around his hand. Then he said, 'Hal, I'm getting you out of this jackpot, and I'm doing it right now. You hear?' And then he sorta half-pulled me into a fast walk and we headed into the storm."

"So, how did you both get busted up?"

"We walked for a few minutes, and we decided the rope wasn't working. He'd pull forward, I'd jerk back—it was kind of a mess. So he untied me, and told me to stay as close as I could. We ran into that same rock field we hit coming up the hill—remember that one? We had to climb over some beauts, I'll tell you. And that's where it happened. Mr. Holden had just gone over a four-footer, and I was right behind him. I made it to the top of the rock, and then I lost my footing. Ice, wind, I don't know."

Hal choked up. "I just lost it," he said. "I fell down and forward and crashed onto his back. He went down like a stone, and hit his head hard against a boulder. It's awful steep there. We started to tumble down the embankment, on the ice between the rocks. I remember banging against the first rock, and my leg twisting under me, and I heard the bone snap, and then I hit my head against another rock, and I was out."

I poured some warm soup into a tin cup and held it against Hal's lips.

"Next thing I know," said Hal, "I was under those blankets you guys set up outside the cave."

"That rock field is at least three hundred yards down the slope," I said. "And he carried you all the way up? With his dislocated shoulder? I don't see how he did it."

"He promised to get me out of there, Martin. It's pretty clear he keeps his word."

•••

54

GARY AND PATRICK RETURNED from their trip to the food cache about the same time that Mr. Holden and the 'X' team finished their work. Gary's news wasn't good; they'd found the wooden boxes with the food stores easily enough, but a black bear had beaten them to it.

"There wasn't much left," said Gary. "The bear tore the flour sack open, and scattered the dried beans and rice everywhere. We scooped a couple pounds of beans out of the snow. There was some canned beef and salmon, a tin of cocoa and some dried milk. But that's it. No bread or cheese or syrup."

"We'll make do," said Mr. Holden. "Beats the heck out of what we ate yesterday, that's for sure. Patrick, you're up to bat. You've still got to prepare one meal for the troop, remember? See what you can do—and make it snappy!"

"We laid out quite a sign on the southwest slope," said Mr. Holden. "That big fat 'X' can be seen all the way to the Rockies. Gary, did you lay out an arrow pointed uphill from the camp site?"

"Yep, we did. Patrick even carved the words 'cave ¼ mile' on one of the sticks," said Gary.

"Good job. Forrestal, how are your patients?"

"I'm okay," said Hal. "I'll walk out of this cave if I have to."

"Toby's about the same," I said. "Fever one minute, cold the next."

"The weather is holding steady," said Mr. Holden. "That means there will be a team coming up the mountain later today or tomorrow early. They'll probably have to make the trip from Sisters to the trailhead on horseback—the road will be snowed over. Our job is to stay as dry and warm as we can, and to keep Hal and Toby settled. As long as the sky is clear, we'll keep one of you on watch outside, say, one hour per watch."

With both teams back, it was time for Perry and I to head upslope to gather more firewood for the cooking of a proper meal. Soon, we were lined up with our mess plates. I'm not sure what a four-star restaurant would have called Patrick's concoction of boiled beans topped with canned beef and salmon, but nothing ever looked so good as that hot pile of mush. Even Toby was able to get a little down.

With the weather holding, and our stomachs full, we sat around the fire in much better spirits. To keep us busy, Mr. Holden reduced the outside sentry watch to thirty-minute intervals, and organized us into teams for a Scoutcraft competition. First, we did one-hand knot-tying, where two of us stood face to face, each holding a rope in our right hand, with our left hand in our pocket. On Mr. Holden's signal, we had to tie our ropes together using just one hand each. The slipknot was easy. So was tying the square knot. But complex knots like the sheet bend and timber hitch were just about impossible. It was the first time any of us had laughed in a couple days.

The morning dragged on, with no sign of the rescue team from Sisters. We knew that with good weather, it was only a matter of time before they arrived. We took our turns at sentry duty, and tended to Hal and Toby.

I was cleaning my mess kit as Eddy slid back into the cave after his watch. Mr. Holden and some of the others were packing up gear in preparation for our descent. Suddenly, a peal of thunder from outside the cave broke the calm. I froze. The thunder continued, and loud cracking noises began. The walls of the cave shook, and dust and rocks rained down from the cave ceiling. Mr. Holden raced over to Hal, and crouched over him to shield his body from the rock shower. Gary did the same for Toby, who had dug himself deep into his sleeping bag.

"Get over against the walls!" shouted Mr. Holden.

Wade and I raced to the cave wall and hugged against it as tightly as we could. Rocks tumbled down, and a few hit my back, but the worst of it missed me. I couldn't see Eddy or Patrick—and where was Perry? The thunder grew louder, the shaking intensified, and amidst the shouts and confusion I could barely make out Mr. Holden and Gary, but I knew they were getting smashed by the falling rocks. The horrifying realization that we were being buried alive rang out in my mind. I closed my eyes, and for the first time since the whole ordeal began, I prayed.

Then, as suddenly as it had begun, the roar disappeared. The last rocks fell to the floor. Heavy dust, moaning, and crying filled the air. Eddy and Patrick pulled themselves away from the opposite wall. All of us were covered with dirt. All of us were shaking.

Mr. Holden and Gary were kneeling beside Hal and Toby. Holden was bleeding from his forehead, and there was blood on Gary's head and neck. They had protected our injured, but at a price.

I tried to assess the damage. Across the cave, Mr. Holden was cradling Hal's head in his arms. I'm not sure he knew how badly he was bleeding. I went over to him. "Come on, Mr. Holden," I said. "You need to sit back so we can doctor you up. You, too, Gary."

He gently lowered Hal's head on the pillow, and slid back against a boulder.

"Thanks, Martin," he said. "What's the situation?"

"We're okay," chimed in Patrick and Eddy.

"Me too," said Wade.

"I'll make it," said Gary. He held a towel against the back of his head. "Doesn't really hurt, just a little blood."

Patrick opened the first aid bag, and handed Mr. Holden a gauze patch to staunch the flow of blood from his forehead.

"We all accounted for?" asked the Scoutmaster.

"Everybody's here," said Wade. "Except Perry—he's outside on watch."

Mr. Holden dropped the gauze pad and ran to the cave entrance. He got down on his hands and knees, and then turned to us. "I can't get out—there's snow blocking the way. Somebody grab me a trenching shovel."

Patrick took him a shovel, while I grabbed a bandage roll. "We need to wrap you up first, Mr. Holden—you won't be able to see."

"Alright," he said. "Patrick, you lay down and see how far you can stick the shovel out into the snow."

Patrick began working, and I bandaged Mr. Holden's head.

"Mr. Holden," called Hal from across the cave. "Was that an avalanche?"

"I expect it was. There's no way to tell how much snow and ice just fell off this mountain and on top of us."

"What about Perry?" I said.

"Let's hope he's trying to dig his way in right now," said Mr. Holden. "He had the advantage of seeing this thing start; he should have had time to get behind cover."

The last dust settled to the cave floor. Wade and Eddy fueled the fire, and Mr. Holden patched Gary's head wound. Patrick continued probing the snowfall at the entrance, trying to gauge how much we had to dig through to get outside.

"How's Toby?" asked Mr. Holden.

"His fever's back," I said. "Hotter than ever."

"Keep a cool cloth on his forehead, Martin. Hal, you okay?"

"I'm alright," Hal said. "Wouldn't mind a little more aspirin, though. I think my leg is swelling up."

Mr. Holden pulled back Hal's blanket. I could see his right leg through torn trousers. It was a deep black-purple, and double the size of his left leg from his hip to his knee. I winced. I couldn't imagine the pain he must be feeling.

I checked on Patrick. He had pulled twenty or thirty shovels full of snow into the cave, but the weight of the soft snow above kept pushing the opening closed each time he tried to expand it. He tossed the small shovel aside. "Not much point in this," he said.

We went over beside Mr. Holden and Hal, and sat on the ground. Holden gave Hal two aspirin, and bundled him back up.

"I can't get enough headway on that snow to get out the door," said Patrick.

"I sort of expected it would be like that," said Mr. Holden. "Judging from the sound and commotion in here, I'd guess that avalanche pretty much dumped the whole mountain on our doorstep."

Patrick slid over next to me. His dirt-crusted face made him look like an old man, and his hands were blistered from the ferocity with which he had been digging. "I don't know, Martin," he said in a hushed voice. "This is real bad."

Eddy and Wade joined us. Wade had been struck on the face by at least one rock, and a dark bruise was forming along his jaw. We sat, arms on our knees, watching the fire in silence.

Gary took the shovel from Patrick. "We keep digging," he said.

"What's the point?" asked Eddy. "We can't get through…there could be a hundred tons of snow on top of us."

"Then I guess I'd better get started," said Gary.

Mr. Holden called us together. Gary had swathed his forehead in bandages, but dark blood had already begun to seep through. I opened another large gauze pad and taped it to the old bandage, then wrapped more bandage around Mr. Holden's head.

"Let's get some things straight, boys," he said. "Eddy's right about one thing—we may not be able to dig our way out. At least not right now. But there is a big melt on outside, and that avalanche probably carried away the heaviest layer of snow. That, plus the July sun is going to take care of the rest pretty quick."

He ran his hand through his hair, something I'd seen my dad do when he was thinking carefully about what he was saying. "This isn't the end of the road, or the end of anything for any of us, and that includes you, O'Hagan."

Patrick nodded.

"Heck, son, we survived your cooking, which means you punched your First Class ticket. That's worth something. And as for this being a tight spot, well, it sure enough is, that's no lie. But so what if it is? Do any of you think this will be the last time in your life when you find yourself up against it? I promise you, this isn't the big one. You'll all—we'll all face that one in God's own time, but I'm here to tell you that this isn't *anybody's* time. You boys understand that?"

He tended the fire, and passed around a pail of water and a washcloth for us to wipe the dirt from our faces. I put another wet towel on Toby's forehead, and got some water for Hal to sip. Gary handed off the shovel to Eddy, and joined us by the fire.

"We have been knocked for a loop, no doubt about it," Mr. Holden said. "But we've been knocked down, not out. Big difference. If you're knocked down you can still look up, and by gosh, if you can look up you can get up, and if you can get up you can get something done. You have a choice to make, each one of you. You can huddle up and cry. You can complain and look for someone to blame for everything that's been dropped on our plates these past few days. Or you can buck up, and contribute everything you've got to help get us out of this cave and back down this mountain. I can't make that choice for you."

"I'm worried about Perry," I said.

"Yeah, well, we should all be worried about that little shaver," said Mr. Holden. "But, to tell you the truth, my guess is that he's out there perched on a tall rock, worried about us."

"So we dig?" asked Wade.

"We dig," said Mr. Holden. "And we take care of Hal and Toby and we clean up this mess, and we sort and pack our gear, because we're getting out of here soon. Anybody need an assignment?"

We shook our heads and prepared to get to work. "One more thing, boys," said Mr. Holden. "You know, for the first half of your life it seems like people are always telling you what you should do. And for the second half, they tell you what you should have done. The best way to live, as far as I can tell, is to decide for yourself, and then do it. Don't worry about what anybody else says. Make up your own mind, and do right. Everything else will fall into place."

Patrick shot me a grin, and the troop got to work.

•••

SEVERAL HOURS LATER, Eddy shouted from his station at the cave entrance. His shovel clattered to the rock floor as he ran to us.

"I hear people!" he shouted. "There's people outside."

Mr. Holden told Wade to stay with Hal and Toby. The rest of us ran up to the cave mouth. There was quite a puddle of water from the snowmelt, but as we lay down and scooted near the opening, none of us minded a bit.

"Can you hear 'em?" said Patrick.

"Quiet!" said Mr. Holden. "Don't anybody even breathe."

We strained to hear through the mountain of snow that covered our cave. At first, I thought I was hearing the wind, or maybe some far off birdsong. But then I made out spoken words, and shouts.

"They're here, right over here!" It was Perry's voice.

"That's Perry!" Eddy yelled. "That chowderhead made it through the avalanche!"

"Forrestal," said Mr. Holden. "Grab me the longest pole you can find."

I rummaged through the woodpile and found a branch about eight feet long. I slid it to Mr. Holden, and he started to shove it out through the snow-covered opening. When he couldn't push it any farther with his good arm, he swung around and pushed against it with his boot. In a minute the branch disappeared into the snow. Mr. Holden scooted back and sat on his knees. I held my breath.

Then, just like that, the branch was pushed back into the cave from the outside.

I shouted. We all shouted. Patrick slapped me hard on the back.

"Let's all move back so they can get in," said Mr. Holden.

We moved back far enough to stand up. A minute later the snow at the mouth of the cave began to move, and a hand poked through. A man on his hands and knees wiggled through the opening, and stood up right in front of us.

I was too happy—too astonished—to talk. No one else could, either. We just stood there in the pale firelight for a few seconds, soaking it all in. We were rescued!

The man—a huge fellow in a green mackinaw jacket—stuck his hand out to Mr. Holden. "Deputy Sheriff Garcia," he said. "I'm glad to finally make your acquaintance."

Mr. Holden shook the deputy's hand. His mouth was pursed, and his eyes were shining, but he didn't say a word. For the first time in days, our Scout leader was speechless.

•••

THE CAVE FILLED UP in short order. Two more deputies, Scout leaders from all over Central Oregon, and, best news of all, Doc Wilson from Sisters, all poured in. Flashlights lit up the cave, blankets were distributed, and the wet, moldy smell gave way to the aroma of fresh coffee and sandwiches.

Then, in crawled Perry. We swarmed around him, slapping his back, and yanking his cap down over his eyes.

"What happened out there?" asked Gary.

"Well, I saw it coming, that's for sure," said Perry. "This mountain started to shake and rumble before the snow cut loose. I climbed about fifteen feet up one of those rock pillars, and squashed myself into a niche in the stone. The snow slammed into the rocks like a freighter hitting a lighthouse, but in a minute it was all over, and I just climbed down. I couldn't get back into the cave, so I figured I'd better head down the mountain. An hour later, I met these folks on their way up."

Deputy Garcia and Mr. Holden assembled everybody a few minutes later. The doctor and his assistant gave Hal a shot of morphine for pain, and reset the splint we had placed on his fractured leg. They put Hal and Toby on stretchers and carried them to the cave entrance as Garcia detailed the evacuation plan.

Before we moved out, I took one last look around the cave that had saved our lives, and then crawled out behind Patrick. So much snow had been dumped by the avalanche that we had to climb up a forty-five-degree snow tunnel.

An unfamiliar landscape greeted me. Snow was piled above boulders and trees, and most of the landmarks I had grown accustomed to in the past few days had vanished.

The deputies were already headed down the slope with Hal and Toby. The doctor stayed behind to check on the last of us—including me—in better light. In the excitement since the avalanche I hadn't paid much attention to the fact that my cheek had swollen up again. I couldn't see out of one eye. "We're going to have to drain this down at base camp," said

Doctor Wilson.

I sighed. "Yeah, I sort of expected that."

"You're going to sport a handsome scar," he said, "but, other than that, you're going to be just fine." He moved on to check Wade's frostbite and Gary's head injuries.

I leaned against a rock and took in the scene. The air was still, the temperature was rising, fog shrouded the higher elevations of the mountain, and a scattering of clouds slipped high above in the bright blue sky. Miles down the mountain I could make out a road, and the alfalfa hay and peppermint farms we had passed on the way to the trailhead—how long ago? Just a week? Miles down and a lifetime ago, it seemed.

Mr. Holden and Deputy Garcia were the last to climb out of the cave. Holden hadn't shaved or washed in days, his clothes were rumpled and grimy, and the bandage wrapped around his head was stained with blood and dust. His bad arm was still supported by Patrick's makeshift sling. There were deep circles under his eyes—he hadn't slept since we arrived at the cave. He gave me a nod, and then joined the rescue team.

One by one, my friends began the trek to safety. Wade and a Scout leader from Metolius headed out first, followed by Eddy and Doc Wilson. As Gary walked past he said, "We'll do this again next year, Forrestal. Count on it."

Mr. Holden and I were the last to go. I knew that it was a tradition in the military for the leader to be the first one to step onto the battlefield, and the last one to leave. My Scoutmaster was a man bound by such traditions. Even at fourteen, I recognized that it was only by virtue of his leadership and unrelenting determination that we were walking down that mountain instead of being buried under it.

I watched my friends wind their way down the trail through knee-high snow. A minute later the last Scout rounded an icy cornice, and disappeared. I looked back at the massive granite cliff that had sheltered us, then at Mr. Holden. He slung his rucksack over his good shoulder, and smiled at me.

"Let's go home, Martin."

HONESTY

THE OVERSIZED DISPLAY on the nightstand clock shone a bright 2:38 AM. I had been awake for hours since completing the narrative of my Scouting adventure. I switched on the lamp, and picked up the battered legal pad with my original notes for the project. I looked at the list of fifteen values, and for the first time I saw each of them as an independent volume in an encyclopedia of one man's life. Why does it matter that my recollections and observations, my fears and hopes and secrets and triumphs and regrets live on?

I examined my face in the bedside mirror. I stared deep into my own eyes. At eighty-two, with advanced prostate cancer spreading to every cell in my body, the end of my life was a forgone conclusion. I had undertaken this project not to deny the inevitable, but to imbue that inevitability with a meaning that would, I hoped, transcend the mere physical boundaries of my life.

I understood that for some of my family and friends my values project was just "Martin's way of dealing with it all." I hoped it would amount to something else altogether. Something meaningful. Something lasting. And, if I could pull it off, something of value, the same way that the work of an artist increases in value when he dies. That was the theory, at least.

What had kept me up tonight was a conversation I had yesterday with my six-year-old granddaughter, Gwen. She had ignored my son and daughter-in-law's instructions to sit quietly on a chair beside my bed while they went for coffee, and instead hopped up with me. She squeezed through the tubes and wires connecting me to monitors and IVs, and settled in nice and comfy.

"Do you like my dress?" she asked. "It's the brightest colors I have. Everybody says bright colors make you feel better."

"Honey, you're prettier than a bag of striped candy," I said. "And those colors make me feel better just by being next to them."

"I hope so, Grampa, because Mommy and Daddy said you had something wrong with you that nothing could make better, and Momma said that you have to go to heaven real soon. I told them to not believe that. I don't believe it. Is it okay with you if I don't believe that you won't get better, Grampa, and you won't ever go away?"

I held her tight. Just then, my son Eric and his wife Rachel appeared in the door. I could see my son was agitated at Gwen for having disobeyed parental instructions. I gave him my best "back off" glare, something I don't think I've had the occasion to use in many years. It still works. They stood silently while Gwen and I finished our conversation.

I brushed her hair back. "Gwen, in our family we believe that no one ever really goes away. We believe that our souls go to heaven, and that someday, all of us will be together forever and ever. But honey, the body I live in is tired, it's worn out, and it needs to rest. Mom and Dad told you the truth."

"You mean you have to go away like Peterborough did?"

"Well, I don't know that it's the same for Grampa as for your pet rabbit, but, yes, all pets must die someday, Gwen. So do all flowers, and so do I."

"Because God says so?"

"Because it is part of the plan He has for all of us."

"Grampa, I don't think I like that plan. You could get a new plan, couldn't you?"

I chuckled. "I'm just fine with the plan I have, young lady."

"Honest to gosh?" she asked.

"Scout's honor, honey."

"Okay, Grampa. You can keep your plan then."

Rachel leaned against the doorframe. Her eyes were moist. Eric stirred his coffee, and stared at the floor.

"Time for you to be getting along home now," I said.

She planted her best smooch on my cheek, hugged me hard as she could, and clambered down off the hospital bed. And there she waited, her hands grasping the aluminum side railing. Her brow wrinkled, and her mouth pulled into a little half-frown. I'd seen that look before when she wasn't happy with how the bedtime story I was reading turned out. Gwen was a natural literary critic.

"Yes?" I said. "Something on your mind?"

"Grampa, are you afraid to die?"

That's a brave question—no adult, not even my wife, had broached the subject with me—and also a natural one for a six-year-old to ask. It took me a moment to respond.

"No honey, I'm not afraid to die."

"But why not? Isn't it scary?"

"I'm not afraid to die, Gwen, because I wasn't afraid to be born. Does that make sense?"

With maturity and timing that only an innocent commands, my granddaughter closed the conversation. "Oh, Grampa, you are so silly. Of course you weren't afraid to be born, you weren't even here yet!"

I got the laugh I wanted, and another kiss, to boot. She happily gathered her things. Eric and Rachel said their goodbyes and then stepped out into the hall to talk with Connie. As they left, I reclined my bed, and pushed the button for the nurse. The pain in my back was sharpening. I needed more of the pain medication I was trying hard to avoid.

A few minutes later I heard the sound of feet coming down the corridor. Gwen—not my nurse—popped around the door. She ran to my side and handed me a piece of folded paper.

"I made you this, silly Grampa," she giggled.

I unfolded the paper and glanced at the sketch.

"You made this just now?"

"Yep. While Mom and Dad were talking with Grandma."

She blew me a kiss with both hands, and turned to go.

I shook my head and smiled. I could picture her sitting on the ground in the hall in her bright little dress scribbling furiously with a crayon. Pretty focused work for a six-year-old. I watched as Gwen scooted out the door to catch up to her parents. She'll get a scolding for this, I thought. And I don't think she'll care at all.

The paper contained a sketch of a little stick-figure girl—labeled 'Gwen'—standing next to two headstones. One headstone was inscribed 'Peterborough.' The other said 'Grampa.' The little girl was smiling, and pointing up to the sky where two birds soared upward to the sun.

I've heard many definitions of honesty in my time. But I'd never thought about honesty in its purest, most innocent form. Not until this.

•••

"YOU ARE STILL AWAKE?"

Leticia San Remo, the brightest smile to ever grace the nursing profession, leaned over my bed.

"Isn't it enough that your chart notes say that you talk to yourself all day long? You must rest, or give up your day job!" She checked my temp, and adjusted the IV flow rate. "And why is my favorite patient up at 2:45 in the morning? Something on our delicious menu not agreeing with your digestion?"

"I wouldn't mind if the dietician added some food from your homeland to the menu around here, Leticia. Then I'd probably sleep like a baby."

"Sleep? After Filipino food? Mr. Forrestal, you haven't been watching the Food Network. Our food is spicy and strong, like our people. You eat it to dance, to sing, to make love. But never to sleep!"

"I know your food. And I love it."

"You have been to the Philippines?"

"To Manila. Right after World War II."

She put another pillow behind my head, and checked my pulse.

"And you didn't marry a Filipino girl? What, were you blind?"

"Plenty of folks would say I am. But in the marriage department, I think I did just fine."

"So, what keeps you awake at this hour? Is your pain returning?"

"It's not the pain, Leticia. It's this." I pointed to my notepad and digital recorder.

"Yes, the other nurses talk about your project. When I work a day shift, you will have to tell me about it. Right now—you must sleep."

I planned to talk with my friend and attorney Tarrell the next day about the value of honesty. I wanted to go beyond the simple "honesty is the best policy" idea, and consider the way that honesty plays out in real people's lives—mine included. I had seen innocent honesty in action today as my granddaughter grappled with the reality of my impending death. There were still conversations I needed to have with Connie about that subject. Those talks would call for the intimate honesty between a husband and wife that takes a lifetime to build.

Looming over all my plans, of course, was the calendar. For each of the values I was summing up through the stories of my own life, I also hoped to be able to talk with anyone and everyone who would give me a little of their time. That included the nurses and technicians who were with me every hour of the day and night. Right now, that was Leticia.

"May I ask you something?" I said.

Nurse San Remo leaned against the handrail. "It is slow tonight. Too many healthy people out there. One question, then you rest."

She pulled a chair close to my bed. "I have never been interviewed by a writer," she said.

"And you will still have that distinction after tonight, I'm afraid. I'm not a writer. I'm a lumberman, have been all my life. Only now—"

The nurse smiled. "Now you think it is a good time for a career change?"

"Something like that. Let me tell you what I'm doing."

I gave her a quick overview of my project, and read the list of values aloud.

"And where are you now?" she asked.

"I'm talking about the value of honesty," I said. "Interested?"

"Mr. Forrestal, I have been married twice, and divorced twice. Honesty—or the lack of it—is a subject on which I am pretty much the world champ."

"So how about I agree not to ask you about that particular subject—men, I mean."

"You may ask about anything. If it's about men, just make sure I'm not holding anything sharp in my hands at the moment."

"It's a deal." I took a deep breath. "Leticia, you know that I am going to die soon."

Her smile evaporated, replaced by a professional mask.

"Is this part of your study of honesty?"

"In a way."

She shifted in her chair, and flipped my chart cover open.

"I know your condition, Mr. Forrestal. And I know the usual prognosis in a case like this."

I didn't speak. I just looked at her.

Finally she said, "Yes, I know you are dying."

"Please, don't misunderstand—I don't mean to seem disrespectful. You are a real professional, and I appreciate your skills. I also value your character, and the honesty you have shown me since I arrived."

Her smile came back. "I am not offended. But I always think of myself as being in the life business, not the death business. Most patients in your condi—at your stage, don't want to talk about death."

"They're afraid?" I asked.

"They are many things: scared, in denial, angry, desperate."

"Maybe *you* should write a book," I said.

She stood up. "I'm sure I should. Now go to sleep."

•••

I SLEPT BETTER than I had in days. When I woke, sunlight was streaming into my room. My IV line had gotten tangled in my pajamas during the night, and as I started to sort it out, I realized that Connie had arrived early. She was listening to my digital recorder through earphones, her eyes half closed. Gwen's drawing was open on her lap.

I cleared my throat. Her eyes opened. "Good morning yourself," she said.

"What's it like at home today?" I asked.

"The rhoddies are in full bloom, and the hydrangeas are starting to pop. Eric is coming over this afternoon to fertilize the lawn—and to haul off a branch that fell from the big cedar the other day."

"Have you ordered your onion sets?"

"It's still a little early for onions, my dear. I don't even have the garden tilled yet. I don't know—"

"You don't know what—if you're going to do a garden this year?"

Connie blinked several times, and held a tissue to one eye. "I have never, in my life, done a garden without you, Martin. I don't think I want to."

"And if Gram doesn't do a garden, who will teach Gwen and Jimmy to do theirs? Eric and Rachel don't garden. The kids are old enough to help plant and weed. Remember last summer when Gwen put that huge ear of fresh corn on her plate, and insisted on eating it all because she had planted

68

it, and watered it and picked it and shucked it and helped you to cook it?"

"She was a sight, that's for sure," said Connie. "All that butter on her face. And wearing your big straw hat."

"Did you look at her drawing?"

Connie held up the sketch. "I did. And I was just listening to your description of it on the recorder."

"I'm going to have to quit recording, aren't I, or we won't have anything to talk about."

Connie picked up the tiny device. "Why didn't I discover these things years ago?" she said. "I could have saved a lot of energy, and just left you a message now and then."

A lab tech came in to draw blood, and a moment later my breakfast was delivered. Connie drew her chair closer to my bed to make sure I ate.

"Connie. About Gwen's drawing," I said. "What do you think she was saying?"

"That life goes on," my wife said. "Forever. Oh, and maybe that Grampa is just as important to her as her rabbit was."

"I'll take the compliment," I said. "But life *does* go on, Connie. And there's no better way for a child to learn that than by standing in good soil in a proper garden and getting their hands dirty planting seeds and starts. When they tend to their own crops, and fight off the bugs, and when the plants bud, and they get to see the strawberries ripen red and plump and juicy, and the pumpkins flower and grow bigger and bigger, and when they go out before dinner and pick the lettuce and munch a snow pea right on the spot, and rinse the dirt off the summer squash, Connie, that's miraculous stuff."

Connie brushed her hand across my face. "Martin, you lied to me when you asked me to marry you."

"Really?"

"You told me you were in the lumber business. You should have told me that you were a poet who happened to sell wood."

I kissed her hand. "But it's true, honey. When the days cool and grow shorter, and the kids harvest that last fall tomato, and the plants begin to wither and die, and they pull out the dead plants to prepare for the new ones when spring returns, then they've seen the whole magical cycle of life, haven't they, just the way it has been since time began. We don't have to make up stories about what's happening to me—or why."

I had to pause to catch my breath for a moment before I could continue. "The best way—the most honest way—to teach Gwen and Jimmy about life and death is for you to take them out into the garden and let them work the earth. Let them plant, and let them watch the miracle happen right in front of their eyes. And next fall? When that last sweet salad has been harvested, and the garden is all brown and dull and the song birds have moved on to better pickings, tell them it's the same way with humans, and the lives we live. We have seasons, too, just like those plants, and we grow and blossom and produce a bounty of our own, until our fall comes, and our winter sets in. That's the truth of it, Connie. It's not complicated. It's honest."

A nurse stepped into the room, sponge bath gear in hand. "Am I interrupting?" she asked.

Connie moved away from my bed. "Oh, I think Johnnie Appleseed is about done for the moment," she said. "Aren't you, dear?"

•••

BATHED, SHAVED, COMBED AND FED, I began my fourth full day in the hospital. Connie gathered her things and headed down to the quiet solarium to make phone calls. When I gave her the final list of people who I hoped would come to see me over the next two weeks, she was surprised at some of the names, especially that of my former business partner, who I had not spoken to for over thirty years.

Each name on that list was more than a person; they were either the physical embodiment of one of the values on my list, or the inspiration for my own self-discovery of a particular value I hold dear. I could dictate the stories of those long gone, like that of Nate Holden. But when possible, I wanted to be able to talk to—and thank in person—the people from whom I have learned the most important lessons in life. At age 82, of course, the list of people who were still around was getting shorter.

Nurse Marsden came into the room for morning inspection. "Good morning, Martin. What does your day hold in store?"

"I'm meeting with my attorney, if that's any indicator. And my wife is going to wheel me out of here for a walk in the park across the street. All in all, not a bad schedule."

She applied some topical cream around the IV needle on my forearm, and re-taped it tightly.

"You asked yesterday if we could move your bed so that you could see out the window. I spoke with maintenance, and they'll have someone come in this afternoon while you're down in therapy. Sound good?"

"No, it sounds wonderful. Thank you."

She put a fresh glass of water on the nightstand. "Enjoy the view."

•••

My attorney arrived an hour later, accompanied by his guide dog and by his paralegal assistant. Tarrell Knowles had been blind since birth, a disability that more than a few opposing attorneys in civil litigation had learned the hard way should not be mistaken for weakness. Tarrell was a ferocious courtroom lawyer whose love of the law was matched only by his zeal for winning.

"Do we need Andrew?" asked Tarrell as his assistant settled him into a chair by my bed.

"No, not for this," I said. "Andrew, thanks for coming down."

"Sure thing, Mr. Forrestal. I'll grab a hot chocolate and be downstairs if you guys need me."

Tarrell sat quietly for a moment, fiddling with the hem of his jacket.

"Not like you to be at a loss for words, Tarrell," I said.

"Well Martin, this isn't exactly my favorite kind of visit. Give me a minute to warm up to it, will you?"

"Tarrell, do you remember that fishing trip we took back in the mid-seventies, when we went out on the rock jetty at Newport?"

"Yeah, I'm afraid so."

"When I baited your line and you cast out along the rocks, you got an immediate hit."

"The wolf eel?"

"Yep. I recall you were convinced that you had a big rock cod on your hook, and you wouldn't believe me when I told you to loosen your drag so I could cut the line before that six-foot monster landed in our laps."

"I thought you were making it up. Didn't I make you describe it to me before I would agree to let go the line?"

"You did. Just like a doggone attorney. You thought I was kidding you."

"Actually, I thought the beer was talking," Tarrell said. "When you said

I had a six-foot eel with a head the size of a volleyball that looked like Frankenstein on my line, what was I supposed to think?"

"Just the same, you pulled that darned thing out of the water and flopped it right up on the rock next to your boot, which it chomped, of course."

"At which point I became a believer—he bit clean through into my toes. I never knew a creature could have a bottom set of teeth, a top set, and a third set on the roof of its mouth."

"Funniest part for me," I said, "was chopping his body from his head with my hatchet, only to have that head stay clamped onto your boot. We had to lay you down and wriggle that boot off your foot, and the eel still wouldn't let go! I had to hold my lighter against his head until he let loose, didn't I? What a story."

"To this day, my wife doesn't buy it," said Tarrell. "Even with the razor-teeth marks on the boot, she didn't believe it. Can't say I blame her."

A pain stabbed deep in my abdomen, and I sucked my breath in.

"You okay?" asked Tarrell.

"Just give me a minute." I pushed the button to raise the bed a little higher.

"Martin, if this is a bad time…"

I laughed. "I'm afraid bad time is about the only time I have left, old friend," I said.

"Alright, Martin, but if this gets to be too much, just let me know." He sat back in his chair. "Now, other than reliving old fishing tales, what did you have on your mind?"

"First, I want to make sure that the trust revisions and the college fund plan for my grandkids are all complete and in place."

"Been done for months, Martin."

"And everything for Connie, she won't have to go through too much legal paperwork after I'm gone?"

"It will be seamless, Martin—everything is in place. You don't need to worry. We've got it all covered."

"Good. Tarrell, I think Connie has told you about my values project."

"A little. You're doing a recording for your family, aren't you?"

"Something like that. I decided—or rather, I came to the conclusion—that this old man had one last job to do, one last measure of value to share. It's partly why I asked you here today. These values I'm writing about—or recording, really—mean more to me than anything else I'm leaving to my family. I'm wrapping stories from my life around each value, and I'm talking to people like yourself who have been an example to me of a particular value in action."

Tarrell leaned forward. "I'm on your list? Is it okay for me to ask what value it is that you ascribe to an old blind curmudgeon at law?"

"I wish you could see me smiling, my friend. I can't tell you how pleased I am to be able to tell you this directly. Tarrell, you have been, these past thirty years and more, my friend and my advisor. In both capacities you have been absolutely, scrupulously, sometimes even irritatingly honest. You have always told me what I needed to hear—not what I wanted to hear— about my business and myself. I have relied on your honesty more than you know. It has guided me, inspired me, kept me accountable to my family and myself, and just plain helped to make my life better—cleaner, easier, more comfortable. Your honesty has been a great gift to me, Tarrell, a great gift."

He shook his head, and laughed. "Martin, you teach me something new every time we meet. And only you would have the gumption to use the words 'attorney' and 'honest' in the same sentence."

A technician came in to change out a line on the panel behind my bed, and Tarrell and I sat in silence while he did his work. When he left, Tarrell had more questions about my project.

"You're sure you are up to this?" he asked.

"I may be short on time, Tarrell, but I'm still long on ideas. Look, I'm not leaving a huge estate, nobody's going to quit work and live a life of leisure with what they'll be getting when my money is disbursed, or even when Connie goes. Maybe I could have been a rich man if that had been my goal, but it wasn't, and I'm not."

Tarrell squeezed his eyelids tightly, something I knew he did when he was weighing his words carefully. "I have a different definition of wealth than you do," he said. "It has nothing to do with money, and everything to do with value. You have touched so many people in your life, and set so many positive ripples in motion. Those ripples move out and touch other things. Generations from now people will still be benefiting from your passage through this world. That's wealth, pal. Not the stuff. Not the money."

"When the train gets near the end of the track," I said, "a man spends a lot of time thinking about what might have been. My grandfather used to say that you are not old until your regrets take the place of your dreams.

Never really understood that until the day the doctor gave me the news."

"Taking self-honesty to new heights, are you Martin?" said Tarrell.

"More than you know. And today I've been talking to everybody I can get my hands on about the subject."

"And what's the consensus been? Is it still a good idea, being honest, I mean?"

I took a sip of ice water and poured a glass for Tarrell. "At the end of the day, honesty is everything," I said. "When you come right down to it, it's really the only thing that defines who we are."

The sound of traffic outside my window ceased, and for a moment, it was quiet.

"You know, Martin, plenty of people, and not just lawyers, would argue that there is no such a thing as knowable, objective truth. Past events are what we make of them now."

"I don't know that I can go along with that idea, Tarrell. Sounds like a way to rationalize bad behavior, or to justify rewriting history. A thing is honest or it is not. If we gave up on that concept, I think our society would just plain collapse."

Tarrell smiled.

"The good news," I said, "is that there will always be people like you out there to make sure that doesn't happen."

"Don't get me wrong, Martin. Being honest is good business for a lawyer. We don't win cases with lies—no matter what some folks think. I can't tell you what it is that glues our system together and keeps it working, but the fact is, it does, warts and all."

We spent a few minutes catching up on family news, and then Tarrell's assistant arrived to take him to his next appointment. As he stood to go, Tarrell leaned over my bed and took hold of my hand.

"I have another answer to your question about honesty, Martin. At the end of the day, I believe that honesty is the thread that connects man directly to God. When you are honest, it is the only time that you and God can see each other clearly."

He took his guide dog's leash. "I will miss you, my friend. I will never go fishing again, or hoist a great glass of wine, or engage in spirited debate with anyone, without thinking of you. I knew when I first met you that inside that timber man's body lurked the soul of a poet and scholar."

Tears welled in my eyes. "Thank you Tarrell, for all you've done, for all you've been, to me and my family. Thank you for looking after Constance, too."

"She will want for nothing, Martin. Now, rest."

And then I was alone. For a moment I couldn't even hear the usual noises from the hospital corridor. There was only the sound of the IV pump, and my own sniffling.

I reached for the recorder. I wanted to get all of my thoughts about honesty and the conversations of the past day down while they were fresh in my mind. But a wave of exhaustion poured over me, and I felt myself drifting toward sleep. A face hovered above me as I nodded off, but I'm not sure if it was Connie, or a nurse, or an angel.

HONOR

NURSE MARSDEN WAS TRUE to her word. When I returned from therapy yesterday, my bed and all of its assorted equipment had been turned toward the windows. I woke this morning to the sight of a giant blue heron swooping over masses of white cherry blossoms on the state capitol mall. The mirror on the wall next to the washbasin still afforded me a view of the hallway and anyone stepping into my room. It was just right.

I sorted through my notes, and found the paragraphs I had written earlier about the next value on my list—honor. I was glad to address this value, mostly because it would give me the opportunity to talk about the most honorable man I ever knew—my father.

I know that each succeeding generation of old venerables like me tends to find fault with their children for turning their backs upon many of the values, principles, traditions and behavioral codes by which their parents and grandparents lived. Some of that concern was overblown, to be sure. And yet, the amateur historian in me also knew that social change had occurred at a snail's pace prior to the Industrial Revolution. A peasant in fourteenth century England lived pretty much the way his ancestors had lived three centuries earlier. They farmed with the same implements, lived in the same kinds of houses, ate the same food, died of the same diseases and adhered to the same ideals, superstitions and values, generation after generation.

I didn't believe that the fundamental nature of the individual had changed since the Middle Ages—or since cave man days, for that matter. We are the products of our biology and our surroundings every bit as much as the stone masons who built the pyramids four thousand years ago. Our humanity is our humanity, as it has always been. What is different, earth shaking in fact, is a phenomena that has bubbled up from nothing to become the defining characteristic of all human life—literally during my lifetime. The game changer now is the *pace* of change. Changes in the characteristic customs and conventions of societies that once took centuries to seep into the general culture now take place in a few short decades. Advances in technology have changed our world with blistering speed. We are experiencing exponential technological leaps—each advancement taking us higher and further—faster and faster. And while I have no doubt that most of that progress is for the good, the truth is that if you strip away the trappings of modern life, take away our forced-air heating and air conditioning, turn off our computers, close the futuristic airports and hospitals, and pull us out of our luxurious automobiles, we are more like that fourteenth century peasant than we might want to admit. At least we are as far as the drive to fulfill our basic needs for food and shelter, and our common desire to be in relationships with one another and with our Creator.

This is partially why I have felt like my generation was right for lamenting the steady erosion of some of the core values that had inspired and sustained people since the dawn of civilization.

The value of honor is a case in point. Honor was, for millennia, one of the foundational values of virtually every culture on earth. Humankind's earliest epic poems, sagas far older than Homer's *Iliad* and *Odyssey*, celebrated heroes for whom the true test of honor was how much they would risk to keep their honor intact. One of my boyhood heroes was Achilles, the Greek warrior who fought upon the dusty plains of Troy in accordance with a code of honor that was eons old by the time he was taught its meaning. That code, which required absolute integrity of belief and action, was little changed three thousand years later when I sat in the balcony at the Elsinore Theatre to watch Roy Rogers fight against the rustlers and stagecoach robbers—who usually outnumbered him by at least five to one. The bronze sword may have been replaced by a six-shooter, but the hero answered the call of honor with the same sense of duty.

I was steeped in stories of honor when I was a boy. I read and reread the tales of King Arthur and the Knights of the Round Table until the only thing holding that book together was tape and glue. Patrick and I regularly acted out the eleventh century legend of Roland and Oliver, the knights who gladly sacrificed their lives to warn Charlemagne's army of a sneak attack by the Saracens. We'd toss a coin to see who got to be Roland, because at the close of the story, just as the villainous Saracen army was about to pounce upon the unsuspecting Charlemagne, the young knight blows three warning calls on his ivory tusk horn with such force that his lungs burst. Roland and Oliver die dramatically—and in our recreation, loudly, since we used to borrow my dad's beaten up old trumpet for the grand finale—all in the name of honor.

I fear the value of honor might be headed for societal extinction. I know that it is alive and well in the military, and among the few real cowboys who still ride the open range. But I don't see it taught in school, or celebrated in songs and stories. In fact, the opposite seems to be true; the outward manifestation of honorable behavior is often ridiculed in the media and by the mainstream culture at large as being hopelessly out of touch with contemporary norms. As for honor in politics or business, I'd say that the term "endangered species" fits those categories pretty well. Would anyone argue today that the value of honor is a significant component in the education of young people? In my opinion, that's not just an oversight; it is a tragedy.

It is the duty of the old duffers like myself for whom honor is a core value to tell our stories, to describe how we learned about honor, what it meant in our own lives, and why we think that every boy and girl should hear the classic stories at their parents' knee.

•••

MY FATHER, CHET FORRESTAL, was a plainspoken man. He was tall and solid, with unruly brown hair that defied all tidying efforts. He loved his God, his wife and boys, his country, and his lumber business, pretty much in that order. He went out of his way to find the good in people, but he did not wear rose-colored glasses.

My father was a carpenter's mate on the battleship USS Delaware during the first World War. His most harrowing memory of his service had nothing to do with battle, though. A duty ensign caught a seaman in the act of stealing another sailor's wallet from a locker one morning. The ship's captain convened a hearing at noon, found the seaman guilty as charged, and ordered that he be hanged from a mast on the quarterdeck before sunset. My father and most of the crew were ordered to assemble on deck for the execution. The captain spoke briefly. A thief would not be tolerated onboard a ship at war, he said. In battle, men must be able to trust one another completely. With that, the command was given, and the thief was summarily hung. It was the only death my father witnessed during the war.

I began doing small jobs at the lumberyard when I was eight. Mostly I would run messages from the sawyers or the yard boss across the u-shaped lumberyard, up the outside stairs and into my father's office. The office was long and narrow, with a bank of windows looking down upon the operation. From my father's vantage point you could see the entire process of turning a freshly cut tree into dimension lumber. Log trucks arrived daily, and each de-limbed tree was swung by a loader into the spindle-shaped log peeler. The peeler neatly spun and sliced the skin off of the tree, spitting a shower of sticky bark into great piles destined for the plywood mill or the furnace. Then, Tommy the grader evaluated each bare tree and marked it for one of several stacks that were destined for the saws. Once cut into dimension lumber, the boards were air-dried, then either moved into the retail sales yard or loaded onto flatbeds for delivery to construction sites.

When I was thirteen, my father began teaching me the business side of the lumberyard. Half of my work time was spent down in the yard helping with equipment or chasing parts for the mechanic, half was spent up in the office learning about accounting, purchasing, sales, inventory management—everything it took to run a business efficiently.

To my mind, if it was downstairs, it was fun. Upstairs—well, let's just say I enjoyed watching the sixty-inch headsaw slicing into huge trees a heck of a lot more than I enjoyed adding columns of numbers.

One Saturday in October when I was in the seventh grade, I was up in my dad's office sorting through a stack of invoices. I was turning to the file cabinet to put each invoice into the matching customer folder when the fire bell in the yard began to clang.

My dad grabbed his firefighter's turnout coat from the rack beside the door. He raced out, then turned and stuck his head back in the office. "You want to come along on this one, Marty?" he asked.

Oh, boy, did I! I grabbed my jacket from a peg and raced down the stairs behind him. He was the assistant chief of the Salem volunteer fire brigade, which merited a shiny red pickup in a special parking bay in the yard. One of my chores was to start that truck every day, and make sure it was clean, fueled up and ready to go. Dad often drove it to and from the lumberyard. Salem had a unique firefighting set-up; the full-time professional firefighters were responsible only for fires that broke out in the downtown commercial district, where new fire hydrants had been installed only the year before. Fires that broke out beyond the downtown zone were the responsibility of the all-volunteer force.

By the time we hit the bottom of the stairs, Joe Cleary, the chief sawyer, had gotten the call in his shack telling us the location of the fire. Joe passed me a slip of paper as my dad and I jumped into the pickup.

"Where to?" called my dad as he fired up the engine and flipped on the siren.

Before I could finish saying "corner of Center and Cottage," he slipped the truck into gear and we tore out of the yard and onto the street.

"Center and Cottage," repeated my dad. I nodded. It was only a few blocks away. Traffic was light in the gathering twilight, and the air rushing in my open window clean and cold.

"Marty, when the other trucks arrive, you help out, but only when asked, you got that? I don't want you too close to the fire." My heart sunk. I was old enough and big enough to do a fireman's work. I knew how to lay hose, hook it to the pumper, and start the pump to get the water flowing. Before I could argue the point we hit a rut in the road, and my dad's helmet came loose from its hook behind our heads. I leaned back to grab it, only to hear my dad say, "Here we are—oh my God, the bank."

He veered left into the opposite lane, and swung the pickup against the curb directly in front of the burning building, which sat about fifty feet back from the sidewalk. As I hopped out of the truck, two more volunteer firefighting rigs roared up alongside us. The chief was not among them, so my dad began barking orders to the half-dozen men in turnout gear and helmets. A cop arrived, and began stopping traffic from both directions.

Gawkers materialized out of nowhere.

As the firefighters began laying out hose and listening to my dad's instructions for attacking the flames, I stepped back and surveyed the scene. The two-story Valley Farm and Merchants Bank building was the only building on a triple lot. That was the good news. The bad news is that it was three blocks from the nearest fire hydrant. We had only one pumper truck. If that wasn't enough water to douse the flames, my dad's job was simple: keep the fire from spreading to any other buildings.

Suddenly, there was an explosion. The second-story windows of the wood and stone building shattered as the growing inferno sought more oxygen to feed its insatiable appetite. People scattered in all directions, and the firemen lowered their heads so that their helmets would protect them from flying shards of glass. I ducked behind the open door of the pickup.

Orange and blue flames shot out of the upper windows, and licked up to the roof. Then a plate glass window on the first floor blew out, and I felt a blast of superheated air. More sirens heralded the arrival of two more police officers, and an ambulance.

The growing crowd of onlookers was corralled by the police on the other side of the street. I stayed with the pickup, and watched my dad direct the men holding the hoses. The firefighter's axes and picks lay unused on the street. No one had attempted to enter the building. The fire had done most of its damage before the first firefighters arrived. There was nothing worth risking life and limb for at this point.

More police arrived, along with more volunteer firefighters. Their job now was one of containment; the bank building was fully engulfed in flame, and the firemen encircling the building focused only on keeping the fire from spreading. It was completely dark now, and the figures of the firemen moving around the property were outlined in an ember-red glow.

I was replacing gear in the storage bin on the side of the ladder truck when I heard a thundering crash. I turned just in time to see the top floor of the bank fall in on itself in a shower of red and yellow sparks that leapt hundreds of feet into the sky. The collapse of the floor and walls also had the effect of dampening the flames on the first floor. The firemen concentrated their hoses near the ground, and in a few minutes the last of the flames were doused. The building would smolder for a day or more, and a couple of firefighters would remain around the clock to prevent flare-ups, but, for the most part, this fire was over.

The spectators melted away, and a cold wind blew down out of Santiam Canyon. I started to walk over to my father and the group of firefighters he was talking to on the sidewalk when I heard the sound of a car traveling at high speed come to a screeching halt.

A big Buick had spun around the corner and braked hard in front of our truck. The driver leapt out, and rushed over to the sidewalk. He was a short, stocky man in a thick overcoat and fedora hat. Ignoring the firefighters and the hoses that were still spraying water on the smoking rubble, the man raced up to within a few feet of the charred double doors that used to open into the bank.

He yanked his hat from his head, and threw it into what once was the lobby. I heard him yell, "Ruined! Ruined!" and then I saw my father walk up to the man, take him by the elbow, and lead him away from the building.

I edged closer to the firemen and police officers who were arranged in a semi-circle around the man in the overcoat. I stood behind my father. When I finally saw the man's face, the crazy behavior suddenly made sense. He was Arthur Scammon, the founder, president, manager and sole stockholder of what was, until a few minutes ago, the leading business bank in town. Scammon's face was contorted with anger, his fists were balled tightly at his side as if he were about to swing at someone. My dad was closest to him, and for a moment, I thought that this firefight was going to turn into a fistfight.

"You couldn't stop the fire?" Scammon seethed. "You couldn't get here faster? You only had two hoses? *Two hoses?* This is unacceptable, do you hear me? Unacceptable!"

My father answered in a measured voice: "We were here quickly, Mr. Scammon. And we applied all of the people and equipment we have. You built your bank outside the downtown core, knowing full well that there are no fire hydrants here. These men did their job well. No one was hurt, and no other buildings were damaged. In our book, that's a victory."

Scammon looked at my father as if he were a misbehaving child. "A victory?" sputtered the banker. "You call this," he waved one arm in the direction of the ruined building, "a victory? A victory for whom—for you and everyone else who owes me money, Forrestal? Is that what you all think? Scammon's bank is a heap of burnt out rubble, hooray for us, we won't have to pay the SOB what we owe him? Is that what this is about?"

I saw anger and disgust on the faces of the men who had just risked their lives in an attempt to save Scammon's bank. Such an outburst might have been overlooked by someone who was liked or respected in his community, after all, seeing your life's work go up in flame in a matter of minutes has got to be pretty tough to stomach. But even at thirteen, I knew that Arthur Scammon was probably the least liked member of the Salem business community. His reputation for being tough to the point of ruthless was a painful fact of life for his customers, many of whom had no choice but to deal with the Farm and Merchants Bank because they couldn't get loans elsewhere, not in the middle of the Depression. Scammon knew that, and in exchange for what he regarded as his magnanimous generosity in making loans at exorbitant rates of interest, he enforced his contracts with an unbending ferocity, and a complete disregard for civil behavior. He was not a man to cross, people said, not if you wanted to hang onto your home, your business, or your farm.

My father didn't reply in kind. That wasn't his nature. He often said that when you were in a tough spot you should deal with the situation, not the personality. He did that now. "It's been a difficult night for you, Arthur. Go home. We'll clean up here, and a crew will stand guard all night. No one will get close to the building without your say-so. We'll have a report for you to give to your insurance company in a couple of days. That sound okay?"

The mask of fury that stamped Scammon's face made it clear that my father's plan was anything but okay. Still, there was nothing more he could do here. The banker looked at the assembled men and hurled one last insult: "If I hear that any man jack of you has gone into that building without my permission, I promise I'll swear out a warrant and you'll do time in county jail. You got that?"

Without waiting for an answer, Scammon shoved past my father, climbed into his car, slammed the door and sped off into the blackness.

•••

I HADN'T NOTICED that my mother and a few other wives of the volunteer firemen had shown up during Scammon's tirade. They brought plates of egg-salad sandwiches, wedges of apple pie and jugs of hot coffee to the grateful crew. Food has a way of dampening tension, and by the time I wiped the last crumbs of pie from my jacket, I was feeling pretty good. It was going on 7 PM, and most of the firemen had gone home. I helped sweep up the glass that had been blown out of the windows as my dad organized the night watch plan. It was growing colder, another reason I supposed that the onlookers had drifted away as soon as the flames were out. So, I was surprised to see a group of seven or eight men walking towards us from the direction of downtown. They all wore overcoats and hats. As they passed me to join my father, I recognized them as some of the members of the newly formed Salem Businessmen's Association. It was a fancy name to give a group of men who met informally once a month to discuss matters of mutual interest, or, if you believed my mother's interpretation, a bunch of husbands who wanted their wives permission to play a little poker and smoke a cigar now and then.

I saw Len Dodge, the owner of the feed and seed, and my father's best friend. And there was Skip Reardon the druggist, Andy Lewis, who owned a diner, Mr. Tiberon, the undertaker, and Wilson Bump, the barber. I also recognized the owner of the only car dealership in town, plus Sam something-or-other, who had miraculously converted his clandestine speakeasy to a bar and nightclub within twenty-four hours of the repeal of Prohibition.

My father seemed surprised to see them, too. He set down his shovel, and wiped his brow. "Did I miss a meeting?" he said to Len, "or are you fellas here to sign up for the volunteer fire department? We could use you."

"Nothing like that Chet," said Len. "But if you need a hand, you bet, I'm happy to help."

Andy Lewis piped up: "I don't know about the others, but I'm here to enjoy the sight. Wish I could have got here earlier, I woulda roasted me some marshmallows." Several of the men laughed at Andy's remark. My father and Len ignored them.

"When I got the news I thought it might be good idea for our group to see if there was anything we could do to help out," said Len. "So I called everybody and asked them to meet here. We don't want to get in your way, of course."

"I appreciate that," said my father. "We've got the clean up and security mapped out."

"Security for what?" interrupted the undertaker. "Doesn't look to me like there's much to secure."

"That's for Mr. Scammon to decide," said my father.

The car dealer spoke up. His voice was hushed, as if he didn't want to be heard outside of this small group. "Do you suppose everything is burnt up?" He pointed to the heaps of smoking debris. "Could any paper survive that heat?"

"I suppose that the vault provided some protection for the money," said my father. "I think the rule is that as long as they can make out the denomination the Federal Reserve Bank just replaces the note. Beyond that, I have no idea what the insurance company might replace."

"It's an interesting thought, though, isn't it," said Reardon. "I mean, think about it. I'm pretty sure each one of us here has done some kind of business with Scammon—a mortgage, business loan, something."

I saw eight heads nod in the dim light. If you did business in this town, sooner or later you did business at the Valley Farm and Merchants. I understood that. But, what was the druggist getting at?

"Do you figure that Scammon kept all of his contracts in the vault?" continued Mr. Reardon. "What if he kept them out in his office instead, in one of those big wooden file cabinets that lined the wall behind his desk, the ones with our names on the drawers? Do you think those cabinets made it through the fire?"

The ground floor of the bank had burned with the heat of a steam locomotive's firebox for the better part of an hour, I thought. There was no way that a single scrap of paper or sliver of wood could have survived.

"What's that got to do with anything?" my father asked.

From the looks on the other men's faces, I'd say that Reardon's question had a lot to do with everything. I saw lights going on in their heads, wheels turning, mental calculations processed.

Sam the barkeep spoke. "Could have a lot to do with a lot," he said.

Andy Lewis said, "Amen to that, brother."

"You guys are out of line," said Len. "What the heck are you doing even bringing that up? You did business here, you signed the dotted line right over there, and you have an obligation to honor your side of the deal whether there's a piece of paper to prove it or not."

"Says you," muttered the undertaker. Andy and the car dealer nodded in assent.

Several voices spoke at once, but my dad had had enough.

"This is crazy talk," he said. "A man's life just burned to the ground.

How about we recognize that. Now, why don't you all go home. We have a meeting Monday night. We'll talk then. Right now I want to finish up here and get home myself."

Without waiting for a reply he turned back to his shovel. The men walked off in different directions. Len patted my dad on the shoulder as he left and gave me a thumbs-up. I swept up the last of the glass, then put the broom and dustpan away.

My father gave his last instructions to the two firemen who would stand first watch, and then he climbed wearily into the truck.

"You did a fine job tonight, Marty. In a couple of years you'll have your own turnout gear."

I appreciated the compliment, and I was excited at the thought of being a full-fledged volunteer firefighter, but something was gnawing at my insides. The conversation in front of the burnt out bank was playing over and over in my head. I turned to look at my dad. His hands were planted firmly on the steering wheel, and a line of black soot framed his face. He was whistling softly. I was sure that when we got home my mother would have finished her evening chores, and would be in the kitchen at her sewing machine, hemming, mending and repairing clothes she took in to help make ends meet. She seldom knocked off before midnight.

As for my dad, he'd be up before dawn working on his account books. Then down to the lumberyard or up into the Oregon Coast range to negotiate the purchase of more timber. His workday seldom stopped until six or seven. I knew that he liked work, but I also knew that if he had the choice, he'd cut back from seventy-plus hour weeks. As long as he had to pay the bank, though, there would be no rest. Not for him, and not for my mother.

As long as he had to pay the bank.

•••

WE PULLED INTO THE DARKENED LUMBERYARD, and my dad backed the fire truck into its bay. We hopped out, and he waved to the night watchman up in the shack. He slapped a truck fender. "How about washing her after Sunday school tomorrow?"

"Sure, Dad," I said softly.

"What's on your mind, son?"

I paused. "Can I ask you something?"

"Only if you let me fill my pipe first," said my dad. He pulled a pouch of cherry tobacco from his inside pocket and stuffed his pipe. He struck a match against a post, took a puff, and then leaned against the hood of the pickup. "What's on your mind, Martin?"

I shivered in the cold. I was uncertain how to get to my point, so I took a roundabout approach. "Dad, it's about Mr. Reardon and those other men talking about Mr. Scammon tonight. That stuff about not having to pay him back, I mean."

"Idle talk, Martin, that's all it was."

"Dad, last January when you took your timber contracts to the bank, how much did you borrow?"

Each fall he signed contracts with the owners of timber lots that gave him the right to harvest a certain number of trees from their lands the next season. He took those contracts to the bank, and borrowed against them for the operating capital he needed to run both the logging operation and the lumberyard mill. The trick was never to borrow more than the market for finished dimension lumber looked like it could absorb. In the middle of the Depression, that was one difficult trick.

My father tapped his pipe against the fender of the truck, and re-lit. "Since I'm training you on the business side of the operation, I suppose that's a fair question for you to ask," he said. "It's also just *our* business, Forrestal family business only. You understand that?"

I nodded.

"Good," he said. "Last December I signed a note with Mr. Scammon for a credit line of one hundred and twelve thousand dollars, secured by the timber contracts that are worth about twice that amount."

One hundred and twelve thousand dollars! It was an almost unimaginable sum. Why, a new house on a big lot cost under five thousand dollars. A new car was about six hundred dollars. Bread was just eight cents a loaf. And we owed the bank more than one hundred thousand dollars?

My father grinned at the astonished expression on my face. "We don't take it all at once, son. It's a credit line, and I borrow as we go, depending on our monthly needs and our sales. We also make a sizeable payment to the bank each quarter. It's a little like a high-wire balancing act, but we generally come out a little ahead each month. As of this week, our actual outstanding obligation to the bank is about thirty-five thousand dollars."

I would have felt some relief at that lower number, but even thirty-five thousand sounded to me like a king's ransom.

"That all you wanted to ask?" my father said.

I stuck my hands in my pockets, and drew a circle in the sawdust on the ground with the toe of my boot. "There's one other thing," I said. "What Mr. Reardon was saying about all of the contracts burning up in the bank tonight. If our contract burned up, and there aren't any copies anywhere, do we really still owe the money? I mean, I heard what Mr. Dodge said about honoring your obligations whether or not there is a piece of paper that says you have to, but, what does it really mean if the papers are gone? If we had a fire here and you couldn't sell any lumber, could you just tell Mr. Scammon too bad about the loan payments? I mean, not that you wouldn't pay him later and everything, but if there aren't any legal papers that he can enforce, can't you repay him when you feel like it?"

Even as the words passed my lips, I felt a sense of unease in the pit of my stomach. I didn't want my father to think I was suggesting that we cheat anybody—not even a despised old miser like Scammon. On the other hand, times were tough for our family, too, and we were on the edge just like everybody else. Why shouldn't we take advantage where we could if it meant looking out for us? Paying back the loan later than the original contract called for wouldn't really be cheating, would it?

My father pulled his pipe from his mouth. His head turned slightly sideways, and in the weak light I could see that his eyes had narrowed. He had an almost quizzical look on his face, as if he was looking into the face of a stranger. He emptied his pipe on the ground, and returned it to his inside pocket. Then he unbuttoned his turnout coat, and hung it on a sixteen-penny nail jutting out of the post beside him.

We stood in silence for what seemed an eternity. I kept my hands in my pockets, and I continued to stir dirt and sawdust around the parking bay with my boot. At last my father spoke, but not in a way or with the tone I was expecting. I was expecting to be corrected, to be lectured. My dad could inflict more hurt with a few well-chosen words than other dads could do with a willow switch. To my surprise, when he spoke it was in an absolutely calm, even voice.

"That's quite a statement you just made," he finally said. "There's a lot wrapped up in those words. More, I think, than you know." He contemplated me again with that far-away look, and then said, "Do me a favor. Grab a fire bucket and bring it over here."

We kept two-gallon buckets of water on hooks all over the lumberyard. Not enough water to put out a real fire of course, but plenty enough to stop a few sparks from igniting a dry pile of sawdust shavings, a common occurrence around a sawmill. I stepped across the bay and took down a bucket. A little water sloshed onto my shirt as I carried it back to my father, who had moved outside the bay and was now standing directly below the light pole.

He motioned for me to set down the bucket.

"Put your hands together like a cup," my father said, "as tight as you can. Then, dip into the bucket and fill the cup with water. Careful not to spill any."

I cupped my hands tightly, and dipped them into the bucket. The water was cold.

"Now, stretch your arms out a bit—that's right, right about there."

I was standing directly in front of my father, my cupped hands extending about eighteen inches from my body. I was careful not to let a single drop spill between my fingers.

"That's good," said my dad. "Keep your hands cupped like that for a minute, and think about that water like it was a chest of precious jewels, more valuable than anything else in the whole world. Don't open your fingers, don't let even the tiniest drop fall to the ground. You can't let any spill, because that's all there will ever be in your life. It's that important. Do you understand?"

I nodded, but I had no idea what the heck my dad was talking about.

"Marty, what you are holding in your hands is your honor. It's the most valuable possession a man or woman will ever have. It is also one of the easiest possessions we can lose. Once lost, it cannot be restored. It is not the strongest thing in us, but it is the thing that makes us the strongest."

My dad reached over and placed a hand on my shoulder. "Honor elevates us, and makes it possible for us to achieve great things, while never forgetting to be thankful for the small ones. Being an honorable man doesn't mean that the obstacles you will face in life will get any easier, Marty. Honor doesn't make your problems smaller. It makes *you* stronger."

My shoulders were starting to ache from holding my arms at this angle, and from clasping my hands hard to prevent any water from escaping. A few stars were visible outside the cone of light shining from the pole. It had gotten colder, too. I could see my dad's breath in the air as he spoke.

"Here's how it is," he continued. "When you give your word to someone, it is no different than what you are doing right now. Each time you make a promise to a friend, a pledge to your spouse, or a commitment to your country, you bind that assurance with your honor, holding it in your heart just as you are holding that water right now. The same is true of any business agreement you make, or code of conduct you agree to abide by."

He stepped back. "Now, I want you to open your fingers just enough for a few drops to spill."

I loosened my hands a bit, and a few drops of water fell to the ground.

"That was easy, wasn't it," said my father.

I nodded. It was easy.

"And it's that easy to shave a little off a promise, to back off a bit on an agreement, or to argue for changes in a deal after you have signed the contract. It's not hard at all. But when you do, what happens?"

"A little bit of your honor spills out," I replied.

"That's right," said my father. "And if you'll notice, no new honor welled up from anywhere to replace what had been lost. What is spilled stays lost forever. Now, open your fingers enough so that the water drips out steadily."

I opened my fingers again, and allowed a steady stream of droplets to fall to the ground.

"And there goes the honor in your marriage," my dad said, "and the honor in your work." About half of the water in my hands had now fallen to the ground. My father continued. "Now there is no honor in your business commitments, or in your faith. No honor in your relationships with friends, or with your children."

My cup was empty. I let my aching arms drop.

"Your honor defines your character," said my father. "If you choose a dishonorable path—even one that you think you can rationalize away because the consequences of doing so seem so minor—it's just the same as when you opened your fingers a tiny crack a moment ago. Honor does not compromise. Once it's breached, you will not be able to stem the leak."

My dad faced me and put a hand on each of my shoulders. "Think carefully before you commit your honor to anything or anyone, son. And then when you do, never, ever turn away from the pledge you have made.

That pledge is who you are—whether it is your signature on a contract or the marriage vow you make to your wife. Do you understand that?"

I couldn't think of anything to say, so I hugged him, something I didn't do much now that I was a teenager. He gave me a strong embrace in return, and then he said, "and speaking of marriage vows, we'd better get our tails home before your mother thinks you and I are out someplace smoking a cigar."

We decided to walk home. The smell of ripe apples and cherry pipe tobacco wafted heavily through the cold, clear night air. Piles of freshly raked leaves dotted many of the lawns we passed, and through opened curtains we saw several families in their living rooms listening to the radio. My dad picked up the tune he was whistling earlier, and after a minute I joined in. We didn't say a single word during the ten-minute walk home. Even so, it was just about the best time I ever shared with my father.

•••

ON OUR WAY TO CHURCH the morning following the fire, we swung by the site of the bank. The piles of rubble that had been Farm and Merchants were still smoldering. My father got out of the car to talk with the volunteer chief, who had been out of town the night before.

A rope line had been placed around the building, and two firefighters were turning over rocks with their shovels looking for hot spots.

"That's about it," my father said as he got back into the car. "At least for the fire."

"What's wrong, Chet?" asked my mother.

"The chief got word this morning: Scammon didn't have any insurance on the building, I guess he figured he could handle anything that came his way out of his own pocket. And that's not all. The chief interviewed Scammon this morning at his home. Seems that the rumors flying around about him not keeping copies of his contracts and accounts in some other location are true. No copies at his home or in safe deposit boxes in other banks, no filings at the county courthouse. Nothing."

"But, I don't understand," said my mother. "How could a banker of all people not keep copies of all of those important documents? I mean, how will he know who owes him money? And what if someone he has loaned money to just ups and says, 'What money? I never borrowed from you—

where's the signed contract?'"

My father turned his head to me and raised his eyebrows as if to say, see what I mean? "That would seem to be the question of the day," he said as he pulled into the gravel parking lot of our church.

Arthur Scammon and family were not in their usual pew that morning. But they were not absent from the conversation after service. The fire and its aftermath were all that people were talking about as they milled around. We went to breakfast after church, a rare event for the Forrestals in those days. When we got home I intended to do some serious lounging to settle out the full stack of buttermilk pancakes drenched in maple syrup I had downed. But Mom handed me a rake as soon as we got out of the car and pointed me in the direction of the two big-leaf maple trees that were shedding leaves all over the front yard.

I had only raked for a few minutes when my father came out of the house and waved for me to drop the rake. "Let's go for a ride," he said. He handed me a cardboard folder stuffed with papers. We got into the car and began driving toward the south end of town.

"Martin," my father said, "all this talk about Mr. Scammon and the bank has got folks stirred up. I'm no economics expert, but I know that a healthy town needs healthy banks. This Depression we're in proves that."

We crossed the railroad tracks that marked the boundary of downtown, and entered the small enclave of fashionable houses that was known as the Estates.

"Mr. Scammon didn't deal with regular folk; his bank was exclusive to farms and businesses and home mortgages, so he won't have hundreds of small depositors worried about their savings pounding on his door tomorrow morning."

"But what if Mr. Reardon and some of those men who were talking last night just up and refuse to pay back their loans, what then?" I asked.

My father pulled over to the curb and shut off the engine. "Mr. Scammon can take them to court, of course, and he probably will. But that will be a long process, and in the end it will come down to his word, and his memory, against theirs. If enough people do that, it could ruin his bank. And that would leave a big hole in the business community. There aren't exactly a lot of folks opening new banks these days, and probably won't be for a long time. Let's go."

My dad opened the door and got out of the car. It wasn't until I opened my door and looked around that I realized where we were: right in front of Scammon's grand English Tudor style house.

•••

I WAS NERVOUS AS MY DAD RANG THE DOORBELL, and then relieved when it looked like no one was going to answer. He rang again, and then a third time. Finally, the door swung open. Scammon looked awful. He hadn't shaved, his shirt was badly wrinkled, and one suspender lay loose at his side. He smelled of stale tobacco and gin, and his eyes were puffy and red.

"Forrestal," Scammon said slowly, with utter contempt. "I might have known you'd be along. Couple of your friends have already paid their respects." Scammon rubbed one finger across his upper lip. "They said they wanted copies of their notes right now, said they wanted to make sure that my records were accurate. Isn't that a riot. I do this crummy one-horse town the favor of loaning money to its struggling businesses, and this is the thanks I get: first chance they have, they try to destroy me. And now you."

A spray of spittle hit my face. My father hadn't punched the man last night, but I didn't think he would pass up that opportunity again. Instead, my father calmly wiped his face with his sleeve. "Can we come in, Arthur?"

Scammon hesitated. "What about the boy?" he finally said.

"Martin works for me. This is his business, too."

Without a word Scammon turned and walked back into the house. But he didn't slam the door, which we took as an invitation to follow him. He led us into a high-ceilinged, walnut-paneled library. In the center of the room was a massive oak desk, piled high with folders, ledger books and stacks of paper.

The ashtray was overflowing and a half-empty gin bottle sat precariously close to one corner. Scammon sat down, and motioned us to take the two chairs across from him.

"Well," he said. "This is your big day, isn't it Forrestal. I suppose you, too, want to know if the fire burned up any proof that I loaned you money? You were one of my largest accounts, you know. Between you walking out on your obligations and that druggist and undertaker already thumbing their noses at me this morning, I guess you'll get what you want. I'll be ruined, and maybe even go to jail for not keeping duplicate records like the law says."

So, it was true! Scammon had kept only one set of contracts and notes. He had been too cheap to employ a clerk to hand-write duplicate copies to keep offsite.

Scammon rubbed his hand along one unshaven cheek, anticipating the verbal blow he knew he was about to get from my father, the words that would condemn the Valley Farm and Merchants Bank to the scrap heap.

"Martin, please hand me the folder, would you?" asked my father quietly. He untied the string that held the folder closed, and withdrew a thick sheaf of papers. Then he leaned forward, placed his left forearm on the right side of Scammon's desk, and in one fast motion, swept the piles of papers, books, ashtray and gin bottle across the desk and onto the floor. Scammon pushed his chair back in surprise. So did I. I didn't know what my father was up to, but I sure didn't expect this. What the heck was going on?

My father fanned the papers from the folder across Scammon's desk like a card dealer in a casino. The banker's eyes opened wide.

"These are my copies of every note, contract, letter and statement that you and I have ever signed, or that has ever come to me from your bank," said my father. "Everything is here." His tone was calm and measured, completely without anger or emotion. Scammon's expression changed from fear and surprise to disbelief.

Scammon placed his hands palms down on the edge of his desk. He leaned slightly forward, and scanned the papers before him. His lower lip trembled, and he shook his head slowly from side to side. But he didn't say a word.

My father motioned for me to stand up. "I speak for no one but myself, Arthur," said my father. "I entered into agreements with you, and I will honor my side of those deals, to the letter. If you think any documents that you need to rebuild your files might be missing, please let me know. I am more than willing to recreate them exactly as they were."

Scammon folded his hands in his lap, and cast his gaze to the floor. He sat motionless, and silent. My father put his hand on my shoulder and we started to the door. Then he turned and said, "By the way, Arthur, as far as I know, those are the only existing records of the business we have done together. I'd consider it a personal favor after you get your new office organized if you'd have copies made for my files. No big hurry, of course. Good luck now."

I gulped. Was that a gift, or a knockout punch that my dad had just delivered?

With that, we left the office and let ourselves out the front door. My dad put his arm around my shoulder as we headed down the tree-lined walkway. Someone opened the wrought-iron gate near the street and came toward us. It was my dad's friend, Len Dodge, another one of Scammon's business customers. Under his arm he held a cardboard folder, just like the one my dad had dumped on Scammon's desk a few minutes ago. Len smiled as we passed on the walk. He didn't say anything. Neither did my dad. They didn't need to.

Honor speaks for itself.

•••

NURSE MARSDEN POPPED IN to check on me. After she left, Connie, who had joined me when I was in the middle of dictating the story, asked me what had become of Scammon in the months after the fire.

"My father and Len Dodge weren't the only customers who made the trek up Scammon's walkway," I said. "Over the next week, most of his customers gathered up their documents and took them to his house. Scammon rented an office at a competitor's bank building, and slowly began re-building his business."

"Was he a changed man after that?" my wife asked. "I mean, what your father and the others did after the fire was one hundred and eighty degrees away from what Scammon expected. They turned his sour worldview upside down."

"You'd think so," I said. "But that old saying about a leopard not being able to change his spots is true. Or at least partially true in Scammon's case. He was still the toughest businessman in town. Maybe he had to be, what with the Depression and all. No one awarded him any merit badges for kindness for the rest of his days, I can tell you that. But, it's also fair to say that the fire and its aftermath mellowed him some—made him at least more aware of the goodness in people. In fact, he did some things over the next few years that surprised us all."

Connie saw me eyeing the glass of ice water. She held the glass up to me and put the straw in my mouth. The cold water felt good. I had been sitting up for about an hour. I lowered the back of the bed halfway, and to my surprise, I didn't get hit with a wave of pain.

"About six months after the fire," I went on, "a local building contractor showed up at my father's lumberyard. I was doing some filing when he came up the stairs to the office. He had just signed a deal with Scammon to rebuild the bank, and as part of that deal Scammon instructed the contractor to purchase all of the lumber from my father."

"Was it unusual for him to do business with your dad?" asked Connie.

"I'm sure my father expected to be given a shot at bidding the job, but there were other suppliers in town, and plenty of larger outfits up in Portland. Nobody expected that Scammon would just hand the business to us, but that's exactly what he did. In those days, every job counted, and a job that size helped to keep us afloat."

"So he had a conscience after all," Connie said. "Or he just knew he'd stand a better chance of procuring ongoing business in the community if he stood by those men who didn't swing at him when he had one hand tied behind his back. It would be easy to say he was just being pragmatic."

"Well that would make this next one a lot harder to explain," I said. "That same Christmas I received a package in the mail. The return address said it was from Arthur Scammon. At first I thought he'd probably meant it for my father, and written my name by mistake. I opened it at the dinner table with my mom and dad present, just in case. Inside the package was a book that had just been published. It was called *The Sword in the Stone*, by T.H. White. It was all about the young King Arthur. I remember that it had a wonderful illustration of Merlin the Magician on the cover."

"So it was meant for you, and not your father?"

"Yes. I flipped the book open, and there was an inscription: 'To Martin, with best wishes for a memorable read, A. Scammon.' I didn't know what to say. How did he know I enjoyed those kinds of stories? To this day I have no idea."

"So the old dog did learn a few new tricks," mused Connie.

"Which leaves the rest of us some hope," I said. "But then there's the best story of all. Five years later, when I was in the Marines, I got a letter from my mother. She told me that Scammon had been invited to join the Board of Directors of the new hospital that was being built in Salem. He took on the responsibility of managing the finances of the newly formed group, and as part of that job he selected the prime building contractor."

"Don't tell me," said Connie. "He also selected the lumber supplier for the project."

"That he did," I said. "It was the biggest single job my father ever did. Kept the lumberyard and mill humming for more than a year."

"It's a shame all of the old buildings were torn down when they remodeled this place," she said. "There were a lot of memories for your family here."

"Well, that's the thing, honey," I said. "They didn't tear down all of the buildings. The South Wing, the smallest wing, was left standing. They added a new façade and made some minor changes inside, but basically, it's the same as it was in 1944."

My wife looked around the room. "But Martin, *we're* in the South Wing."

I beamed. "And every stick of lumber inside these walls came from my father's lumberyard. Heck, they worked so much overtime that he probably cut and delivered some of the two by fours in these walls himself."

Connie stood up and rapped her knuckles several times on the sheet rock behind my bed. "That's a solid wall, Martin. Those Forrestal men do good work."

COMPASSION

SATURDAY HAS ALWAYS BEEN my favorite day of the week. When I was a kid, it meant getting sprung from school for two days. As a young man, it was all about summer dances at Ayres' pasture barn, movies at the Elsinore, or steelhead fishing on the Siletz River. And when Connie and I had built our lumber business to a place where we only had to work sixty hours a week, Saturday meant knocking off at noon and driving up Santiam Canyon for dinner at the Riverbend Steak House, or trips out into the country around Kings Valley to pick wild blackberries around the pioneer apple orchards.

I'll fess up now and say that as trite as it sounds, the fact that today happens to be Saturday, and yours truly is lodged in room 512 at Willamette Hospital instead of snapping a fishing line tipped with a hand-tied fly in a cool shallows on the river, or digging for fresh clams in the muddy sand at Yachats Beach, is a source of no small irritation to me.

When I was a boy, my dad used to say that Monday through Friday belonged to the bank, and Sunday was the Lord's, but, by gum, Saturday belonged to him, and he was going to make the most of his one seventh ownership of every week. He always slapped his knee when he said something that amused him, followed by a Dutch-rub on the head for me, a good scratch for the dog, or a loving pat on my mother's backside.

Her role in this ongoing comedy would be to roll her eyes, return the pat with a snap of her dish towel, and offer up some variation on, "Oh, Chester, now what would you do with two Saturday's in a week?"

The cherry blossoms in the park, white and frothy only yesterday, were blown away with the April breeze, replaced by masses of deep green leaves. Some of them were Royal Annes, the same as Connie and I have in our backyard. The sweet, ruby-red fruit has been the harbinger of summer for all the years we've lived in our stone and timber house on Carmichael Street. In late June we lean ladders into the trees, and fill bucket after bucket to the brim.

Connie cans cherries for winter, and makes jam and preserves, but it is her cherry pies that I live for. They have a crust so delicate and flaky that if you sailed one off a mountaintop it would take a week to float to the ground. I have told her that every year since we got married. Never saw the need to work up a new compliment—one of the few secrets I know to enjoying a successful marriage is to find out what works and stick with it. Ten or twelve fresh cherry pies per season for over half a century proves my theory, I think.

I expect that I'll miss cherry season this year. Funny how the things that you've taken for granted for so long can take on a new shine when you learn the curtain's about to come down on the play for the last time.

•••

"YOU RECEIVING VISITORS?" It was Doctor McGuire, dressed causally in khakis and a light jacket.

"Come on in, Mac. Your tie and stethoscope at the laundry?"

"Day off, Martin."

"Yeah, I remember Saturdays."

I tried to push myself to a better sitting position, but the back pain that had been increasing since yesterday stopped me cold. I winced. McGuire adjusted my bed, and settled another pillow against my spine.

"That's why I stopped, in Martin."

"To give me a pillow? Medicare covers that now?"

"Maybe it should." Mac pulled a chair around at an angle so he could face me directly. He pulled the baseball cap off his head, and turned it in his hands as he spoke.

"The bone pain you're experiencing is a sign of the progression of the metastatic disease we've talked about," he said.

"It was a theory then," I replied. "The actual experience is something altogether different, I can tell you that."

"We have opioid pain relievers for what you're going through now," he said, "and there are some radioisotopes we'll inject, too. They're pretty effective."

He saw the look in my eyes.

"Yes, I know you don't want to be drugged. I'll keep my end of the deal—I'll try to find a balance between comfort and alertness for you. And you do your part—be honest with me and with your nurses about your pain, and don't forget what I said about Connie. You two have been married long enough that when you feel it, she's going to feel it." He rose from his chair. "I'm your doctor, Martin, and your friend—and Connie's, too. As your doctor I'm telling you I'll help you in every way I can to see that you finish your values project. As your friend," he put his cap back on, "I'm telling you that the first time I find your wife crying her heart out down in the hospital chapel because she can't watch you go through the pain, you'll need a company of hard-ass Marines to keep me and the world's biggest syringe of morphine away from your rear-end. You got that?"

I couldn't help but chuckle. "You learn this speech in a bedside manner course in med school, did you?"

"My delivery might lack a little polish, but I'm hoping you get the picture."

"I've got it, Mac. Listen, can I ask a favor?"

"I'm already late for golf, buddy. Don't know how much more I can do for a guy who hasn't had the good sense to change doctors for all these years. But give me a try."

"Mac, would you take your wife to dinner tonight? To the best darned place in town? Tell her to get dolled up—you do, too. Try that Oregon Pinot I told you about, buy the lady a flower. Would you do that—and on me?"

McGuire put his hand on my shoulder. "I'll take Charlene to dinner, Martin. But I'm going to do it for you, not on you, pal. See you Monday."

•••

McGUIRE WAS OUT THE DOOR, and I began to prepare myself for today's main event.

When I picked up my writing pad this morning, the next value on my list was compassion. My pastor once said that compassion was the basis for all morality. I'm not on a first-name basis with any of the world's great philosophers or theologians. I define compassion as the voice of conscience that speaks to us all day long, in every situation, at every bend in the road. The voice that urges us to recognize what others are experiencing in their lives, and more importantly, the voice that says, "don't just stand there—do something about it!"

Eric would be on his way up in a few minutes. My son—the perfect person for me to hold this conversation with. At forty-seven, Eric is a model of the hyper-driven professional. It would be one thing if his workaholic habits were confined to his office, but the truth is that for him, like for all of us, the pressures of work weigh on the family one way or another. As Emerson said in his essay on self-reliance, "you carry your giants with you, wherever you go." The perfection Eric demands of himself is no less than that he requires of Rachel, and little Gwen and Jimmy. Up against the inflexibility and exactitude of that level of analysis, I hope his family can make it.

I took a sip of the thin protein shake that was to be the mainstay of my lunch diet now, and watched as Eric walked past my door, thumbing furiously away on the keyboard of his phone. A moment later he realized he'd missed his turn. He whipped around and stopped outside my door.

"I'll be right in. I just need to finish sending these specs to the general contractor."

He stood in the doorway for several minutes, texting as fast as his fingers could fly. He'd gained some weight this past year. His eyes looked puffy, and he was pale, even by Oregon standards. When he finished his message, he slipped his phone into his pocket and dropped into the chair next to my bed.

"Hello, Dad. Busy day—the electricians are ready to go into the Broadway building, and I have to get them updates before Monday. You know how it goes."

"I suppose I do, Eric. Good to see you too, by the way. What's your—"

Eric's phone buzzed. "I'll be just a minute, Dad—have to take this call."

He rose and walked out into the corridor. When he returned five minutes later his face was flushed, and he was shaking his head. He flung himself down in the chair.

"Unions! Who the hell gave them the power of God when it comes to approving my specs? It's hard enough when you have to fight the city, and OSHA, and no-growth community groups, but the Unions, my God, they are a kingdom unto themselves. How'd you ever put up with them all those years, Dad?"

I put my hand on my son's arm. "I'm fine, Eric—how are you today?"

A sheepish smile warmed his face, and he let out a long sigh. "Oh, I'm alright. Dad, how do you feel?"

"Do you want the canned response I give to the media, or the version I give to the nurses to talk them into bringing me a cup of coffee now and then, or do you want the plain truth?"

Eric sat up. "Dad, I want to know how you are really feeling."

"I tell you what. You told me you were planning on spending the day here with me. That's fine, I'm looking forward to it. How about you turn that darn phone off? Take a break once in a while and check messages, but, unless you're privy to some top-secret information the doctors aren't sharing with me, my understanding of the situation is that you and I are not going to have that many more opportunities to visit before this old carcass of mine gives up the ghost. Does today work for you or not?"

"Dad, look, I'm sorry, it's just that things are kind of crazy at work right now."

I spoke softly. "And they will be tomorrow, Eric. The day after that, too. And every day for the rest of your life as long as the cart is driving the horse."

"It's not that easy, Dad. I'm the guy who has to juggle thousands of things and keep them from crashing into each other."

"Or?"

"Or the job will slow down, or costs will skyrocket, or we'll get sued—there's a million things that can go wrong, Dad."

"And what's the best thing that can happen if those millions of things go right?"

"Then I bring the job in on time and on budget. Everybody's happy."

"Everybody? Rachel and the kids, too?"

"This isn't about them, Dad."

"Well, I'm glad to hear that your work doesn't affect your family life.

They'll be glad to hear it, too."

"Dad, don't you think I'm a little old for this? I'm working my tail off so my family can have a better life."

"And what do you suppose would be number one on Gwen and Jimmy's list of things that they think would make their lives better? New bikes? A week at Disneyland?"

Eric shook his head. "Dad, you want me to say that what the kids want is more time with me. I know that—but, they're kids, and they don't understand that if I'm going to be able to spend more time with them later, I've got to spend more time at work now. I'm not talking about forever, I'm talking about laying them a solid foundation."

"Any idea how long that might be?"

"Dad, I just don't know. I just don't know how to put a timeframe on building a better future."

I finished my tasteless lunch shake, and set the empty plastic cup on the table.

"You know, Eric, until the doc put his finger here"—I pointed to the date I had circled in red on my nightstand calendar—"and told me that would pretty much be the end of my warranty, I would have agreed with you. I didn't think you could put timeframes on the big things, either. I was wrong. Jimmy starts Little League in a few weeks. You won't be ahead by then, will you? And in six or seven short years Gwen is going to go to her first school dance—will you be ahead then? Or when Jimmy takes his driver's test, or hits his first high school home run? What about when Gwen announces she has a boyfriend, and wants to invite him to dinner? Will you be ahead by then? And what about Rachel, when she puts your untouched dinner into the fridge for the hundredth time because you had an emergency and had to work late? Will a hundred missed dinners be enough for you to get ahead?"

"Dad, I love you. But you just don't understand. It's not something that can be worked out with a few broad generalizations about life, or with a book of happy quotes. Life's just—"

"A lot more complex than that?"

"A lot more."

I changed the height of my bed. "You want some coffee or anything?" I asked.

"I wouldn't mind something. Can we check you out of this motel and head downstairs?"

"I think that can be managed."

I pushed the nurse call button, and arranged for a wheel chair. Eric helped me with my robe and into the chair for the ride down to the second floor solarium.

He left me in front of a bank of alder-framed windows that overlooked the park. Nearby, in the shade of a flowering maple, was the hot dog vendor's cart. I wondered if I could talk Eric into slathering some chili and onions on one of those beauties and smuggling it into my room.

Eric returned with coffee. I'd pay for it tonight, I knew, but that first sip of strong, fresh-ground java sent a wave of satisfaction to every cell in my body.

"Eric, did I ever tell you what my first choice of major was when I started college?"

"Don't think you did. It wasn't business?"

"Oh, no, that looked far too dull for me. No, I wanted to be a geologist, travel the world, explore for oil and diamonds and gold in places that weren't even on the map yet."

"Gee, Dad, when you went to college, that would be just about the entire planet, wouldn't it?"

"Alright, wise guy. It was geology for me, right up until I dropped out at the end of my junior year so your mom and I could get married. I always loved the history of the development of the planet. From a smoking ball of gas, to a green world covered with oceans and lakes and forests and continents. It's an amazing science. And there's one thing I learned in my three years of study that I think I'd like to pass along."

"Just one?"

That made me chuckle. "One's enough if it's an important enough thing, I guess. It happened at the first lecture I attended—Introduction to Geology 101. Professor Jepson. Big guy, a mountain climber I think. The class met in a theatre-style lecture hall, with a wall of blackboards and cork panels that was about fifty feet wide. And every inch of that fifty feet was covered with detailed charts, maps, chemical formulae, technical diagrams and seismographic print outs. I took one look at that wall of data and told myself that my first stop after the lecture was going to be the counselor's office to change my major."

"Sounds intense."

"It was. I was overwhelmed, and I felt about the size of a baby flea on the back of a Great Dane. So did everybody else in the class, I found out later. And that's exactly what Professor Jepson wanted us to feel; a mix of awe, respect and fearfulness in the face of God's most complex creation. And then he did something that impresses me to this day. He raised one of the charts to expose the only blank surface on the wall. On the blackboard underneath he wrote two words in large capital letters: TIME & PRESSURE.

"Jepson looked out over the sea of anxious faces and said, 'To be a geologist, you need to understand only two things—time and pressure. Everything on this planet—and I mean everything—is a product of their interaction.' He swept his arms wide to include the mass of scientific information on the wall. 'The rest of this,' he said, 'is just the language we invented to describe what happens when time and pressure meet. If you pay attention during your journey through life, you will discover that everything that happens to you, and everything you set in motion with others, is also a product of just those two things. Time and pressure.' I can't tell you that this truth all by itself helped me to resolve any of the biggest problems that have stared me in the face over the years, but it sure has helped me to understand why I was where I was, and why other people were where they were."

"Your professor had a way with words," said Eric.

"Well, he sure knew how to chop through the clutter and get down to what really matters, if that's what you mean."

It was time for me to return to my room. As Eric wheeled me back down the corridor I told him that I had a copy of Professor Jepson's memoirs on my desk at home. "Why don't you pick it up this week," I said. "I think you'll enjoy the read."

Eric nodded, and rolled me back to room 512.

•••

CONNIE WAS WAITING for us. She was reading in the window seat, a mug of herbal tea in her hand. She wore a light periwinkle-colored sweater—my favorite.

"Do you boys mind if I sit quietly while you visit?" my wife asked.

I sat on the edge of the bed. "I don't know about that. I was going to tell Eric the story of the first date I ever went on—don't know if I should share the details around his mother. Might be a bit more than she can handle."

"That sound you hear is me rolling my eyes, dear," said Connie. "I'll try not to gasp at the juicy bits."

"Your first date?" he asked. "Why haven't I heard about that before?"

"Maybe because the shame and embarrassment of the event haven't faded over the years?" my wife suggested.

"You read your book, missy," I said. "We men will take it from here."

I settled back into bed, and buzzed for the nurse to re-attach the IV to the shunt in my forearm. Nurse Marsden hooked me up, and rearranged the pillows behind my back. The pain was pretty much constant now, and it seemed to be radiating upward along my spine. That wasn't going to change, I reminded myself. And if Doctor McGuire was right, the pain would only increase from now on.

Eric stepped out in the hall to check messages, but returned almost immediately.

"Nobody needs you?" I asked.

He bent and kissed my forehead—something he hadn't done since he was eight or nine.

"That depends on who you define as nobody" he said. "So, let's hear about the first date. If there's any really good stuff, we'll just send Mom downstairs for ice cream."

Connie tossed a pencil over at Eric. "Not on your life, boys," she said. "I paid full admission for my ticket, and I expect value for my money."

Eric handed me the digital recorder. I adjusted a pillow, took a sip of water, and turned the recorder on.

•••

IT WAS JUNE 1941, two weeks after school let out for the summer. I was fifteen—going on sixteen—as Patrick and I would say when we felt we needed to impress someone, usually a girl. America was entering the last quiet summer before the war. The Oregon spring weather had been mild, but June promised to be the warmest in years. Strawberries would be on early, which meant that old man Takashima would need to hire local pickers to fill in until the Okies came up from the Salinas lettuce fields on their regular vegetable and fruit picking circuit.

Takashima's fields were down along the Luckiamute River, not far from the Pedee sawmill. Patrick and I hitched a ride each morning at 5 AM on the logging company bus—we called it a crummy—on the west side of the Willamette River. The ride out to Pedee with the loggers and mill workers was a lesson in tall-tales, epic swearing and plug tobacco chewing. On the first morning out, we walked to the home of the logger who had invited us to ride along.

The lights were blazing in the window as we walked up to the porch at 4:30 AM. Ralph's wife invited us in, and when we saw the dining room table we were pretty sure the calendar was wrong—it looked like Thanksgiving.

Just three men were seated at the long table: a pair of brothers, Alby and Tucky, and their father, Ralph. They were dressed alike—hickory stripe shirts with cut off sleeves and red suspenders, stagged-off double front jeans, and slippers. Their steel-spiked, calf-high cork boots and tin hats were lined up outside the door.

Laid out on the oak table before them was an enormous spread; two dozen fried eggs were heaped on a platter beside a serving plate covered with a mountain of sausage patties, bacon and ham slices. Alby's wife came out of the kitchen with stacks of pancakes, which she set beside a quart of syrup, a pound of butter and a pot of coffee. There were also a couple jugs of milk, mounds of toast, four jars of homemade jam and an apple pie.

"Steak's up," came a voice from the kitchen. In came Tucky's wife with a platter of venison steak and a cast iron skillet filled to the top with cheese-topped hash browns.

"Got biscuits?" asked Ralph.

"No time this morning, honey," his wife replied.

"Guess we'll get by," her husband said. Then he turned to Patrick and I and said, "Boys, I'm sorry we didn't know for sure you was coming—the wife would've butchered another doe."

Patrick shot me a quizzical glance? Not enough for two more? There was food for ten men on that table, plus a couple of boys, maybe even an entire Scout troop, to boot.

"Uh, we ate already," I said.

The driver dropped us off at 5:30 that morning at the turnoff to Takashima's, a quarter mile from the mill. The row boss didn't hand out crates and boxes until 6 AM, so we wandered down to the river's edge to toss rocks and stir up crawdads. We left our lunch boxes in the shade of a rock close to the water, and got in line with the other pickers just before the field boss rang the work bell.

Most of the pickers were teenagers, but there were plenty of families, too. A family of five or six could make a healthy income working berries and beans in early summer, before moving on to moss, fern and chitum bark in the early fall.

Each picker was assigned a double row, about one hundred yards in length. You picked one side of the row to the end, then turned and worked back on the other side. We were paid two cents per box, with twelve boxes in a case. When the case was full we took it to the row boss, who checked a random box for rocks or greenies, and then punched our row ticket with his special punch. Each punch was worth twenty-four cents at the end of the day.

Mr. Takashima's strawberry fields covered twenty-five acres. The warm, sweet smell of that many ripe berries is as strong as drugstore perfume— but infinitely more enjoyable. At noon, everybody headed down to the river, where we took off our shoes and cooled our feet in the water before returning to work. The fields shut down at 3 PM sharp, at which time we'd knock around the river until the mill whistle blew. Then we'd scramble up to the highway and wait for the driver to take us back to Salem.

On Monday of our second week picking, Patrick had to stay home to help his father at the hardware store. I made the bus ride out to Pedee without him, gathered my boxes and wooden flat, and headed for the end of my row on the south side of the field. What happened next was summed up best by my friend Mario, whose Sicilian father owned the butcher shop downtown.

"Martin," he said when I told him my tale, "you've been struck by the thunderbolt!"

And I had. Just as I bent over and set to work picking, I heard an unfamiliar laugh. I swung my head in the direction of the sound, over toward the river. The morning sun was just peeking above the South Salem hills, spilling golden light through the cottonwoods across the river in a glittering shower.

And there she was. As pretty as a pony. Sandy hair, cornflower blue eyes. Most of the women wore aprons over long cotton dresses to the fields.

She had on a man's shirt and corduroy trousers. She had just squished an overripe strawberry on her sister's arm, and it looked like a berry war was about to break out. The girl's father gently intervened and directed them back to work, but before she turned away, she looked down the row and smiled at me.

The thunderbolt didn't just hit me, it knocked me over. Every detail of that moment is etched in my memory; rows of berry-laden bushes spilling down to a deep green river, the soft morning sky, the chatter and singing of dozens of berry pickers, and Mr. Takashima in his broad-brimmed straw hat handing a piece of candy to a six-year-old two rows down. I can still smell the aromas of ripe fruit and river water, and the rich, brown earth. I can see the silver flash of an osprey diving for an unlucky trout, and hear the row boss shouting that a load of cardboard boxes were available at the counting table.

Five seconds. That's all it was. Almost seventy years on, it is one of the strongest memories I possess.

Her name, I learned later, was Megan Hazelton. Her family was from Oklahoma, and they'd pulled off the picking circuit last year and settled in the mill town of Philomath, about a half hour south of Takashima's fields. I didn't have the vinegar to talk to her, but the next day when Patrick learned of my plight, he invited us to sit with her family at lunch along the mossy riverbank.

And so it went on Tuesday, Wednesday, and Thursday. I don't think I said more than a dozen words to Megan those three days, and what few I managed I'm sure were as jumbled as an unfinished jigsaw puzzle. But it didn't seem to matter. She and I would sit after lunch and dangle our toes in the river, or toss pebbles at branches as they floated by. I wasn't sure if I was in love; but what ever I was in, I was in up to my eyeballs.

Then, on Friday, Megan dropped a bombshell: Philomath High School was having its annual summer BBQ and dance Saturday night. She wondered if I might like to join she and her sisters there? I felt like I'd been sat on by an elephant—the air was knocked out of my lungs. I couldn't speak, so Megan's father kindly threw me a life preserver.

"It's okay, boy—you just need to say yep or nope. It's just a visit—it's not a date."

I collected myself enough to nod in acceptance, and watched in teenage bewilderment as Megan and her sisters ran laughing back to their rows.

•••

I DON'T RECALL A THING about the drive back to Salem that afternoon. It was a blur. As for the wait from Friday to the dance on Saturday, my mood swung between complete exhilaration and a sense of utter foreboding. My mom and dad were about as helpful and supportive as my friend Patrick once they learned the news, too. The more agitated I became, the more they all ramped up the teasing. Good-natured or not, it made for a bumpy twenty-four hours.

Tragedy struck about a half-hour before I had to jump the bus for Philomath. I discovered that my one and only dress shirt had a small tear in the middle of the back. I stood in the center of my room looking at that shirt for what seemed like hours. In my drawer I had a couple of old school shirts, my Scout uniform shirt, and a sweater. I wasn't due for any new clothes until the start of the school year—seven weeks off. I could borrow one of my dad's, I supposed. Not that his would be much better.

There was a knock at my door. It was my mother. "This is a big night, isn't it Martin," she said.

"It's just a visit. It's not a date."

"Oh," she said, smiling knowingly. "Right. Well, do you have everything you need? Clean socks? Do you need me to iron your shirt or brush off your jacket?"

"Nah, I'll be fine, Mom. But thanks for asking."

"Alright. I'll let you get ready." She kissed my forehead, and left my room.

I reviewed my wardrobe choices one last time, and decided to wear the dress shirt with the hole in the back. I'd have to keep my jacket on, but that shouldn't be a problem.

Another knock. I was getting a little testy.

"I'm busy," I said. "I'll be downstairs in a minute."

But the door opened anyway. It was my mother again. She was holding a brown-paper parcel tied with string.

"Martin, I know you said you had everything you needed, dear—oh, my, you're wearing that shirt?"

"Pretty much what I have mom," I said.

"Well I don't know that that's quite true," replied my mother.

She placed the parcel on my bed, and untied the string. Then she held up a brand new long-sleeve blue cotton shirt and a pair of summer weight khaki trousers. I didn't know what to say. Money was in short supply that year. My dad's lumber business had slowed to a crawl, and Mom was doing seamstress work to help make ends meet. My strawberry picking money had to go for school next fall. How was she able to buy these clothes?

My eyes watered. "Mom, I don't, I can't—Mom, we don't have money for new clothes right now."

My mother hugged me, and sat down beside me on the bed.

"Martin, whatever should become of you and this young lady of yours, I know this: you will remember this day for the rest of your life. Everything about it. My cookie jar was getting a little heavy with money anyway, and Mr. Sanders was having a sale at the haberdasher's, so don't you give it another thought. Now I'm going to give these a quick press—you get your face washed and your hair brushed. It's your first date. You ought to look the part." She squeezed my shoulder and bustled off to iron my new clothes.

How many nights I came home from working at O'Hagan's Hardware or from high school events to find her in the kitchen at that cranky old Pfaff sewing machine. There would be a pile of torn trousers and frayed dresses on the floor, Glen Miller playing on the radio, and the teakettle would be warm from her last cup. Sometimes the arthritis in her hands was so bad that my father had to pour hot water on them so she could bend her fingers enough to work. But when I stepped through that door, she would set her work aside and turn off the machine. That was my signal to pull up a dining room chair and talk about the events of the day. She would ask all about my adventures, my friends, my plans, what I was reading and why I enjoyed a particular book. And when my eyes grew heavy and I headed for bed, the whispering of the teakettle and the rhythmic whirring of the sewing machine would sing me to sleep.

•••

I left my house at 2:30 sharp on Saturday for the three-hour trip to Philomath. My mother told me how handsome I looked in my new get up, and waved from the porch as I walked to the bus stop. I didn't argue the point—there is something about a set of new clothes that changes your outlook on pretty near everything.

The bus headed west to Dallas, where I transferred to the Corvallis line for the ride through timber and farm country down to Philomath. I settled in behind the driver. Across from me was an elderly man, slicked up about as much as I was. He wore a dog-eared fedora and a threadbare suit that might have been fashionable at the turn of the century. His tie had been cleaned so many times with naptha to remove the grease spatters that I could smell the chemicals. In his lap the old gentleman held a huge bouquet of store-bought flowers. There were easily three or four days of berry picking income in that bunch, I thought.

The old man nodded at me as I sat down, and he grinned when he recognized a kindred Saturday spirit turned out in his finest doing-the-town splendor. We did stand out, I'm sure, that well-dressed old man and this stylish boy at the front of a bus filled with Siletz Indians, loggers, fruit pickers and mill workers headed home from the early Saturday shift.

"Going to see your girl?" the old man asked.

The idea of "having a girl" puffed me up some, and I answered with a bravado that was new to me. "Sure am. She's in Philomath. We're going to a dance. How 'bout you?"

He held up his flowers. "Same here—not the dance part, though. Going to see my girl, just the same."

"That's quite a bouquet," I said. I entertained a question for a minute, wondering what an old boy in his seventies was doing in the dating business, but I thought better of it, and let it slide.

"Isn't that a fact—nothing a woman loves more, that's the truth of it," he said. "My Gladys, especially. What are you taking to your girl?"

The question floored me. What was I taking her? Was I supposed to take her something? Would she be expecting a gift? Flowers? Candy? This whole girl thing was pretty new to me, but I suddenly had the feeling that I'd just flunked the first and most important test for admission into the fraternity of guys who had girls.

"Uh, nothing this trip," was the best I could do.

"That so," said the old man. "Guess things have changed a bit since I started to court Gladys. Never knew a woman though who didn't 'spect a little something special when her fella swung 'round to pick her up. You must have landed yourself one of those understanding type of gals."

Had I? I felt a chill go up my arms, and I stuck my hands in my pockets to warm them up. In my left pocket was exactly enough money to get into the Philomath dance and to buy my return bus ticket tomorrow, with fifty cents left over for a soda and a hot dog. I would be spending the night at my cousin's house outside town, but that was the only free part of this adventure.

The old man reached across the aisle, and gave me a pat on the back. "Good on you, youngster. 'Bout time things changed and we men were allowed to keep a few extra dollars in our pockets." He chuckled.

I sunk into a black misery. As the bus rattled down the narrow highway through stands of Douglas fir past homestead clearings and fenced meadows, I considered my options. I could get off the bus at the Valsetz logging camp turnoff—and find myself a new job—or I could soldier on and make the best of it, knowing full well that Megan would probably not give me so much as a howdy-do the next time I saw her out at Takashima's.

How could I have been such a dope?

The driver pulled into the wayside at the Valsetz turnoff. We waited as a couple of folks got off the bus and a woman and her baby climbed on board to claim their seats.

I made up my mind. I had come this far, it just didn't make sense to turn back. Anyway, maybe I could find a little trinket of some kind before the dance, something to let Megan know I was not a complete slug.

The bus pulled back onto the road. I kept my hands jammed into my pockets, my chin on my chest. I felt like I was heading to an execution at the state penitentiary instead of to a dance with my girl.

The old man spoke over the clatter of the bus. "Son," he said, "could be it's not my business, but I can't help noticing you all a'sudden don't look too much like a feller on his way to see a beautiful young thing. I've seen treed coons look happier knowin' they was about to get et by the hounds."

"Lot on my mind, that's all," I said.

"Well I hope to sunshine so, thinking on dancing and all," he replied. He set the bouquet on the seat, pulled out a penknife, and cut off a plug of tobacco. He offered me one.

"No, thanks all the same."

"What's your name, boy?"

"Martin. Martin Forrestal."

"Well now, let me see if I can figure this here mystery out, Martin Forrestal. A young buck gets hisself prettied up for a date with his best gal, and he climbs on board the bus with a smile wider than my Aunt Letty's backside—and that's saying something, width wise, I mean." He chuckled. "Anyways, this young feller has got excited writ all over his mug, eyes shining bright, tappin' his foot like Tommy Dorsey's band was on board this very bus—bet you didn't know you was doing that, did you? And then, before you knowed it, why, you'd a thought some darn barber'd just shaved him bald and set his britches on fire in front of the lady's church bazzar."

The old boy finished, and looked at me expectantly. I didn't have an answer, and the one I might have come back with would only have hurt his feelings, so I kept it to myself. Out of the corner of my eye, I saw the old man doff his fedora, and scratch his head as if he were doing some pretty deep thinking. It looked like he wasn't done with me.

We rounded a tight turn a little too fast, and the old man's hat fell into the aisle. I picked it up, and handed it to him. "Thanks, boy." He looked down at the floor for a second, then raised his head and gave me a knowing wink. "Say, being as we're both sort of on the same mission and all, I wonder if I might ask you a question?"

I was getting pretty tired of this one-sided conversation, and wanted to get back to stewing in my own despair, so if I could wrap up my new found friendship with this old coot by answering one more question— well, let 'er rip.

"No. Don't mind at all."

The woman behind me pulled her window down, and a burst of air rushed into the bus. Several other people followed suit, and the noise made it a little hard to hear the man as he shouted his question:

"Jest exactly how many times you been out with this gal of yours?"

I frowned. "Never. This is the first time," I said.

He cupped an ear. "What's that? Can't hear you!"

"Never!" I yelled. "I've never taken her out, never taken any girl out, for that matter. This is my first time." I turned my head and saw that the woman in the seat behind me was leaning forward so as not to miss a word of this dandy little opera. The old man scooted close to the edge of his seat. He leaned across the aisle. "I'm truly sorry, son," he said in a soft voice. "Please accept an old fool's apology. I knew directly when I asked you what you was bringing to your gal that I'd dropped a hornet down your shorts. I'm sorry, boy. I should know better than to tease, 'specially when it comes to love. Love ain't no laughing matter, that's for sure."

He picked his flowers up, slid back over by the window, and stared out at the passing trees and meadows. I shook my head. Just how many more people could I possibly upset in one day, I wondered? The old guy was just trying to make talk, and I'd managed to drop the proverbial cowpie into the Sunday punchbowl.

I moved across the aisle and sat down beside him. He turned toward me with a distant look in his eyes.

"You don't need to apologize," I said. "I'm the big-shot who thought he had this girl thing all figured out. Don't pay me any mind."

The old man's eyes lit up, and a smile creased his weathered face. "Son, I've discovered that pretty much all the advice anybody gives you on the big things in life is usually about as useful as" —he noticed the woman and little girl behind us and thought better of his choice of expressions—"well, about as useful as udders on a bull, if you'll pardon my French. That said, you might want to take this here advice to heart: ain't no man ever, and I mean ever, has lived long enough to figure out women. Won't ever be, that's for sure. So jes' put that little thought to bed—for good."

I smiled. "Are you saying you haven't got your Gladys figured out?"

His smile faded, replaced by a wistful expression. "No, Martin, that's something I was never able to get done, not in fifty long, wonderful, God-blessed years. Not by a long shot."

I was trying to figure out what the heck he meant when the driver called out, "Your stop, Mr. Sanford."

The bus slowed, and came to a halt on the curve of a sweeping hill. To the west a vast stand of virgin timber sloped down into a valley that stretched forty-five miles to the Oregon coast. On the east side a bramble-covered stump farm rolled up into the hills. There wasn't a house or a farm or any kind of building or business around; there hadn't been for several miles. There was just the forest, and a rutted dirt logging road that wound up a ridge before it disappeared in a thicket of brushy chestnut and blackberries.

I stood up so the old man could get off. Where was he going? Was someone picking him up? Did Gladys drive? He thanked the driver, and then turned to me, a slightly embarrassed look on his face.

"Never did this for a fella," he said quietly. "Least not on purpose." He handed me the huge bouquet of flowers. "Your gal deserves these," he said. "Maybe they'll get you to off to a good start."

I was too startled to reply. The driver cranked the door open, and the old man stepped down to the landing.

"Gladys and me, we had ourselves a good start," he said. "And a good start is half the battle, Mr. Martin Forrestal." He tipped his hat. "God bless you, son." He climbed off the bus, and trudged slowly in the direction of the logging road.

I watched him walk away. The driver said, "You gotta sit down, now, so we can leave."

I sat down, and looked behind me, around the bus. The other passengers were all going about their own business. No one seemed to think it odd that an over-dressed old gent was getting off the bus in the literal middle of nowhere. As the driver shifted out of low and geared back up to cruising speed, I craned my neck to see if I could catch a glimpse of the old man, but he was already lost amid the fir and cedar trees lining the log trail.

I sat there for several minutes, looking at the flowers, a mass of gladiolas and daffodils and irises, mixed with fresh fern. In the exact center of the bunch was a single, deep-red rose.

I leaned forward. "Excuse me," I said to the driver.

"Yeah, buddy, what is it?"

"About the old man?"

"Mr. Sanford. You must be somebody special, him giving you Gladys' flowers and all. That was really something."

"You know Gladys?"

The driver looked at me in the rearview mirror as if I was crazy.

"Of course I don't know Gladys. Nobody does—except that old man."

"I don't understand," I said. "He said he was coming out here to see his favorite girl, his Gladys—doesn't she ever meet him at the bus stop?"

"Doesn't she ever what? Boy, are you plumb loco? Don't you know what's up that logging road?"

"No."

"Son, that there's the Pedee Cemetery. Oldest one in these parts, been there since before the War Between the States. That's where Gladys lives, boy."

I held the bouquet tightly, trying hard to figure this all out.

"How long has she been gone?"

"Couple years now. Three, I guess. The old boy would come out here every day of the week if he could."

"Why doesn't he?"

The driver glanced back at me. "He can't afford bus fare more than once a month or so. He's a pensioner—Spanish American War if I'm not wrong. I don't figure they ever had much, but when she got sick what little they did have went to the doctor and the hospital and the funeral home. You know how it is. The old boy lives in a shack out by the quarry. Collects scrap metal and rags to buy his beans and bacon—and a bus ticket every time he can."

"But, the flowers," I said. "They must cost seven or eight bucks."

"At least," said the driver, then leaned back and yelled, "Kings Valley coming up!"

"How did he earn enough to get flowers like these?"

"There's more to it than that," said the driver. "There ain't no florist in Dallas. He's got to take the morning bus into Salem for that, then back to Dallas, and then out to the cemetery."

I did a little calculating in my head. "It must take him a couple weeks of full-time work to pay for the tickets and the flowers."

The driver shrugged.

The bus pulled into Kings Valley, and stopped at the general merchandise. The people getting on the bus smiled knowingly at me.

I went on to the dance and had pretty much the most wonderful first date anybody in North America had ever experienced.

There was no second date. Megan's family pulled up stakes and moved to California a few weeks later. I went on another date with a very nice cousin of Patrick's later that summer, but it wasn't the same. No date would ever be the same.

•••

I SHUT OFF THE RECORDER and put it on my bedside table. That one had felt good to tell. I looked at Eric.

"That was a beautiful story, Dad." He seemed genuinely moved. "I really liked hearing more about Grandma. She had a big, big heart. And so did that old man. What a character."

"Old Man Sanford? He was the sort of man you never forget."

"Why have I never heard this story before now?" Eric wondered.

I wondered for a minute, too. "I guess I didn't realize I hadn't shared it with you. I know I told your mother, though."

"You had," Connie said, "though I distinctly don't remember you including any of that business about a 'pony' and 'lightning' striking you."

I looked to my son. "You see, a man can never win."

"Dear," I said to Connie, "if you search hard, do you think you might find, in the depths of your kind heart, enough benevolence to forgive this old man his foolish first boyhood infatuation?"

She waited a moment. Her face twisted into a look of deep contemplation. "Maybe," she deadpanned, struggling hard to restrain a laugh. Then she couldn't restrain it, and we all laughed.

We laughed a lot together over the next few hours. Eric and Connie stayed with me through what the hospital claimed was dinner. We talked further about my parents, and some of my experiences picking in the fields to earn spending money when I was a boy. It was especially enjoyable to spend this time with Eric. I don't think he so much as glanced at his phone again the rest of the time we were together.

As he and Connie were getting ready to leave, he turned to me.

"Dad, what ever came of you and that old man, what was his name? Sanford?"

"I never did have the good fortune of running across his path again. But some years later I heard that he and Gladys could be found together, there in that ancient cemetery. Thanking him is on my to-do list. I think I'll be able to check that one off before long."

RESPONSIBILITY

SLEEP IS A GREAT LUXURY. Until I was diagnosed with prostate cancer last year, I never gave getting sleep a second thought. I have dozed deep and easy on the decks of warships tossing on the waves of the South Pacific, on fir branches on the sides of mountains, and through all of the assorted high-stress adventures that normal life throws at a person. Even on those blessedly rare nights when my hard-headed approach to some issue or another with Connie found me huffing off to the couch in the den with a pillow and blanket in an attempt to look like I'd won the encounter, I have always enjoyed great sleep.

Until now. The combination of having my routine turned upside down, the effects of a host of medications on my body, and living in the round-the-clock organized chaos that is a modern hospital have achieved what war and work and kids and marital reality never could—I'm not sleeping worth a darn.

My Marine Corps company commander used to say that sleep was a weapon. Of course, it was a weapon he seemed to take delight in not letting us use very often. But he was right.

The nursing staff has attempted various remedies—some more pleasant than others—but so far nothing has helped. The quality of one's stay in the hospital seems to boil down to the number of prods, pokes, sticks, squeezes and assorted insertions you undergo in an average day. Twenty-two was my count yesterday, by the way. Five-star rating in anybody's travel book, I'd say.

Not being able to sleep does have its benefits, though. When I decided to spend what time I have left focusing on this little values project, I didn't think I had a prayer of getting it all done. Not in the timeframe Doc McGuire was talking about. And not with eighty-two years of stories to sort out, distill and record. It still looks daunting, but I didn't know when I launched this project that I'd have a few extra hours every day to get the job done. "Small blessings," my mother would say. Take all you can get.

•••

I LOOKED AT THE CLOCK. It was 6 AM, Sunday morning, about four hours since I dozed off. There were clouds outside my window, dark and thickening. Rain had been a little shy this year, and the snow pack in the Cascades was light. Farmers would be happy to see this storm. Connie would be in after church, and maybe I'd get a visit later with Rachel and the kids.

I raised my bed to its maximum angle, and swung my legs over the side. Leticia had unhooked me from the IV, so I had a few hours of mobility. I stood slowly, pulled on my robe, and shuffled closer to the window. I'd discovered that I could lean on the back of a chair, and stand by the window for as long as fifteen or twenty minutes—another one of those small blessings.

Beyond the cherry tree, I could see into the park, across the creek and all the way to the white marble façade of the state capital building. I was especially glad to have a great view of the figure on top of the building; the twenty-two foot tall, gold-gilt statue of the Oregon Pioneer. My family and I attended the statue unveiling ceremony in 1938. As a lifelong lumberman, it warms my heart to look up at that broad-shouldered fellow with his ax ready at his side. Axes built my state, and made possible the revenue to build the schools and roads and bridges and water systems. Most folks these days have forgotten that—and I figure there are those who'd like to see him replaced with a statue of a slender computer programmer holding out a microchip instead of an ax—but for the ones who remember history, that pioneer is a true representation of who made our comfortable lives possible. Grit and steel and determination and courage—that's what the pioneer stands for.

"You thinking of escaping?"

I turned to see Nurse Marsden coming into the room.

"I'll wait until you take a day off to slip away," I said. "Wouldn't want to put a black mark on your record."

She handed me a small plastic cup with three pills—patriotic red, white and blue today. "This floor will be at max population by the end of the day," she said. "So if you'd like to blow this joint, be my guest. We can use the room."

I turned to walk back to my bed, only to be hit by a sudden wave of pain and nausea. I clutched my abdomen, fighting the urge to throw up. My temples throbbed, and I felt like a hot poker was being pushed through my back and into my gut. I sank to my knees, dizzy, disoriented. I heard Nurse Marsden's voice, far away and faint, but I couldn't make out what she was saying. The pain intensified, and I slumped to the ground on my side and pulled my knees up against my chest. My vision blurred, but I could make out feet all around me, and there were many voices talking at the same time. I felt myself being lifted, and then laid down, and then an oxygen mask was attached to my face. I could tell my IV shunt was being attached, and I felt a wave of comforting warmth wash over me. The pain began to lessen, my eyes closed, and I slept.

It was nearly noon before I came to. Connie sat next to me, reading a book. The oxygen mask was gone, but two new IV towers with half-filled drip bags now loomed above me. Sure enough, a shunt had been inserted into each of my arms. I also had a patch on my chest with a wire running to an unfamiliar monitor.

"What hit me?" I whispered.

Connie came close, and took my hand.

"The on-call doctor just left. You're doing fine, darling. You just over did it."

"I walked ten feet and stood by the window for five minutes," I said.

She squeezed my hand, and kissed me. "The nurse asked me to call her when you woke up. Do me a favor—stay in bed, would you?"

A minute later Nurse Marsden came in. "How's the pain?" she asked.

"Tolerable. No, it's better than that," I answered. "I'm feeling okay, a little woozy, but better. Sorry about that."

"Well, let that be a lesson to you to not walk away from a woman in the middle of a conversation," she said. "We like to get the last word in, don't we Mrs. Forrestal."

She checked my temperature and blood pressure, and unhooked the heart monitor.

"We'll remove one IV this afternoon," she said. "But you aren't going exploring any more today. Got it?"

"I have an important visitor coming by in a couple of hours."

"I'd rather you rested," said the nurse. "But, if you keep it short, I guess that will be alright."

She left, and Connie went off to call Eric and Rachel. My head had cleared, and the dizziness subsided. Many more episodes like that, I thought, and I wouldn't be able to do any more recording. Speaking of that, where was the digital recorder? I was too weak to sit up, or even to raise my arms. When my dear friend Lois Greaves arrived, I'd have to ask Connie to do the recording.

•••

OUR FRIENDSHIP WITH LOIS began by accident. I was flipping though the Sunday Oregonian one summer morning and was about to turn a page without reading any of the articles when something in a photograph caught my eye. A tall, stately, fortyish black woman with over-sized glasses was smiling for the camera. She looked a little uncomfortable having her photo taken. She stood in front of a classroom chalkboard with two words written on it in large, bold print: "You're responsible."

Responsible? That got my attention. The article headline was "Longtime Portland Teacher: Public Schools Have Deserted Our Children," with the sub-head, "Lois Greaves announces opening of new academy."

Now, they really had my attention. According to the article, Greaves had been a highly respected middle school English teacher in the Portland public system for over twenty years. She described how the quality of education for her mostly black students had declined year after year. A host of causes, some of them social, some political, many economic, had left the neighborhoods of Northeast Portland blighted. The public schools, Greaves said, fought a valiant battle for a long time. But little by little, the schools began to unravel just as the neighborhoods around them did. "The glue that holds neighborhoods together just melted over the years," she was quoted as saying.

"Families broke down, businesses left, crime spiraled out of control, politicians lined their pockets with money slated for neighborhood improvement, and who suffered most? The children. And how did the school district respond? By disassembling the very framework of learning, support, discipline, structure and achievement-orientation that the schools needed now more desperately than ever."

According to Greaves, as the neighborhood crumbled and the social structure that rewarded hard work and individual responsibility faded away, the public schools were all that stood in the gap between hope and chaos. But instead of recognizing its societal obligation as a bulwark against crime, corruption, neighborhood decay and diminished expectations, said Greaves, the schools instead threw in the towel in the name of social and political progress.

"Standards were gutted," she said. "The art of teaching began to take a back seat to the function of warehousing children. The ideal of academic excellence was forgotten. Basic concepts like personal responsibility were no longer mentioned in classes, let alone consciously taught."

What I found most interesting was her description of the "final straw" that led her to the decision to walk away from her secure public employment and risk everything on the startup of a small private school.

"The school board issued a directive this year regarding students and language," she said. "We were told, English teachers in particular, that we were no longer to insist that students use—or even strive to use—proper English in their written work, or in their spoken language. To correct grammatical errors, misspellings, mispronunciations, malapropisms, and double negatives, the board said, would constitute an infringement of the students' personal, civic and cultural rights."

"They took away the one tool that I knew—the one that anyone who cared about these children knew—could make the difference between success and failure in their lives. A strong command of the English language is the key to opening every door of possibility out there," she said in the article. "And the school board was pretending that wasn't true. Never mind that they would never allow their own children to use the kind of street vernacular they were defending. Never mind that their directive was going to have the net effect of condemning a generation of children to poverty and hopelessness. I couldn't, I wouldn't stand by and watch these children be sacrificed upon the altar of such misguided policies."

She left public teaching that June. She found a neighborhood church willing to rent three empty rooms to her, and she cashed in her retirement, borrowed a little from family, and was planning to open her own little K-6 school in the fall.

"I don't know how I'm going to do it," she admitted to the reporter. "But these children need someone to take on the responsibility of providing them a good education. The public schools have given up any notion of responsibility for anything other than collecting tax money for each classroom seat they fill. I'm not going to shuffle this responsibility on to anyone else—it's mine, and I'm going to accept it."

I read and reread the article. The second time through, I caught something I had missed earlier: the reporter made mention of the shoddy condition of the rooms that Mrs. Greaves was turning into classrooms.

Maybe there was something I could do.

I called the reporter first thing Monday. She told me that Greaves was holding a community information meeting Wednesday evening as a way of looking for people who might want to teach, volunteer or donate labor or money to the project. I followed up with a call to the church pastor, who, as it happened, had worked in construction while going to college. He told me exactly what kinds of building material Greaves needed to make those rooms habitable.

That Wednesday afternoon I climbed into the cab of our biggest flat bed. Packed on the truck's deck was a load of two by fours and two by sixes, pressure treated posts, four by eight plywood, sheet rock, windows, insulation, interior and exterior doors, flashing, floor tiles, roofing materials, and enough paint, nails, and other materials to refurbish those three old rooms into brand-spanking new classrooms.

Another of my yard guys followed in the smaller flatbed with the forklift for unloading the materials. The article hadn't pulled any punches—it was a rough neighborhood. Boarded up houses, a seedy motel, empty storefronts and trash-strewn lots surrounded the tiny school complex. It was clear, as we pulled into the parking lot, that there would be a lot of work ahead.

Lois was leading a group of about fifty people from the church sanctuary over to the dilapidated little building that was going to become her school. I picked her out just as she spotted our trucks. She approached us, scanned the piles of building materials strapped on the flatbed, and sized up the situation in an instant. I can't describe the beauty of the smile she beamed up to us.

"You young men wouldn't be looking for a nice place to unload all that wonderful stuff, now would you?"

That was the beginning of one of the most important and rewarding friendships Connie and I have ever known. That fall, with no real funding, the barest of supplies, money for only a handful of paid teachers (she herself took no salary for the first three years) and a couple dozen parent volunteers, Lois opened the school she called The Academy.

Some worried about how the community would take to her notion of a school where personal responsibility and academic excellence were the watchwords. A place where the murky educational and behavioral shallows of the public school system were replaced by rigorous academic standards rooted firmly in a no-holds-barred moral compass. The worry didn't last long: Lois received more than four hundred applications for the seventy student openings that first year.

Over the years, the school grew large enough to purchase the entire church property for its current K-12 student population of four hundred fifty children.

For Connie and I, working with Lois and the students and staff at The Academy has been a lifelong labor of love. We have funded one student scholarship per year for over twenty years. We also employed three students as full-time summer interns at the lumberyard. Connie took on the task of finding free summer housing for the interns, and when I sold the business to my foreman four years ago, the sale came with a stipulation that he continue the internships as long as he owned the yard.

When I identified responsibility as one of the values I wanted to touch upon, Lois' was the first—and only—name that came to mind.

•••

A LAB TECH CAME IN for another blood draw, and the on-call doctor dropped in to check my progress since my episode that morning. I was feeling much better. He okayed the removal of the second IV, and told me I could eat anytime I wished. Despite my very reasonable argument, though, he did not approve my request to send someone over to the park to get a Polish dog with mustard and sauerkraut.

I looked at the clock on the far wall. It was just now two o'clock.

"I always wondered what you did with your time off." The sound of that familiar voice was music to my ears.

Lois stood in the doorway next to Connie. She wore a long, plum-colored dress and her trademark square-framed glasses. She carried a flowering plant, and a two-foot wide roll of paper wrapped with red ribbon.

"This is actually about twenty-seventh on my list of vacation spots, Lois, but the view is good and the room service is fast."

I raised my bed, and gathered a hug and kiss from Lois while Connie pulled up another chair. Lois radiates energy like a dynamo at a hydroelectric plant. I had the notion that if you attached a couple of wires to her you could light up a small city. And at age seventy-two, she showed no sign of slowing down. Lois unfurled the paper, and she and Connie stretched it out to about six feet in length. It was covered with signatures, notes, and drawings.

"It's signed by every student in the school," she said, "plus the teachers. Look at what the middle school math students wrote."

I leaned forward to read a bright blue headline. It said: "Thanks a 10^{10}, Mr. Forrestal, for all you do for us." I shook my head. Thanks a million, indeed. Those kids had no idea how much they had added to my life over the years. Connie and Lois put the banner up next to the window.

"A lot of people are praying for you, Martin," said Lois when she sat back down. "My Friday night Bible study ladies have got you and Connie covered."

I took her hand. "I wondered why I jolted out of a deep sleep last Friday—should have known it was you."

We caught up on school news and on Lois' plans to fly to Baltimore in a couple of weeks to attend her oldest grandson's graduation from medical school. He was one of the many miraculous stories to come out of The Academy.

Connie and I told her about the scholarship endowment we had created. Starting in the fall, it would fund an ongoing year of tuition and books to two students chosen by the staff on the basis of that child's demonstration of leadership and determination. We decided that it would be called the Nate R. Holden Scholarship.

"I didn't think you'd let anything be named after you Martin," Lois said.

She smiled. "But you know, we could paint your name on the wall of the new cafeteria—you supplied the materials, after all."

"And have the kids connect my memory with school food? I think I'll pass, all the same."

Connie poured some fresh ice water for me and picked the digital recorder up. She turned it on.

"I told Lois about your values project, Martin," Connie said. "She's happy to pitch in."

"You really don't know how to just sit back, do you," said Lois. "All these years, you're always making something happen. Didn't retire until you were what, seventy-eight? And when you weren't working you were building a greenhouse for Connie, or coaching Little League or painting a classroom at my school, or taking a bunch of my students steelhead fishing up on the Siletz. How is it that you didn't take up golf or bowling or something? Martin, honey, for a man who is so cheerful all the time, I confess I don't know when it was that you were just having some fun."

I coughed into my water glass. "No fun? Lois, it's all been fun. I have been blessed with the love of a good woman, I have a son and daughter-in-law, wonderful grandkids, a business that I'm passionate about, and pretty darn good health all my life. Best of all, I have had the opportunity to do a few things that I think have made a difference to the world, or at least to one little corner of the world. No fun? You're wrong about that."

Lois laughed. "Does he always go on like this?" she asked Connie.

"These days? Pretty much all the time."

"You read the list of values I'm talking about?" I asked Lois.

"I did, just a few minutes ago in the lobby when Connie and I had a visit."

"So I suppose the value I want to talk to you about isn't exactly a mystery?"

"No mystery, Martin. And I'm honored you asked me."

I pushed on the controls to adjust my bed again.

"Connie, could you please shove another pillow behind me?" I asked.

When Connie was done, I noticed tears in Lois' eyes.

"Not time for those yet," I said.

Lois wiped her eyes with a tissue. "I'll decide when it's time, young man. Now, you just get on with your questions."

"It's not like an interview, Lois. At least, that's not the way I think about this project of mine. It's more like…"

"A testament?"

"I suppose so. In fact, that's not a bad description at all. A testament. That's as good a description as any I've come up with. But I don't want it to end up as just a pile of paper gathering dust on a shelf somewhere—not that kind of testament. My hope is that what I'm doing here can be put together in some kind of form that my family, and other people, too, can learn from."

"A living testament, that's what you mean" said Lois.

"I do. At first, you know, I was a little intimidated to take on this task, not because I wasn't sure I could finish it, but because—and this sounds almost silly to me now—because I was worried that what I had to say just wouldn't stack up against all the great words and ideas expressed by the great minds of all time. I'm no Einstein, for heaven's sake."

"And Al was no Martin Forrestal," said Connie.

"Well, you know, that's almost the conclusion I came to," I said. "I do have something to say that's important. We all do. But if we start to compare ourselves to the giants of literature and philosophy and science and all their classic works, the party's over. We won't get a word written. And if you look at it that way, why would you even try?"

"So what made you decide to go ahead?" asked Lois.

"A couple things. First, I have a responsibility to my family. That's number one. And then, this was my life, my story and my lessons learned. Patton wasn't by my side during the war. And Freud didn't help me through the tough spots in my marriage."

Connie smiled. "I'll confirm that one," she said.

"My responsibility is to tell my story my way to the people who will appreciate it—and the people who could potentially benefit from it the most. I don't need to be Hemmingway or Fitzgerald. I need to be me."

"It's wonderful that now they'll have something personal, a part of who you are, with them always," Lois said. "I know I would dearly love to have something my grandmother wrote or recorded. I only have a few old photographs."

"Connie, would you get my wallet out of the drawer?" I asked. "I want to show something to Lois."

Connie gave me my wallet and I pulled out a laminated scrap of paper. It was about an inch and a half wide, and six inches long. The paper was ragged on both sides, as if it had been torn hastily from a larger piece of paper. The plastic laminate protected the writing on the paper. It was a list, scribed in pencil in a neat, precise hand. I handed it to Lois.

"What do you make of this?" I asked.

She began to read out loud. "Lettuce, hamburger, cheese, bread, salt—it's a grocery list," she said. "With prices. Oh, my, hamburger six cents a pound?"

"Read a little more," I said.

"…trousers for Martin, thirty-one by thirty-four inches, two dollars twenty-five cents. Blue cotton shirt, a dollar ninety-five. More shopping— honey, you were a skinny thing, weren't you?"

I took the list back from Lois. "A few years after my father died, my mother was preparing to move in with us. While she was out one afternoon, her house caught fire. It burned to the ground, and she lost just about every possession she and my dad had accumulated during their years together. No one was hurt, and her cats were safe, and we were all thankful for that. But a fire burns more than the building—it burns a lifetime of memories."

"When the smoke settled and we got her moved in," I continued, "everything the fire department had been able to save came with her in two cardboard boxes. Mother died six months later."

"When Connie and I finally went through the boxes, we found mostly old bills and magazines. Hardly worth saving. But there was one thing, the only thing I have written by my mother, the only proof I have that she ever put pencil to paper."

I held up the scrap of paper.

"This is it—a shopping list. There's a story behind the shirt and trousers, but even if it said tomato sauce and peanut butter instead of pants and shirt, it wouldn't matter to me. This list is the only written expression of anything that I have from my mother. And, as silly as I'm sure it sounds, this darn thing is a treasure to me."

"Let me see that again," said Lois. "A shopping list." She read it again. "No, I don't think it's silly, Martin. Not at all."

"And just think how I would have felt if I had discovered her journals in those boxes," I said, "someplace where she wrote about her life and her struggles and her triumphs. What would that mean to me, and to my children and theirs? She had a treasure to give, just like my father did, just like yours did. But they didn't leave it."

"You mentioned other motivations," Lois said, "for deciding to take on this project. What were they?"

"'Motivations' might not be the best word. But I was really emboldened by something Mark Twain once said to a reporter. Twain was at the height of his fame, probably the best-known living author in the world. The reporter asked the old bird how he compared his works to those of the pantheon of giants, like Dante or Cervantes—'the truly great writers.' Twain thought a minute, and then said, 'There's no question that the works of those men is like the finest, rarest, most expensive wine, while my work is more like, well, more like water.' Twain paused a moment, and then dropped his punch line: 'Of course now,' he said slowly, 'everybody drinks water.'"

Lois and Connie chuckled.

"I hope I'm giving my family something that is a part of them already, something as natural as the air they breathe and, to borrow Twain's line, as natural as the water they drink. So it's not rare wine—so what? It's me, and I'm a part of them. That's why I'm doing this. It's my responsibility, and it's my heirs' birthright."

"Oh, he does get fired up, doesn't he?" Lois said to Connie.

My wife gave me a quiet smile. "He does," she said, "at that. But then I'd say that's why you two are such good friends, Lois. Getting fired up over the things that are worth getting fired up for is what you have always been about."

"Well, the furnace is getting a bit creaky," said Lois, "but the fire is just as hot as ever. Nobody is going to do for my students what needs to be done except them, and I don't see that fact changing any time soon. And nothing but a hot fire can keep The Academy going."

•••

WE SAT QUIETLY without talking for a couple of minutes, something I have found that only the best of friends can do. Then Connie excused herself to make a coffee run, and Lois and I began to talk about her school.

"Is it any different today," I asked, "than it was when you began?"

"In what way?"

"Well, how do your new students today take it when they learn that the only operating rule you have in your school is, 'You're Responsible?'"

"Oh, a lot of the children are more mystified than ever. Today, most of them are coming from schools where the rules of conduct take up a twenty-page booklet. When they find out what that level of responsibility really means—that they and they alone are responsible for their own lives—some of them are pretty shocked. Some even get angry. A few never get it at all and leave the school."

"Because, truly, no one has required that?"

Lois shook her head. "Because they haven't had the great privilege of discovering that inside the cover of that one simple concept lies the answer to every dream they will ever have, every treasure they ever seek, and every problem they will ever face."

Lois leaned back in her chair. "It is a process—more of a process with some than with others, that's for sure. But we start them young. The kindergarteners are required to keep their personal work areas clean; they each have assigned chores to help out the teacher with classroom management; and they even do cleanup and weed picking on the school grounds. Everybody has responsibilities, and those lists get longer year-by-year. And every student knows what their fellow students are responsible for, at all grade levels. By the time a child has gone from first grade to high school with us, they know those signs all over the school that say 'You're Responsible,' mean a whole lot of things. Young men learn it includes being respectful to young ladies, and they all learn that a family is a treasure to be cared for, not a situational comedy or drama to be walked into and out of like a revolving door. They learn that they have more control over their own destinies than any other human being on the planet, no matter how powerful or rich or famous that person might be. And it's a positive reinforcement thing. When one of the kids sees most of the other kids around them carrying their own weight, the child not doing her part is going to be mighty lonely mighty fast. That's the worst punishment for a child, believe me."

She chuckled. "People ask me sometimes, 'What do you do to build them up?' I tell them, 'I don't build them up. They build themselves up.' It's a basic law of human nature: esteem flows naturally from the performance of esteemable acts. Let me take that a step further: esteem flows only from the performance of esteemable acts. By practicing responsibility in all of their dealings, the students are naturally building up their own stores of true self-esteem with everything they do. Real self-esteem doesn't come from people telling you how wonderful you are. Children who are fed that all through school feel cheated when they wake up one morning to find themselves living in public housing without an education, without a good job, without a clue. 'Wait,' they say, 'I'm special—aren't I? My teachers told me so. TV told me so. Everybody told me I'm special—so why did I end up here in this crummy place?' How can they be anything but angry at a system that told them day after day that what they accomplished or failed at was far less important than how they felt about themselves?"

Lois was sitting so upright in her chair she looked like she might float out of it. "Being accountable, practicing responsibility," she continued, with a full head of steam, "that is the antidote. And that is the ultimate form of self-love—which is, sadly, in short supply with a number of our students before they get to The Academy. They are confused, they've been set up for failure. A lot of them don't believe, deep down, that they are capable. We tell them they are capable of exactly as little or as much as they believe they can do. And then with every single positive act—with every weed a kindergartener pulls, with every encouragement an eighth grader offers to a fifth grader, with every chemistry project a senior completes—each child proves to himself that he can do more—more for himself, more for his friends, more for his family, more for his community. Our students learn that personal responsibility and civic duty go hand in hand. We teach that freedom and responsibility are interdependent values, for individuals as well as for the nation. Can't have one without the other. And these children understand they have a responsibility to help those who need a hand up, and an equal responsibility to correct those who need correction."

"And how is all that translating into the community these days?" I asked. "Things have gotten better up there, but those are still some pretty mean streets."

"It's tough, no question," said Lois. "I've seen second graders cross a busy street so they didn't have to walk around an addict crashed on the sidewalk. Prostitutes ply their trade behind deserted buildings and in cars within a hundred feet of the school grounds. The kids know it. They don't hide from it—they can't, it smacks them in the face every day when they step out of their doors to walk to school. They know there are limits to what their personal responsibility is towards others, and they know that their number one responsibility is to make it to school and back home safely, every day. That's a big load to put on the back of a seven-year-old child, but we don't do them any favors by hiding from it. We don't want them to close their eyes to the misery around them; for now, we just want them to navigate around it."

Connie returned with coffee for herself and Lois. I got more ice water.

"Once they have proven to themselves that they are capable of being responsible, it provides them with power," Lois went on. "Not empowerment—that's a silly PC concept that takes the raw strength out of the idea of power. You can't em-power anything or anyone. But you can give a child the tools to deal with the bad, even to change it, and to shape her life in such a way that she can see the results of her actions every single day. Responsibility is a tool."

We were interrupted by the entrance of Nurse Marsden and a tech, who removed the IV line and shunt from my right arm. Connie and Lois huddled in a corner of the room while I was being re-configured. My nurse told Connie and Lois that I was going to have to rest for the next several hours.

"I'm sorry our visit has to end, Lois," I said. "I don't think you were revved up all the way yet."

She sat beside my bed, and took my hand in hers. She closed her eyes, and began to rock slowly back and forth. As she did, she hummed "Amazing Grace," sweet and low and whispery. Tears formed at the corners of her closed eyes, but she didn't wipe them. She prayed and hummed and held my hand tight. When she opened her eyes, she said, "I have a confession to make, Martin, something I should have told you and Connie about years ago."

"You don't need to confess anything to me, Lois. Don't you dare."

"Hush. This has been on my conscience for a long time." She sat up straight, and folded her hands in her lap. "Over the years, you donated a lot of supplies to the school. My, that first day you drove into the parking lot with that big shiny truck full of lumber and doors, I thought an angel had fallen from heaven and landed in my lap. About ten years ago, I hit a financial wall. We had grown pretty fast, and one morning the school secretary told me the bank was on the phone, and they told me we were broke. I had to have thirty-five hundred dollars, and I had to have it like yesterday to keep the sheriff from locking the front door."

"Why didn't you call me?" I asked.

"Now I told you to hush, you hush," Lois said. "I've knocked on your door, and everyone else's these past thirty years more times than I care to remember. This time, I needed to figure things out for myself." She dabbed here eyes with the tissue. "I was looking out at the playground, watching the little ones at recess, racking my brain, praying to the Lord, when my eyes settled on something I realized I could sell quick and easy. Martin, it was a load of building materials and a concrete mixer your men had delivered a few days earlier. A big load. It was for our new gym, and there was probably ten thousand dollars worth of donated material sitting there."

Connie couldn't stand the suspense. "What did you do, Lois?"

"Not two blocks down the street, Mr. Patel was remodeling his motel, and doing a nice job, too. No more trash there, he run's a clean place. Anyway, I got myself down there, and made him an offer. 'That pile of materials for three thousand five hundred dollars. No questions, no negotiating, take it or leave it.' He and his son came over to see what was there, and a half hour later I had my check, and the bank had theirs."

Her head drooped as she reached out her hand and put it on my shoulder. "I stole from you, my friends. I am so ashamed. That's why it took us another year to build the gym."

I pushed the button for my bed to go higher. Connie didn't say a word. She was waiting for my cue. Lois was crying into her tissue, staring at the floor. I thought about this extraordinary woman sailing down that busy street and into that man's office and making the pitch for that pile of lumber and materials, and started to chuckle. My chuckle turned to laughter, and in a few seconds I was laughing so hard my stomach hurt.

Lois and Connie were astonished—at first. Then Connie joined in, and finally Lois stopped her sobbing and began to laugh as well. We made such a ruckus that Nurse Marsden popped her head in to make sure everything was okay.

I shook my head, and smiled at Lois. "Everything is great," I told the nurse. "Absolutely couldn't be better."

We pulled ourselves together, and I said my goodbyes with Lois. She stood at my side and held my hand and prayed for me. Then she kissed my cheek, and she was gone.

•••

WHEN CONNIE GOT BACK from walking Lois to the lobby, she was carrying a package.

"You won't like this Martin, but I'm afraid it's out of your hands, so you had better just get used to the idea right now."

She unwrapped a large framed photo, turned it right side up, and laid it on my lap. It was a color shot of the gymnasium at The Academy, and looked like it was taken from the top of a tall ladder. The entire student body was assembled in front of the gym, boys in white shirts and black slacks, girls in blue skirts and white blouses, and the faculty, with Lois Greaves front and center.

Connie said, "This was taken yesterday."

Everyone in the picture was smiling up at the camera, but their bodies were turned slightly, and they were all pointing at something on the building behind them. Stretched above the gym's double doors was a shiny new banner. In three-foot letters were the words: MARTIN FORRESTAL GYMNASIUM. Under that, in smaller letters, it said, HE WAS RESPONSIBLE.

"Lois thought you'd put up a fuss if she gave it to you in person," said Connie. "The banner is temporary until they can have a permanent sign made. You don't mind if I contribute to the effort, do you?"

I held the photo tight against my chest.

"Connie, I'm tired of getting choked up every day," I finally said. "I don't know what to say."

"You don't have to say anything, Martin. Not a word."

But I had to. "He was responsible," I read.

Connie leaned over and wiped a tear from my cheek. "You are, my darling."

Family Unity

My family history is made up in equal parts of heroes and villains and saints and sinners—which is to say that it is like most family histories. My grandmother liked to say that families are like circuses, where acts whirl away non-stop in three interlocking rings, while eager lines of clowns and lion-tamers and acrobats waited in the wings to go on stage as soon as the ringmaster (or mistress in her case) blew the whistle.

She knew what she was talking about. There is no other institution in life—at least none that we willingly put up with—that is at once the source of such great joy and deep misery, such heartbreak and heartwarming edification as the family. Whatever else we do in life, whatever we accomplish, however far we rise or fall, everything we do begins, as it will surely end, with family.

I do not buy into the notion, proffered sanctimoniously from all sides of the political and religious spectrum, that the family is an endangered species. The family structure survived the sweep of the Mongol hordes across Asia, and the brutal repression of the Roman Empire, and the horrendous genocide of Stalin and Hitler and Mao. It pulled through the Renaissance and the Inquisition and the conquest and subjugation of the New World, and the Black Death and the Great Flu pandemic and the

Great Depression, and a thousand other calamities visited upon it by the forces of nature and the abuses of humankind.

The family unit, as an institution, will, I am sure, similarly persevere through the nuclear age, and the clash of civilizations, and the battle over the environment, and yes, even the Internet, and whatever is to come next.

I believe this not only because I have faith in the biological imperative that God programmed into every cell in our body that pre-disposes us to want to be a part of a family, but because from a purely practical standpoint, there is simply no alternative organization that can deliver the goods the way that the family can.

For whom do we go to work every day? For whom do we struggle and achieve? For whom do we sacrifice, and take risks and save and hope and pray? For family. Always.

I know the family is under assault, as it has always been under assault since the dawn of time. I've lived too long to look at life through rose-colored glasses. I know what parents go through trying to find a good school and a safe neighborhood and positive influences for their children. I see the cultural swamp with its moral quicksand and its seductive siren call aimed at capturing and destroying innocence and wonder and hopefulness. I see the enemy clearly. But, I have seen enemies before.

Family has always been important to me. The older one gets, the less the treasures of the outside world beckon, and the more the warmth and welcome of family draws you close.

And, yes, I am more inclined to think of family, and in particular of the value of family unity, as my life ebbs toward that still, quiet place beyond. I expect it is the same with anyone upon whom fortune has bestowed the great blessing of knowing when your number is to be called. Truth be told, if the dark angel had materialized in my bedroom one night and offered me a choice between an immediate departure or a three week stay of execution before the big event, I would probably have taken the fast track. Dying suddenly, unexpectedly, by accident or stroke may be kinder in some respects, in that the whole business is over in an instant, with little time to suffer. A long hospital stay could mean putting my family through the exhausting experience of a deathbed vigil that could last for weeks. Why not take the express train, and let them get about healing and rebuilding all the sooner?

But then I had my late night epiphany, my realization that this old man

137

had one last thing to share with those he loved. Through my stories, I hope and believe that generations of my family will find strength and solace, hope and inspiration. The price of giving that gift will be a few weeks of discomfort for me, and, I know, a difficult time for those I love.

Great gifts really do come at great cost.

•••

IT OCCURRED TO ME this morning that I will be the first Forrestal man in family history to die in bed. That made me laugh. Chance has had a lot to do with that, the whims of fortune and all. But it is also a generational reality. Old boys like me have fathers and grandfathers who lived in a far more dangerous world, where death was seldom far beyond the horizon.

My great-grandfather Bart Forrestal and his brother Noble are classic examples of the swiftness with which Forrestal men have meet their demises. When they returned from service in the Civil War, Noble and Bart packed up their families and left Ohio for the Montana Territory. Before leaving, Noble secured a contract with the Army to establish a sawmill to supply timber for the construction of a new Army outpost in Eastern Montana, at the confluence of the Missouri and Yellowstone Rivers.

Fort Buford was one of the military posts established to protect overland and river routes used by immigrants settling the West. Noble and Bart arrived in Montana in May 1866, and quickly assembled their sawmill. They built houses for their families first, and then began construction of the fort stockade and service buildings.

The Sioux had slightly different plans for the future of the Yellowstone Valley, however. In December 1866, a Hunkpapa Sioux war party led by Chief Sitting Bull attacked a work party near the sawmill. Seven settlers, including twenty-four-year-old Noble Forrestal, were killed in the raid.

His brother Bart continued operation of the sawmill, and he prospered as the Army contracted for more new outposts to help put down the Sioux resistance. When the Northern Pacific Railroad pushed into the Yellowstone Valley in 1871, and on into the Black Hills three years later, Bart made a small fortune manufacturing wooden rail trestles. But he should have learned from Noble's experience and done his business from the safety and comfort of his fashionable home in Sidney, Montana. Instead, he ventured into the Black Hills in the fall of 1874 to see first hand what kind of progress the railroad was making.

It was a fateful decision. Bart was camped on the banks of Turtle Creek with a survey crew when a band of Sioux warriors attacked his party and cut them to ribbons. He left behind a wife and three children, including my grandfather, Jake. Bart Forrestal's widow was no businesswoman, but before her sawmill went bust, she bought a six hundred forty-acre spread outside of Sidney, on the banks of the Yellowstone River, which she worked tirelessly until her death.

Grandfather Jake grew up on the ranch, and built it into a prosperous cattle operation. My father was born on the ranch. My sister and I were born in a house there on a bluff overlooking the river that my father built in 1917 as a wedding gift for my mother.

I have only a few memories of Grandfather Jake, but they are tales worth telling. The Depression hit eastern Montana hard, and my Dad's lumber business all but dried up. He heard that things didn't look so bleak in Oregon, so we packed up the Ford pickup and pointed toward Salem, in the heart of the Willamette Valley. It was just Dad, Mom and me. I never met my sister, who died of diphtheria in 1919, six years before I was born.

Dad wasted no time starting up a small lumber mill in Salem, where he and my mother pretty much lived for the next few years. I spent more time playing in mounds of wood chips and clambering over piles of dimension lumber then other kids did at playgrounds or parks. Most parents today would think twice about letting their seven-year-old (in his Zorro mask) play near the business end of a whirring saw blade, or run under a shower of sticky bark raining down from a log peeler. The timber fallers and millwrights and log truck drivers kept an eye on me as I sailed around my personal pirate island, though. No boy was ever in better hands.

•••

In the spring of 1933, we drove back to Montana to visit Grandfather Jake. It was the first time off from their business that my parents had taken in two years. I was eight, and I was as anxious as all get out to ride horses, shoot the .22, and just maybe see some real-life cowboys. My mother tried to burst that bubble gently, telling me that nowadays cowboys only existed in the movies. She'd never say that again after this trip.

By the time we reached the family ranch, the winter thaw was complete, and flowers were starting to pop up along the sweeping drive that stretched from the county road up to Granddad's front door. His sprawling two-story house had a fresh coat of paint, and Grandmother Gwen's greenhouse was packed full of vegetable starts for their garden. The Montana sky was wide and blue and cloudless.

When we pulled up to the house, though, we didn't get the reception we expected. Jake was standing out on the covered porch talking in an animated fashion with Gwen. On the porch railing in front of him was his Colt revolver and his .30-06 rifle, with a scope. His horse was saddled and tied to the hitch post. It looked like he was going hunting. Didn't he know we were coming?

My dad tooted the horn, and we piled out of the car. Jake and Gwen came down off the porch for a round of backslaps and hugs, Mom and Grandma headed right into the house to set the world in order.

Grandfather Jake was a tall, big-shouldered man with a handlebar moustache and bright green eyes. Like my father, he worked as hard as any man alive, but he also knew how to blow off steam. Some of my earliest memories are of him playing fiddle or guitar in front of the great stone fireplace in his living room, and of Grandma snatching the bottle from him when he'd had one snoot too many to play in tune.

I raced around with their dog in the front yard while Dad and Grandfather Jake got into some serious conversation of their own on the porch. Mom and Grandma soon joined them, and the conversation grew lively.

"By God, they can't do it," fumed Grandfather Jake, "law or no law, they're not taking Samuel's place, or Jacob's either, or anybody's in this valley. Not today and not tomorrow. And if we have to face 'em down with pistols, that's exactly what we'll do."

"Dad, you can't do that," said my father, "you'll go to jail. You can't hogtie the sheriff and arrest the county judge, for pete's sake."

"I've been trying to tell him that all morning," said my grandmother, "but the old fool won't listen. Thinks Montana is still the Wild West."

"Wife," growled Grandfather Jake, "this is the west, and I can sure as straight tell you that today it's going to get one hell of a lot wilder. The sheriff made that certain, not us."

"Jake, stop now—the boy," my grandmother said.

Grandfather Jake gave me a wink. "Oh, he'll be alright. Heckfire, when I was his age I'd be going along on this little soiree."

"Well, then thank goodness for progress," said Grandma.

I went up on the porch. The grownups had all settled into chairs, and Jake took up his revolver and checked the chambers. I could see it was loaded.

"Granddad, what's going on?" I asked. "Is somebody in trouble?"

He brushed his hand through my hair. "By hornswoggle, laddie, it's good to see you. Sorry for all the ruckus. Is somebody in trouble? Well, now, fact is, somebody is in trouble. My own two nephews, and a couple of friends of theirs, too."

He gave the cylinder of his revolver a spin, and slipped it into his holster. That filled my brain with all kinds of possibilities. I'd seen plenty of Westerns at the Elsinore—I knew just what a pistol like that was capable of, from routing a war party of Indians to taking down a couple dozen cattle rustlers—all without a single reload. This vacation of ours was looking more promising by the minute.

My father sat quietly. Something was clearly bothering him. He turned to Jake and said, "Dad, any of my stuff still upstairs?"

Jake slapped my dad on the knee. "By God, son, you bet, and what isn't in that closet, I'll get for you. Come on then."

The men went into the house. Mom shot Grandma a troubled look.

"Mom, what's going on?" I asked again. Somebody ought to pass a law that says that just because you're a kid doesn't give adults the right to leave you in the dark when there's big stuff going on. And when Granddad is loading his rifle and revolver and saddling his best horse, that's the kind of stuff an eight-year-old is pretty much an expert on, so why not let him in on it all?

But, "That's enough now young man," was the only answer my mother gave. "We'll get some lunch—you play outside with the dog."

They returned with a plate of sandwiches and a jug of lemonade. Neither said a word while we ate. I sat on the steps, skulking, taking small bites, and feeling like the pirate who is late for his own ship's departure, forced to stand on the dock and watch as the sails fill out and the skull and crossbones are raised and the ship slides over the horizon to adventure without him.

Then I noticed a cloud of dust off to the west. There was no road out there, and town was in the opposite direction. It wasn't the weather—the sky was clear blue. Maybe a farmer with a tractor was kicking up the dust? Whatever it was, it was getting bigger.

"Grandma. What's that?" I pointed to the cloud of dust heading our direction.

"Oh, my," she said. "They really are coming. I prayed they wouldn't, but there they are."

Before my mother could respond, we heard noises at the side of the house. What I saw made me drop my sandwich on the ground, much to the dog's delight. Around the corner came my dad and Grandfather Jake. Gone were Dad's khaki trousers and sweater. He was wearing jeans and a leather vest over a blue woolen shirt with a neckerchief. He had boots on—boots with spurs! What was that on his belt? A six-gun? My dad was wearing a six-gun!

My chest was swollen with pride at the realization that my dad was, in fact, not the mild-mannered small-town lumberman I had come to know, but an honest-to-gosh, one hundred percent gun-toting, bad-guy-whacking American cowboy. Best of all, he had a weathered Stetson hat on his head. He held leather reins in one hand, attached to a beauty of a chestnut gelding. Behind the saddle was a rifle scabbard holding a Winchester lever-action .30-30.

I ran to my father's side. He smiled and handed me the reins. I don't think I've ever been so proud in my life. I had no idea what was afoot, but walking between my father and my grandfather made me feel like I was a part of something very big, and very important.

My father went up on the porch, and held my mother tight. Grandfather Jake swung up into his saddle. A thundering sound rolled ahead of the dust cloud, sweeping down the piney-ridge a hundred yards out. I could finally see a line of men on horseback, riding toward us at a fast gallop. They'd be here in a minute.

My father came down from the porch, and bent down in front of me. "Martin," he said, "there's something your granddad and I have to do. You see that line of riders out there?"

"Yes, Dad, I do."

"They're each and every one of them family. Some are our family, cousins and such. And some are the family of other folks we're going to help right now." He put his hands on my shoulders. "Fighting is a terrible thing, Son. But sometimes, it has to be done. I hope you never have to fight, Martin, but if you do, make sure that what you're fighting for is worth the price you may have to pay. Do you understand that?"

I nodded my head, but I really had no idea what he meant. I figured he was going to fight, and all of a sudden I felt empty inside. This didn't feel like how I felt at the movies when the heroes were riding off to fight the rustlers.

The riders pulled up to the split-rail fence twenty yards from the house. My father stood up. I grabbed his sleeve.

"Dad—what are you fighting for?"

He put his hand behind my neck, and smiled. "For family, Marty. Take care of your mom now."

With that, he mounted his horse, checked his rifle scabbard, nodded at my mother, and trotted forward to join the other men. Grandfather Jake took something from his vest pocket, and leaned down from his saddle.

"This is an Indian arrowhead, Martin. Genuine Sioux, found it myself up along the Musselshell. Probably belonged to old Sitting Bull hisself."

That was all he offered by way of explanation. He handed me the flint arrowhead, galloped over to the line of riders, and swung around to face the house.

•••

I CAN SEE THAT ROW OF MEN on horseback at that fence as clear in my mind right now as if they were lined up outside my hospital window this morning. There was no breeze, and for a minute the only sound was the breathing of two-dozen horses and the creak of saddle leather. They were ranchers and farmers all, not lawmen or professional soldiers. Some were no older than fifteen or sixteen. Each one had a sidearm and a rifle. Their faces were serious. There was no small talk, no joking. I looked at my father, sitting tall and strong in his saddle, the brim of his hat cocked back just a bit. He sat easy, as if riding off to war was something he did every day. He was thirty-eight years old. I never saw him handsomer, and I never loved him as fiercely as I did at that moment.

Then, one of the men, an older gentleman with long white hair spilling out from under his hat, shouted, "Okay, boys, let's give them city marshals a Montana welcome." He wheeled his horse, and raced off ahead of the rest of the riders. Then the air was filled with whistles and whoops and war cries, and the riders galloped off toward the low hills in the west.

I stood silent as they rode away. In a few minutes the sounds of horse's hooves faded, and then the riders and their cloud of dust disappeared into the lodgepole pines on the far horizon. I joined my mother and grandmother on the porch. Both were crying. I sat on the wood deck beside my mother's chair.

"Mom," I said, "I'm old enough to know what's going on."

She put her hand on my arm. "I expect that you are, son. Let's go in the house."

We joined my grandmother at the slab oak dining table in the kitchen. Grandma poured tea for Mom and herself, and put a plate of butterscotch cookies in front of me.

"Martin," Grandma began, "you know that these are very difficult times. This Depression has put people all across the valley out of work, and a lot of people have lost their homes and farms to the banks, because they can't make their mortgage payments. What's gone and happened now is that Mr. Roosevelt, the President of these United States, and the Board of Governors in charge of all the banks in the country, have declared something called a bank holiday. Every bank in the country is going to shut down in two days, and they'll stay shut until Mr. Roosevelt gets some of this mess figured out."

I nodded. Sounded like a big mess.

"What that means for the banks," she went on, "is that they won't be able to get the court to issue any new foreclosure orders. The sheriff has to have an order signed by a judge before they can throw a family off its place, and sell their land and possessions at a special sale called an auction."

My grandmother called the dog up beside us, and poured more tea for my mother.

"So what's happened here in our county—probably a lot of counties," she continued, "is that the sheriff and the banks and the judges have been working in cahoots to get as many foreclosure orders completed and served as they can before the bank holiday begins. Looks like they're even jumping the gun, and trying to take properties that don't legally go into default for weeks or even months yet. When the judge signs that piece of paper, Martin, the sheriff can march up to your door and make you walk right out into the yard and off the property. And he doesn't have to let you take a stick of furniture with you. Off you go, at the point of a gun, and the bank takes the place and sells it to somebody for cheap."

"Is that what happened to your nephews?" I asked.

"Yes, we got word that the sheriff and his deputies are spreading out all over the valley today trying to serve foreclosure papers on seven or eight more families, Samuel and Jacob's included. The men who just rode out of here are fathers and brothers and cousins and even grandfathers of the families that the sheriff wants to throw off their land."

I had been holding the same cookie for several minutes without taking a bite. I think I understood the bank and the foreclosure part, but the sheriff was the law. What were my dad and Grandfather Jake and those other men going to do?

My mother solved my cookie dilemma. "Eat," she said.

I gulped my cookie, and washed it down with fresh, sweet milk.

"What they're going to do, I'm not so sure of," said Grandma with a heavy sigh. "I pray it doesn't come to it, but those boys strapped on their guns for a reason, and when it comes to protecting family, I guess there's pretty much nothing a man—or a woman—won't do to see that their family is alright."

We sat at the table for a long time. As the afternoon sun dipped toward the western hills, the air began to cool, and my grandmother asked me to build a fire. I fetched an armload of fir from the woodshed, and split some kindling on the back porch. In a few minutes, a fire was crackling in the great stone fireplace. I added some oak, and sat back on the floor to enjoy my work. The head of a bison my grandfather shot with his Sharps .50 caliber looked down on me from above the fireplace mantle. I could smell sourdough biscuits and herb-laced chicken in the oven. Those smells, plus the warmth of the fire and the ticking of the mantle clock brought me a little relief from worry about Dad and Grandfather Jake.

My mother finally gave up pacing around the house, and took a comforter and a cup of coffee out onto the front porch, where she parked herself in Grandma's rocker. The sun dipped below an orange cloud, and the sky faded through blue to purple and on to black. I took a plate of food out to my mother, but she set it on the porch rail and kept her eyes fixed to the west.

I grabbed a blanket and sat next to her. She ran her hand through my hair, and smiled wordlessly. Dad had told me to look after her. I didn't know what else to do.

•••

SEVERAL HOURS PASSED. I don't know how long I was asleep, but when I woke the sky was alight with more stars than I imagined could be in the heavens, shining so brightly you didn't need a flashlight to walk out into the prairie night.

Then I heard hollering and the clapping of horse's hooves.

"Hello to the house!" I heard my grandfather yell. "Uncork a jug—we're home!"

"Ruth, Martin, we're back!" I heard my father shout, and then their horses plunged out of the blackness and were right at the porch.

My mother actually leapt over the railing and into my father's arms while he was still in his saddle. And what a kiss! Never saw anything like that at the Saturday matinees.

Grandmother bustled out the door, wiped her eyes, and then spoke in a tone as normal as apple pie. "Jake Forrestal, you get down off that animal and take off those boots, and get into this house. There's chores to be done!" She turned and gave me a wink, and whisked back into the house, slamming the door behind her.

Grandfather Jake swung down out of his saddle, and tied his sweaty horse to the rail. "The woman's crazy about me, don't you think Martin?"

My father dropped Mom softly to the ground, and then swung his leg over his horse and flew off in one effortless motion. He kissed me on the top of my head. "Good on you for taking care of your mother while we were gone," he said.

Grandfather Jake sent me to the bunkhouse to rouse the ranch hand to take care of the horses. Then I raced back to join my family beside the fireplace to hear the tale of the Great Foreclosure Raid of '33, as it was to become known in Forrestal family lore.

Dad and Grandfather Jake sat in leather armchairs close to the hearth. They were silent as they wolfed down plates of chicken and biscuits. Finally, Grandma had all she could take.

"Well, land o'mighty, are either one of you two gunslingers going to tell us what happened, or do we have to read about it in the paper?"

Grandfather Jake wiped his mouth with his sleeve. "I'm a little parched, my darling," he said. "Would you be getting me my favorite glass?"

146

Grandma fetched his lead crystal drinking glass, and Grandfather Jake poured a couple fingers of whiskey and sipped deep.

"Oh, Marty, what a day," he began. "What a glorious day." He leaned over and kissed his wife on the cheek, and then did the same to my mother.

"We high-tailed it out of here and over to Samuel's spread," he said. "We heard that was going to be the sheriff's first stop. And sure enough, no more than ten minutes after we rode up to my nephew's place we saw the Sheriff's brown and white Chevrolet and two other sedans wheel around the bend through a stand of white oak. Them boys parked outside Samuel's fence and eased out of their automobiles just like they was going to Sunday church dinner." He laughed at the thought.

"We were lined up abreast on our horses just inside the fence—all twenty-six of us," he continued. "It was pretty clear that Sheriff Clark wasn't too pleased with our welcoming committee. He walked up to the fence gate with them four deputies of his right behind him, all bunched up like a warren of prairie dogs. Pasty-faced fellows, with smooth hands and nice white shirts under their jackets."

"Did they have guns, Granddad?" I asked.

Jake finished his whiskey. "That they did, boy. The Sheriff pulled back his jacket from off of his big belly, so's I would be sure to see the little pea-shooter he had tucked in his belt. One of his boys had a shotgun, and one had a .30-30. The other boys carried side arms."

"Did the deputies look like desperados?" I wanted to know.

"Desper-whats?" Grandfather Jake asked. "You mean did they look like they could handle themselves in a scrap?"

"Yes, that's it."

"Well, now, if you believe that sitting behind a desk whittlin' and chewing and jawboning all day makes you a better—what'd you call it? Desperado? I can tell you this, Martin, when a man has a loaded gun pointed anywhere in your direction, you need to pay attention, even if the only shooting he's ever done is at paper targets."

"So what did you do?" my mother asked.

Grandfather Jake poured another belt. "I was getting to that, don't rush me now. So, the way it was looking was this: we was lined up on our horses in front of Samuel's place looking down at those five county boys. And they were looking up and down the line of riders facing them and getting a little nervous. Then the Sheriff waddled up to the gate and hollered out at me: 'Jake Forrestal, what the hell do you think you're doing?' He pulled a sheet of paper out of his vest pocket and waved it in the air for everybody to see. 'All you men: this here is a lawful order signed by Judge Crider,' he said. 'It authorizes me to put Samuel Forrestal off this property forthwith, and assigns the property and everything attached to it to the Richland County Bank. So you men back off, and go home right now or my deputies and I will have to arrest you for interfering with the law.'"

My father laughed. "This is my favorite part—you mind if I pick it up here?"

"You go right ahead, son," said Grandfather Jake. "You miss anything, I'll fill 'er in."

"Okay," my dad went on, "so then Dad says, 'or you'll arrest us? The five of you will arrest all twenty-six of us? That the way you see this here party going?' And the Sheriff replies, 'I'm the law Jake, and my boys here are all armed and they can take care of themselves, so don't you go stirring up a hornet's nest.'"

My father chuckled before he continued. "'Your boys can take care of themselves, you say?' Dad said to him. 'Sheriff, you see them two youngsters on the cow ponies there at the end of the line? Those are the Rupp brothers. Each one can shoot the tip of a tail off a muskrat at a hundred yards. And they're the worst shots here!' We all laughed at that one except the Sheriff, of course. His faced turned about twelve shades of purple, and his eyes began to bulge out. He wasn't used to no one—except maybe his wife—giving him the ol' what for."

Granddad slapped his knee at that, and shouted, "Wahoo!"

I shouted, too, although I didn't have a clue what "the ol' what for" was .

"So the Sheriff walked right up to the fence," my father went on, "and said, 'Jake, I'm coming through this here gate, and I'm serving your nephew these court papers, and by God, you will stand down or I will personally slap the cuffs on you and haul your Irish arse to jail.'"

"Chester!" my mother said. "Your language!"

"Now Ruth," said Granddad, "no need to get your petticoats in a bunch—it's what the man said, after all."

"What happened then, Dad?" I asked.

"Well, like I said, the Sheriff told Granddad to back down, or he'd haul him to jail."

"And what did Granddad do?"

"He sat straight up in his saddle, looked down at the Sheriff, and said in a voice loud enough for everyone to hear: 'You come through that gate, Myron, and I'll send you to hell!'"

"Jake, you didn't say that!" said Grandma.

"I sure did," replied Grandfather Jake.

"The Sheriff is named Myron?" my mother asked. "What kind of name is that for a Sheriff?"

Grandfather Jake laughed, and tossed back another shot. "Pretty much says it all, don't it?"

"The sheriff might be a fool," said my father, "but he can count. Five guns against twenty-six aren't very good odds."

"And besides," added my grandfather with a conspiratorial wink, "that was also twenty-six votes he might not be getting come November when he's up for re-election."

"Myron stood down," said my father. "He wadded the court order up and stuck it in his pocket and stomped back to his car. He flung the door open, and shouted 'none of you men had better show up on Main Street anytime soon.' And then just to show us he meant business, he flipped on his red light and siren as he drove off."

"Was that a 'wahoo,' too, Granddad?" I asked.

"And them some, Martin, my boy."

"We split up the riders into four companies and spread out to the other ranches," said my father, "just to make sure old Myron didn't decide to try his luck elsewhere. But he never showed up, and so here we are."

I had scooted over on the floor between Dad and Granddad as they talked. The dog lay beside me, with his head on my lap. Mom snuggled in Dad's chair tight beside him, and Grandma pulled her chair close beside Grandad's and held his hand. She held his drinking hand, I noticed, which prevented him for reaching for the jug again.

We sat there for another hour, watching the fire, listening to the spring tree frogs and crickets along the river, and telling more stories about the Forrestal clan. I discovered that night what it meant to be part of a community of people called a family, where the links forged by birth and blood are stronger than any steel known to man.

"Make sure if you have to fight that what you're fighting for is worth the price," my father had said. I leaned closer to my parents, and looked out the window to the star-swept Montana sky. I pledged to myself that for as long as I lived I would face any enemy and pay any price to keep my family safe.

•••

I TURNED THE RECORDER OFF, and stretched. It was Monday morning, coming up on 8 AM. Connie would be here soon with Rachel. They were going to show me how Rachel was storing my recordings on the computer, and the archiving system they had developed for the dozens of stories I was spinning each day.

My brother Peter was coming in from Montana with his wife, Marjorie, as well. I was excited to see them both. My dad used to joke that they wanted to name Peter "Whoops," because he was born in 1937, twelve years after me, and nobody was expecting another Forrestal to come along after that long a stretch, especially my mother.

Peter was only five when I went off to war, so we didn't get to do much growing up together. He'd follow me down the street on his red scooter when I delivered newspapers, and I used to take him fishing for blue gill out at Ayres' pond.

He broke his collarbone one summer when he tried to copy Patrick and I as we played Tarzan in a thicket of viney maple. When you find a good bunch of these trees growing in a patch fifteen or twenty feet high, you can shimmy up between two of them, and then throw yourself onto another tree. The perfect tree will bend way down without breaking, close enough for you to push off the ground with your feet and spring back up into the air. If you get the right momentum going you can spring from tree to tree, like a chimpanzee in a jungle.

We weren't watching Peter closely enough, and the little guy managed to climb up a viney trunk about eight feet above the ground. I heard him cut loose with a Tarzan yell, and turned my head just in time to see that he didn't really understand the physics of viney maple springing: he just let out his best "ah-e-o-e-ah," and then dropped straight down on the hard dirt.

When I came back from the War I was twenty-years-old, and things felt a bit different at home. I moved back in with my parents in Salem, but only long enough to find a place of my own out by the river. I was going to work for my dad at the lumberyard, but I was a grown man now, and I needed to be by myself for a while. My folks understood—God bless them. But it was hard on Peter not to have his big brother around every day. I visited often, and had dinner with them every Sunday, and I took Peter to ball games and the park, but it was more like we were friends than brothers.

Peter moved back to the family homestead in Montana after his stint in the Army. He went to college and majored in accounting, and then on to work for the state as an economist. But bureaucracy wasn't in his blood, and he left state employment after a few years and bought a run down little hardware store in Kalispell. He'd worked for Patrick's father at O'Hagan's Hardware while he was in high school, just like his big brother, and the business stuck. He married Marjorie right after he bought the store, and together they built it into the biggest hardware and sporting goods retailer in the county. Peter would turn seventy this year—still a pup, and still working full time.

• • •

THE HOSPITAL WAS BUSY TODAY—just as Nurse Marsden had predicted. I finished my breakfast and laid back to rest for a minute. When I opened my eyes, I thought I'd just napped for a minute or two. But when my eyes focused on the clock it said 12:15. I gave myself a little slap on the side of my face.

"Hey, big brother, let me do that for you!"

It was Peter. He and Marjorie had been there for an hour, visiting quietly with Connie on the sofa while I dozed.

"Well, I am a heck of a host, now aren't I," I said. "Get on over here and slap the other cheek, would you?"

They pulled chairs close to my bed, and we spent a couple of hours catching up on the news of their three children and grandchildren, and the store and Montana politics.

Connie and Marjorie left for the house around dinnertime. Peter wasn't hungry—probably because he got a good look at what was under the meal cover on my tray.

"Peter," I asked, "do you have a memory of one especially great day with our family when we were kids? One that really stands out?"

"That's easy," my brother replied. "It would be that Easter out at the cousins' place in Kings Valley. I was ten or eleven."

"That was the Easter when we had the big softball game in the pasture?"

"That was the one. The weather was perfect," Peter remembered. "I went down with Dad on Friday to mow the pasture with Uncle Rich's tractor. What a beautiful setting, that dark green grass and that enormous hay barn surrounded by the apple trees. And the big oak down on the riverbank, the one with the rope swing? It felt like skydiving when you got swinging on that thing, and when you dropped down into the river on a hot August day, boy that was great."

"It was a heck of a softball game, too," I remembered. "Grandparents played on the same team as the squirts, which made for some pretty interesting fielding and base running. Remember when Great Aunt Esther was running from second to third and slipped in the cowpie? What was she, sixty-five or seventy?"

"She was a sport, that's for sure," Peter said. "How about when Dad knocked the ball up into the big willow, and Mom wanted to prove she could still climb a tree and told all of us kids to stay put while she went up after it. I didn't think she could do it, but she grabbed that lower branch and scooted up that thing faster than one of those tree-topping lumberjacks at the Timber Carnival."

"There must have been a hundred people there that weekend. Mom's relatives, and Dad's—I think that's the most family we ever had in one place at one time."

"You know what the best part was, Martin? When Dad and the other grown-ups headed out the door Saturday night to hide those twenty-five-dozen colored eggs."

"I don't know who thought up that little treasure-planting expedition," I said, "but they should have won an award. Wasn't the golden prize egg on top of a rock in the middle of the river?"

"It was—and I think it was at least five feet deep at that spot. I remember when somebody shouted they could see it, and everybody ran down to the river bank, and there it was, thirty or forty yards from shore, in a strong current on top of that rock, shining like the golden fleece from Jason and the Argonauts."

"And Grandma said it was too dangerous for the kids to swim out there. It was pretty funny watching all those grown-ups diving in for it."

"That's right—and Dad and his cousin Todd got there at the same time and started wrestling around in the water, until Mom's uncle, Gordon swam up between them and stole it away. Geez, he must have been seventy-five, easy."

An unfamiliar nurse came into the room. Peter sat over by the window as she introduced herself, and got familiar with the Martin Forrestal pinch, poke and prod routine. When the nurse left, Peter asked me if there was anything he could do for me, or for Connie.

"You know, there is," I said. I dusted off my legal pad, and read my list of values to my brother.

"And you're how far along with this?" he asked.

I pointed to the seventh line on the yellow sheet. "Right here," I said. "Family unity."

Peter sat down, and took a sip of his soda. "Is that why you asked me about my memory of one perfect day?"

"Yes, in a way it is. I would have put that day pretty high on my own list, by the way. Every doggone relative for a thousand miles was there in that meadow. Remember all the bonfires we built that night? You and some of the other shrimps made your way from fire to fire begging for toasted marshmallows like street urchins out of a Dickens novel. And the music! Guitars and fiddles and harmonicas and mandolins…there was some sweet singing that night."

"Yeah, when Uncle Rich wasn't belting out a Navy sea-shanty. I never knew there were that many rhyming cusswords."

"It was a perfect couple of days, Peter. The best. So how come we never had a family get-together like that one again? Seems like the only time more than a few of our family members are in one place at one time is for weddings and funerals."

"Martin, I think a day like that Easter is a providential event, don't you? Luck and timing and coincidence. You could never plan something like that out."

"I don't know about that. Oh, I don't think any of the older ladies would volunteer to slide into a cowpie for the children's amusement, but as for the rest of it, just getting everybody together would be a great start. After all, if you still have such powerful memories of that family event sixty years later, wouldn't you want to do whatever you could to give your own children and grandchildren a similar experience?"

I shifted in my bed, and Peter helped me rearrange the pillows. "Are you talking about some kind of family reunion?" Peter asked.

"Sort of, but more than that, too," I said. "Some kind of family meeting, where the old duffers like you and me could share the stories of our lives, and talk with the grandkids about the things that really mattered to us, things that made a difference in our lives that could make a difference in their lives, too."

"Is that why you're doing this project, to share at family gatherings?"

"That's sure one way the stories could be shared. Wish I could do it in person, but I'm afraid my travel agent won't be booking any trips to Montana for me this year."

Peter's eyes misted. "Ah, Martin" he said, "I wish we'd gotten together more often—spent more time just sitting out on the deck watching the river flow past. Where have the years gotten to?"

"It does all go by too fast, doesn't it. Like one of those books with the picture down in the corner that you flip really fast to watch the monkey dance."

We sat quietly for a while. Connie called to say she'd be along in a few minutes to take Peter back to our house for the night.

"Martin, I'm going to do something about your perfect day idea," Peter finally said.

"I'll get in touch with everybody, and have Marjorie start working the phone to look for dates. We can have them up to our cabin on the Madison River. Set up a few tents, roll in another grill, get out the canoe. I'll bet we could round up thirty or forty people, easy."

"Let me toss a couple more ideas at you, Peter." I held my list of values up. "I wouldn't be surprised to find that a lot of what I'm talking about in my project is pretty important to other members of our family, too. Maybe there's a way you can get that conversation rolling, and identify values and stories we all share. They could form a mighty powerful roadmap for the Forrestal family in the future."

Peter laid his hand on top of mine. "You have been doing some thinking, haven't you big brother?"

"That's pretty much all I can do these days, Peter. But, you know what? It took cancer and a red-letter date on the calendar to get my mind focused on all of this. I've always tried to live a good life. But sometimes I just got so busy with the busy part of living that I didn't pay enough attention to what matters most in the long run."

I sat up as straight as I could, and looked my brother in the eyes. "I wasn't much of an older brother to you, Peter. So, I hope you'll forgive me if I want to pass along one last piece of advice to my younger brother."

Peter's head was bowed, and he was sniffling. "Anything, Martin."

I squeezed his hand.

"Don't wait," I said.

WORK

PETER AND MARJORIE WATCHED me eat my dinner. Then they left with Connie. They would return in the morning. After they had gone, and I had finished what I could of the meal, Leticia untethered me from my IV, and I slept until 1 AM.

I watched the digital clock dial flip minute by minute for a half an hour. I wasn't falling back asleep, and I wasn't getting any younger. I swung my legs out of bed and put on my robe and slippers. I shuffled out the door and walked down the corridor past the nurse's station.

The doors of most of the rooms I passed were open, with curtains pulled for a little privacy. The smell of disinfectant and the yellow cast of the ceiling lights mixed with the muffled sounds of late night TV. I heard an occasional cough or half-murmured sentence spoken by other patients whose sleep patterns, like mine, were mangled by medication.

The nurses on duty paid no attention to an old man on his evening rounds. I saw an electrician carrying a stepladder toward the elevator, and a lab tech hurrying her plastic tray of specimens to the basement pathology office. Neither acknowledged me as they passed. It occurred to me that you could probably ride buck-naked on the back of an ostrich through the halls of most hospitals at this hour of the night and no one would give you a second glance.

At the end of the hall was what I half-jokingly called the intersection of life and death. I could go left and walk across the elevated sky bridge to the hospital birthing center, or turn right and walk past the surgical intensive care unit.

I veered right, skirting the automatic double doors that swung into the surgical recovery area. The small, glass walled waiting room across the hall was always occupied. Tonight an elderly woman sat vigil on a hard plastic chair and a middle-aged couple used one another's shoulders for pillows as they waited, as everyone in this room waited, for the news that would either break their heart or give them hope. I nodded at the silver-haired woman as I passed, and she replied with a weary half-smile. I prayed that Connie would be spared such loneliness when my time came.

Leticia was making notes at the station outside my door when I completed my walk. She looked up from her work and smiled at me. "Making the rounds?"

"I figured I might as well use these old legs while I can get away with it."

"Are you ready to call it a day?" she asked.

"Maybe. How about you?"

She closed the metal notepad, and put the pen in her side pocket. "You mean, am I ready to call it a night?" she said with a smile. "Not if I have to round up any more of my patients like cattle out on the range."

"Nice to know you hold your customers in such high esteem," I said. I suddenly felt very tired. I stood by my bed and let Leticia help me remove my robe and slippers.

"You love your work, don't you," I said as she settled me back into bed.

"Does it show?"

"With every step you take. My mother used to say that a person was a success if they got up in the morning and went to bed at night, and in between they did what they wanted to do."

Leticia adjusted my pillows. "Your mother was right. I'm one of those lucky people who is able to do the work that she wants to."

A wave of exhaustion swept over me. I tried to fight it, but it was no use. As I drifted toward sleep, I heard Leticia ask, "And did you find the work that gave your life meaning, Martin?"

"You know, I believe I did," I whispered, and I was out.

•••

CONNIE ARRIVED WITH PETER AND MARJORIE shortly after I finished my breakfast. The spring sun shone brightly through the windows as they settled in with coffee and a basket of vanilla scones Connie had baked. Knowing my wife, I'm sure she'd made enough for the nurses on the floor, too.

She picked up my yellow notepad, and read through the values that I had drawn a line through to indicate my work for each was complete. "Leadership. Determination. Honesty, honor and compassion. Responsibility. Family unity. This is so worthwhile. I think everyone should do something like this and share it with their own families. I've been listening to some of the recordings at our house—I've known you for more than forty years, but after listening to your stories I feel like I'm just getting to know you."

"It is something of a liberating experience, I'll tell you that," I said. "I never thought I'd say anything like that, but it really is."

"Because maybe you've been a frustrated writer all your life?" asked Peter.

"Gosh no, that's not it. It's just that when I pick the recorder up, or when I make a note, I start with only one objective: to commit an act of truth. From there it's as easy as—" A spasm of pain tore through my back, cutting me off. Tears filled my eyes. I sucked in my breath, and turned toward the wall.

"Martin, honey, are you okay?" asked Connie. "Peter, get the nurse."

Nurse Marsden arrived a minute later, and Peter and Marjorie moved out into the hall. Connie stood by the bed, holding my hand.

"Martin, I'm going to ask your doctor for permission to place a self-regulating morphine pump beside you," said my nurse as she administered a pain reliever into my IV. "You'll be able to adjust it yourself as your pain level requires. Is that alright with you? Do you want me to lower your bed?"

"Yes to the pump," I answered, "but I'll keep the bed upright for now."

My pain subsided, and the nurse left. When my brother and Marjorie returned a minute later, their faces were lined with worry. When they sat down they remained quiet, like people visiting a funeral home. This won't do, I thought.

"Peter, do you remember what Grandfather Jake used to say about worrying?"

"Don't think I do—the man had a quote for every occasion though, didn't he?"

"He did, and this was one of his best: when he'd see our dad all balled up with worry, or when Grandma was in the middle of one her moods, pacing back and forth across the floor in front of the fireplace, he'd raise his glass and say, 'Woman, get busy: there's only one cure for worry that's better than whiskey, and that's work.'"

Connie raised an eyebrow. "And was it whiskey in the glass he was raising when he'd say that?" she asked.

"Probably so," I replied. "But the old boy was right—if you want to abolish your worry, there's no better way than to get to work. The two can't occupy the same mind at the same time—it violates a fundamental law of physics or something."

"You think we're worried?" asked my brother.

I managed a small laugh. "I tell you what; if you and Marjorie will help me out for a bit, we'll just see."

"What have you got in mind?" asked my brother.

I took my notepad from Connie and pointed to the next value on the list: work.

"You can help me get started on the next value; it might not ease your worry, but it sure would lighten my load to get a little help. This is a huge topic."

Peter finished his coffee, and pulled his chair closer to my bed. "I'd like that," he said. "I've been wondering where you get the ideas for this project. Yesterday when we talked about family unity it seemed as though you had spent a lot of time planning it out."

I chuckled. "Peter, even a broken clock is right twice a day. I don't really have a plan, and I'm not a writer. I figured the inspiration would just come once I'd developed my list. And so far, it has."

"But your stories are perfect," said Marjorie. "They illuminate each value you are talking about in a way that anyone can appreciate."

"That's kind of you. It's not anything magical, though. I've been on this planet for fourscore and two years, and that ought to be long enough to have had a few experiences worth sharing."

"But your stories are extraordinary," Marjorie protested. "My life sounds dull by comparison."

"I think that's where you're wrong, Marge. You have your own stories, we all do, and if you would just take the time to start sifting through them, I'll bet you dollars to doughnuts that yours will be every bit as powerful and meaningful as anything that's happened in my life. Just think about the adventures you have shared with my little brother! Start with how you two met, and the way you struggled for years to build your business. Or about the year you were flooded out, and had to start from scratch, or that winter night when your pickup slid off the canyon road in the snow and you tumbled a hundred yards down that rocky slope. Weren't you both thrown from the rig? I remember you saying you thought Peter was dead."

Marjorie's face flushed.

"We all have our stories," I said.

"The secret, or so Martin tells me, is to be absolutely honest," said Connie. "Honest with yourself, and honest with the generations of your family who will read or listen to your story."

"And if that means you have to hide your stories from everybody until after you're gone in order to maintain the family peace for the time being, that's okay, too," I added.

Peter feigned a pained expression: "Even from me?"

"Especially from you," said Connie.

"I have an idea," I said. "What do you say we take a little break, and then you all help me kick this subject off?"

Peter stepped out into the hallway to call his store in Montana, and when the tech came in for her morning blood draw, Connie and Marjorie headed for the powder room down the hall. To my surprise, my son Eric popped in and told me he was taking the rest of the day off. Could he join in? When everyone returned, I elevated the back of my bed as high as it would go, Marjorie held the digital recorder, and we began to talk about work.

•••

PETER WIPED SOME SCONE CRUMBS from his shirt. "I'd like to know: why did you include work as one of your most important values?"

"Well," I said, "I don't know how I couldn't. Work is what humans do. It's what defines us and molds our character."

"Not to mention how we earn the money to put food on the table," added Marjorie.

"That's true," I said, "but I believe that work is more than a process by which we earn a paycheck. When you get down to it, work isn't about making money. In one sense, we work to justify being alive."

"No fair injecting philosophy, dear," said Connie.

I squeezed her hand. "I won't, I promise. But let me ask you all a question: think back on a specific day in your life when you went to bed absolutely satisfied with how you spent your time."

"Are honeymoons fair game?" asked Marjorie.

"Okay, wise gal, except for honeymoons. Everybody thought of one?"

"I've got a couple," said Peter.

"I'm there," said Connie.

"Me too," replied Marjorie.

"I'm just observing for the moment," said Eric, "you all go ahead."

I took a sip of water. "Anybody pick a day when you just lounged around the beach, or slept in the backyard hammock?"

No one spoke.

"Tell me about your day, Peter," I said.

"The first thing that popped into my head was the day Marjorie and I got the keys to the store from the realtor, over thirty years ago. We packed our old station wagon full of cleaning supplies and went down there at daybreak. Man, it was a mess. The previous owners had run it into the ground, and it looked like a bomb had gone off inside."

"A dirt bomb," smiled Marjorie.

"We set to work at about six that morning," Peter continued, "and we didn't stop until ten that night. We scrubbed and chipped and swept and scraped every square inch of that place. When we finished, we stood outside on the sidewalk and looked through the clean windows like a couple of parents staring at their new baby through the window of a maternity ward."

"How'd you feel?" I asked.

Peter grinned. "Like we had built the Great Wall of China in a single day. I was equal parts proud, excited, satisfied and tired."

"And you can still see it fresh in your memory?" I said.

"Marjorie wore coveralls that day—the first and last time she ever did. Her hair was pulled back with a polka-dot scarf, and she had dirt streaks all across her face. I never saw her look prettier."

Marjorie blushed. "You never told me that," she said.

"I'll bet your kids and grandkids don't have a clue how hard you two worked to get that store going. To them, you've always been well off."

"True enough," said my brother.

"And how about your day, Connie," asked Peter. "Was yours a vacation day?"

"Not quite. My parents owned a bakery, and in high school my sister and I took turns going down every other day with my father at 3 AM to start baking. There wasn't money to hire outside help. When I was a senior, my school prom was held on a Friday, but I was scheduled to be at work Saturday morning, and Saturdays were the busiest day of the week. My sister volunteered to work for me, but that Thursday she came down with the flu, and that night, my father got sick, too. So Mom and I went in Friday morning and we did all the prep and the baking, and then I did deliveries to local stores until nine."

Connie poured a glass of water from the pitcher. "I went to school until noon, and then returned to the bakery to help Mom with the lunch rush. Then back to school at 3 because I was on the prom decoration committee. We finished decorating at 6, and I rushed home to get ready for my date to pick me up at 7:30. My dad and my sister were still too sick to get up and around, and Mom was exhausted, but she and I knew we had to be back at the bakery that night because neither of us could mix or bake as fast as my father."

Marjorie held up her scone. "I'm amazed you still like to bake," she said.

Connie laughed and said, "No worries there: Martin wouldn't make it through summer without my cobbler."

She brushed her hand across my forehead before continuing. "My date wasn't very happy about the circumstance, but he was a gentleman, and he took me to the bakery. It was 2:30 in the morning. My mother was late, and my date waited while I called her. She'd been hit by the flu, too. She told me to come home. We would have to close the bakery Saturday. But I couldn't do that. Money was scarce, and if we missed a Saturday, things would be even rougher. I was tired—remember I hadn't slept the night before. But I knew I had to do the work myself. I thought about asking my date to help out, but he seemed pretty anxious to leave. I assured him I'd be okay, and off he went."

"What did your bakery serve?" asked Marjorie.

"Four kinds of bread, a half dozen different doughnuts, dinner rolls, maple bars, bear claws, strudel, cookies—the works."

"And you did it all yourself that night?" Peter asked.

"I started the first batch in the big Hobart mixer about the time I started to cry," remembered Connie. "I was covered head to toe with flour, and when I looked over at my prom dress hanging on a hook in the corner, it made me cry all the harder. And then something amazing happened. I heard pounding on the back door. I went to the window and looked out into the darkness. There was my date, with eight or nine of my friends. He'd gone back to the party, and told everybody about the jam I was in. There they were in gowns and tuxedoes, ready to help."

"What did you do?" asked Peter.

Connie smiled. "I put them to work. Prepping, rolling, baking, frying and decorating. We turned on the radio, and sang, and a couple of the kids even danced on the flour-covered floor. They were wonderful! By the time the sun came up we had enough baked goods to fill most of the shelves in the retail store. We opened at 6 AM sharp, like normal, but there wasn't anything normal about the girls in prom dresses who waited on customers as they arrived that morning."

"Were you tired?" I asked.

"I was beyond tired. I remember standing in the doorway between the kitchen and the retail store just watching my friends work. I started to cry again, but this time it was because I felt so good. And do you know the best part? Around 7:30 my dad showed up. He was still sick, but he'd been worried when he checked my room that morning and I was gone."

Connie paused, and I could see that her eyes had gone misty. "He sized things up pretty fast. He wrapped his arms around me, and he kissed my forehead. Then he said, 'I have never been so proud of my little girl as I am right now.' I won't ever forget that day."

Eric leaned over to his mother and put an arm around her shoulder. "Mom, that's an amazing story," he said. "You need to do this more often."

"Have you ever worked as hard as that again?" I asked.

"I'm sure I have," Connie answered, "but you asked for just one day, right? For me, that was pretty much the best day of my high school years."

"But it was work, not play," I said.

Connie rumpled my hair. "It was life, honey. But I will say this, in my experience the harder I work, the more I live."

•••

"YOUR TURN, MARJORIE," I said. "What's an example of a day in your life when you went to bed absolutely satisfied with how you spent your time?"

Marjorie put her hand on Peter's shoulder. "I have to go with my guy on this one," she said. "I never felt better about what I accomplished in one day, and I never felt closer to Peter than I did on that first day we worked in the store. So I guess I pass."

Connie broke off a small piece of vanilla scone and placed it on a napkin for me. I nibbled at it, and stole a sip of her coffee.

"That makes it your turn," said Peter.

"Can I cheat a little?" I asked.

"Well, it is your game," said Connie. "What did you have in mind?"

I shifted in bed, and took another drink of Connie's coffee. "Like all of you, the best I ever felt in my life was on those days when I had everything to do, and somehow figured out how to get it all done. But as Connie was talking, I remembered one particular workday when I was a teenager that changed my outlook on all kinds of things, and not just work. In fact, as the years passed, the memory of that day grew more and more important to me." I paused, and thought about how to proceed.

"When I think about work as a value that is important to pass on, it's hard to separate the intellectual concept of work from the gut reaction to the word," I began. "I mean, we all have an idea in our heads of what work is, and what it feels like, and why it's so important."

"Tell that to my fourteen-year-old grandson," said Peter, "he'll say 'dude, why do I need to, like, lift stuff and sweat? That's for idiots. I mean, everybody knows that people who work sitting down get paid more than people who work standing up.'"

"Nice impersonation," I said. "Unfortunately, he's right. But only if we define work first and foremost as a physical activity, kind of like in physics where work is defined as the amount of energy transferred by a force. I suppose that's true, assuming 'energy' encompasses other kinds of effort. I'd define work as any focused application of your physical or mental abilities—or both at the same time—toward a specific end. Splitting a cord of fir with an ax is work just like adding a column of numbers is work. They both require focus to achieve the end result."

"Oh, there's an end of my grandson that I'd like to apply some energy to," piped in Peter.

"And there's a formula for that too, if I remember my high school physics," said Connie. "Force equals mass times acceleration, where the force is the impact you kick him in the backside with, the mass is your shoe, and the acceleration is your swing!"

We all laughed.

"Let's hear about that work day of yours now," said Peter. "But there'd better be a lesson in there somewhere."

"Oh, there are plenty," I replied. "In fact, the more I think about this day, the more lessons I pull out of it for myself about work, and what work means, and all the different ways we learn the value of work when we're young."

Marjorie called a halt to the conversation so she could get the recorder ready, and Connie and Eric took a minute to tidy up after the scones and coffee. I looked out the window past the green canopy of the cherry tree to the golden statue on top of the state capital building, and began my story.

•••

IN THE SUMMER OF 1939, I was fourteen years old. Patrick and I worked all the part-time jobs we could find. We stocked shelves at his family's hardware store, cleaned equipment at my dad's lumberyard, we trapped coyote for the seventy-five cent bounty paid by the agriculture department, and picked hops for Mr. Holden (at the rate of one and a half cents per pound—on a good day we could make a dollar and a half!).

We even worked alongside our mothers as extras on a Hollywood movie being filmed up on the McKenzie River, outside Eugene. It was called Abe Lincoln in Illinois, and starred Raymond Massey. Mostly we just stood around in costume, or walked up and down the sidewalk of the town set, or mumbled softly in crowd scenes as the actors did their lines. The pay wasn't much, but it was time with our families, and we got to be in the movies. To this day when I watch that old film I'm still not exactly sure where I am in the crowd scenes, but I can pick Patrick out standing in front of Lincoln's office, and there is a great shot of my mother bustling along the sidewalk, when Abe even tips his hat as she passes!

But there was one job I did that summer that really stands out. I learned more about work than any other single job in my life. It only lasted a day, but that was all it took.

We arrived at the hardware store one morning expecting to do our regular chores. But Patrick's father had other plans for us. Silas Jennings, one of his best customers, farmed and ran a few cattle on one hundred sixty acres outside of Independence, at Buena Vista. His hired man had been injured the day before, and the farmer needed someone to go up on a hill with him and load ten or twelve cords of oak they'd cut and split earlier in the summer. A cord measures four feet wide by four feet high and eight feet long, so it was a good piece of work if we were interested.

When we asked about the pay, Mr. O'Hagan told us not to try to negotiate. The going farm hand rate was one dollar and twenty-five cents for a ten-hour day, and that's all we should ask for.

Jennings' truck pulled to the curb a minute later, and Patrick and I grabbed our lunch buckets and hopped in the back. A half hour later we were standing on the crown of a hill overlooking miles of summer wheat and alfalfa fields. Jennings had cut down and split three great oaks. They lay on the ground in two huge mounds. Beyond the oak I could see the snow-capped line of the Cascade Mountains, where just four weeks earlier we had been trapped by the freak summer storm.

The farmer spit tobacco juice against a truck tire as we contemplated the job.

"There 'tis, boys," he said. "You both know how to drive?"

We nodded—both of us had been driving the truck out at Mr. Holden's farm.

"Alright, then," said Mr. Jennings. "We've got two pickups here. What you'll be doing is to load the wood into the trucks, and then drive down to the woodshed and stack 'er in level cords. Not too big, or too small. My customers expect a fair measure. You boys savvy?"

We nodded again.

"So, how you boys want to bid on this here little job? Flat rate, or negotiate?" He smiled at his own rhyme.

I was prepared to give him the flat rate of a dollar twenty-five per day for each of us, but Patrick suddenly spoke up. "What kind of negotiating would you have in mind?" he asked.

Negotiate? What was Patrick doing? His father had made a point of telling us not to negotiate with Mr. Jennings. I shot Patrick a quizzical glance. He gave me a muted "shush."

Mr. Jennings leaned against the hood of the Dodge and let fly with another wad of chew.

"Why, the kind where we decide whether or not you fellas are up to the job," he said.

That got Patrick's Irish up. "We can do the job, alright, as good as anybody!"

Mr. Jennings looked out across the field. It was not quite 9 AM, but the air was already heating up. He lifted his cap, and wiped a line of sweat from his forehead.

"As good as anybody?" Jennings said. "How 'bout as fast as anybody?"

I gave Patrick a hard look. I didn't like the way this conversation was headed.

"As fast as anybody, sure we can," said my friend. "In fact, I guarantee it."

"Well, now," said Mr. Jennings in a slow drawl. "If you're prepared to offer some guarantees for your work, why I believe we have something to negotiate."

I'd had enough. "Patrick—"

"Martin, just hold on there," Patrick said. "Let's hear Mr. Jennings out."

"Thanks, young fella. It's refreshing that a couple of young bucks like yourselves are confident about their ability to do a fair day's work. That's the true measure of a man, ain't it—you give your word to do your job, and you do it, no matter what."

I really didn't like the sound of the "no matter what" part, but I was getting mighty curious about where this negotiation was headed.

Patrick nodded. "We'll keep our word," he said.

"Fine, boys, that's just fine," said Mr. Jennings. "Let's get to haggling, then."

The old farmer packed a finger of fresh chew in his cheek. Then he led us around the piles of split oak so we could get a better measure of the job before us. He halted when we had completed our slow pass, and adjusted his cap.

"So here's what I propose, boys," he said. "Bein's as how you prefer to negotiate the value of your work instead of charging by the day like other hired hands, how about I pay you based on how fast you are? The faster you are, the more you make, and if you're as fast as you say you are, shoot, you might make twice the day rate I pay my other men."

Twice the rate? As much as two dollars and fifty cents for one day's work? This whole negotiation deal suddenly sounded pretty good—I didn't know why Patrick's dad was so dead set against it. We were both strong, and we both knew how to work. I could keep up with most of the grown men at my father's lumberyard, where there was a hand-lettered sign on the lunchroom wall that said, "Nobody ever drowned in his own sweat."

"That sounds good, Mr. Jennings," I said. "How do we decide what we all mean when we say 'fast?'"

Jennings grinned, and slapped his knee. "I knew I was dealing with some smart fellas right off," he cackled. "Can't recall the last time anybody tried to best me in a negotiation, but it looks like I might have met my match. What do I mean when I say fast?" He paused a moment, and looked down at the ground, as if he was gathering a very important thought. Then he raised his head, and said in a voice completely void of expression, "What would you think about defining 'fast' as the two of you doing the job faster than an old coot like me?"

My heart skipped a beat. I flashed a look at Patrick, and saw that he was trying to hold his excitement back, too. "You mean the both of us together? Can we load wood faster than you can by yourself?" asked Patrick with barely concealed glee.

"Well, boys, I guess that's exactly what I'm saying," replied Mr. Jennings. "See, now, I'm not just impressed with your confidence in yourselves, I also happen to be a bettin' man. The wife doesn't approve, of course, but there are only so many vices that a man my age can enjoy, and a little gamblin' now and then happens to be mine. This hot weather brings out the gamblin' bug something fierce in me, that's for sure. So, how about we make a bit of a gamble out of this here negotiation? You boys game?"

Patrick and I nodded in unison. Bring it on, I thought.

"Then here's what we'll do. Them wood piles are about equal distance from the trucks, wouldn't you say?" said Jennings.

We nodded.

"And I figure there's nine or maybe ten pickup loads here on this hill that's gotta be hauled down the way. Sound right to you boys?"

We nodded again.

"Well, then, let's get to the proposition," said Mr. Jennings. "We'll load up these two pickups right now. You boys load one together, I'll do the other by myself. A full load means right up to the top of the side rails, and from the cab window back to the rear gate."

"Just to make this a sportin' proposition," he drawled, "I'll load one truck all by myself, but I'll still pay you just as if you did it yourselves? That okay by you?"

"Sure it is," said Patrick.

"And so's we're all throwing something into the pot, what are you boys willing to bet on this little contest of ours?"

What are we willing to bet, I thought? Is this something Patrick and I needed to think through? I hesitated for a second—but only for a second. Patrick was right there with me. "Look, Mr. Jennings," said Patrick, "meaning no disrespect, of course, but Martin and I are a heck of a lot younger than you, and it is two against one, and, well, then there's—" he hesitated.

"This?" replied Mr. Jennings, holding up the stump of his right arm.

I should have mentioned that Mr. Jennings wasn't just a dried up, sixty-five-year-old beanpole who looked like a light summer breeze could knock him over. He was also missing his entire right arm from just below the shoulder. He'd got it tangled in a combine blade when he was about our age. That was the biggest reason that this whole gamble sounded like a sure-fire win for Patrick and me—to the point that I was starting to feel a pang of remorse for letting it go this far. Maybe we should back off, and quote a fair day's wage instead of taking advantage of the old boy.

Jennings grinned, and shook his head. "You telling me that you two roughnecks aren't sure you can load one truck faster than an old, broken-down, one-armed cripple? Maybe I didn't hire me the right sort of workers, then. You did tell me you could do a man's work, right? You sure about that?"

Patrick's temper flared. "We can do the job, Mr. Jennings, and to prove it we'll fill our truck before you get yours loaded, or—or we'll do this whole darn job for nothing!"

For nothing? A lump rose in my throat. I thought about protesting, but I took another look at Mr. Jennings. He wasn't just beanpole thin, he was scarecrow thin. And he didn't look sixty-five, he must have been seventy.

Why was I feeling sorry for the old guy? He was the one who came up with this whole cockamamie idea, not us. If he had a problem with gambling, it wasn't our job to straighten him out, was it? Making twice the regular wages for a day's work didn't sound so bad, either. No, I decided it was time for Mr. Jennings to learn his own darn lesson.

"I'm with Patrick," I said. "We'll whip you, or you don't have to pay us for the rest of the job."

Jennings smiled. He spat on the ground, and rubbed it into the dirt with his boot. "Alrightee, boys, get yourselves a swallow of water, and let's have at it!"

Patrick and I pulled our shirts off, put on gloves, and gulped down some cold water.

Mr. Jennings lounged against the tailgate of his truck as we got ready.

"Let me know when we're ready to ring the bell," he said.

The distance between the two pickups was about fifteen feet. It was five feet from the dropped tailgates to the respective piles of split oak. Patrick and I strategized that our best plan would be for one of us to stand at the pile and toss chunks of oak to the other, who would throw them up into the truck in as neat a stack as possible.

"We'll have to get a rhythm going," whispered Patrick—not that he needed to be stealthy, of course, since Mr. Jennings was paying us no mind at all. "How about I feed the wood to you, and you throw it in carefully, so we get a smooth pile from bottom to top?"

"That sounds fine," I said. "Should we maybe switch positions when we're halfway done?"

"Good idea," said Patrick. "That way we'll stay fresh. That old boy is going to wither and collapse after about two minutes!"

"You boys got 'er all figured out?" called Mr. Jennings. "It's going on nine o'clock, and this ain't no bank I'm running."

"We're ready," said Patrick.

"Darn ready," I added.

"Well, then," said Mr. Jennings as he ambled over to his pile, "what say we count to five and have at it?"

I ran my hand through my hair, and edged closer to the rusty tailgate. I held my arms up, spread my legs, and bent at my knees in anticipation of Patrick's first toss. A quarter-mile below the hill where we were standing, a line of cottonwoods marked the meander of the Little Luckimaute River.

A swim in the cool green water would feel good after this little exercise.

•••

MR. JENNINGS SPIT THE LAST of his chew and began a slow count. "One, two, three, four—you boys ready? Five!"

Patrick flung the first chunk of oak before I was ready. It slammed into my stomach and took my breath away, but I caught it. I shook off the blow, and tossed the wood onto the truck bed, where it bounced and clanged against the bed wall beneath the window. Bullseye! In a heartbeat Patrick tossed the second piece, then another and another. After about ten pieces we had a rhythm going.

It took about two seconds for us to complete a cycle: Patrick would grab another piece, fling it in my direction, and I would turn and throw it onto the growing pile in the truck bed. We were cooking.

I couldn't see Mr. Jennings' progress from my vantage point without twisting my head around and missing Patrick's next missile. We kept up a furious pace for the first minute, and the only sounds I heard were the bang of each piece of wood as it landed in the truck. I grinned at Patrick and gave him a quick thumbs-up between catches, but he didn't respond. In fact, the look on his face worried me—his eyes were narrow, and his lips were pursed. Was that determination—or fear?

I caught the next piece, threw it on the pile, and shot him a "what's going on?" look.

He grabbed the next chunk of oak with his right hand, and pointed his left forefinger toward Jennings' truck. I turned my head to see why Patrick looked so concerned.

What I saw made the hair on the back of my neck stand up. I froze for an instant, and missed Patrick's next toss. It grazed my side, smashed into the tailgate, and fell to the ground. I didn't care. I was transfixed.

There is only one word I can use to describe what I saw when I looked over at Mr. Jennings: windmill. Imagine a reed-thin man, six feet tall, dressed in baggy overalls. A shock of white hair on his head, his legs spread wide to compensate for the balance problem caused by a missing arm. He was bent at the waist over his pile of oak, and he was, for the life of me, singing! It sounded like a Civil War battle song, something about following Stonewall Jackson to the gates of perdition, I think.

As striking as that was, what really got my attention was what he was doing with his left arm. It swung in a great smooth arc up above his head, fired down toward the wood pile, scooped up a piece of oak, and tossed it effortlessly into the truck—one seamless movement. It kept swinging like a well-oiled machine in a great circle, around and around, not stopping for a second anywhere along its path. Like a windmill dipping into a stream, Mr. Jennings' long fingers snagged another piece of oak each time they flew past the pile. One whirl of his arm, one piece of wood on the truck.

My heart sank, but Patrick's shout of "Heads up!" brought me back to reality. I caught the next piece, and shouted, "Faster, we've got to go faster." Patrick increased his pace, and I turned and tossed and piled as fast as I could. We'd been at this contest for about three minutes. I was drenched with sweat, and my hands were slippery beneath the gloves. I wanted to pull them off, but to do so would mean losing our rhythm.

Patrick had to shift position to get into a more accessible section of our oak pile, and I took the opportunity to steal a glance in Mr. Jennings' direction. Surely he couldn't keep up that windmill activity. No human could.

But Mr. Jennings defied conventional definition. Not only was he still swinging and grabbing and piling on without so much as a hitch in his motion, he was actually speeding up. That one arm of his flashed in a blur over his head, down to the woodpile, onto the truck and then back up in the air. A windup like that belonged in the Major Leagues.

My quick glance spotted something else, too: in just over three minutes, Mr. Jennings' truck was half full! I grabbed the next piece from Patrick, tossed it into our truck, and sized up our progress. We were only about a third full. Mr. Jennings was whipping us, and good.

Patrick jumped over to load, and I began feeding him pieces of oak from the pile. We poured it on with everything we had. Our pace increased, our truck continued to fill up, and my heart lightened at the thought of passing Mr. Jennings. I couldn't make out how far along he was, but Patrick and I were moving so fast now that I knew it was not possible for that old farmer to beat us.

We moved the way Olympic runners do when they hand their batons off to the homestretch sprinter. A light breeze stirred, and gave us a respite from the August sun, and as we passed the half-full mark, Patrick gave out a victory shout.

And then, a voice said: "Boys, what's the story?" Mr. Jennings materialized at the front of our truck. He pulled his tobacco from an overall pocket, and put a pinch in his mouth. He wasn't even breathing hard. I dropped the piece of oak I had just caught onto the ground.

"No!" Patrick yelled. We raced over to the back of Mr. Jennings' truck. It was full up to the top of the side rails, packed tight from front to back. To make matters worse, the wood was stacked as neat as the books on a schoolteacher's desk.

Mr. Jennings looked into our truck, which was a hair over half-filled. "Not bad, boys, not bad," he said. He spit a load of dark juice on the ground, and while still appraising our pitiful accomplishment said, "It appears you fellas have lost our little bet. Shame about that."

He pulled out a battered pocket watch. "Ten after nine," he said. "Not a bad start. Two loads near done up already. You boys ought to have 'er all done by six or so, don't you think?"

I don't know which of us boys looked more dejected. I hopped into the loaded truck without a word, flung it into gear, and headed down the hill to begin stacking the cords on Mr. Jennings' wood lot. I would have it out with Patrick when we finished. Right now, I was so mad I couldn't see straight.

•••

I LOOKED UP FROM the digital recorder. Peter and Marjorie had started to chuckle about the time I said the word "windmill." Now they were laughing full out, and Connie was wiping a tear from her eye.

"Pretty funny?" I asked.

"Martin, I wish you could have seen your face when you described how you felt the first time you looked over at that old one-armed farmer and realized he was beating the tar out of you two," said Peter. "It's almost as if you were right back there on that hill."

"I think I was," I said. "Isn't it something how you can still get your dander up all these years later?"

"So Dad, what happened after that?" asked Eric.

I lowered the back of my bed about an inch. Sometimes the smallest adjustment could cut the pain.

"Well, we finished hauling and stacking the wood around seven that night, and Mr. Jennings drove us back to town. Patrick and I hadn't said a word to one another since the contest ended. I was still steamed, and more tired than I had ever been in my life. Ten hours of work—and not a penny to show for it. Oh, we kept our word, and didn't ask for pay, and Mr. Jennings kept his word and didn't offer any. To add insult to injury, when he dropped us off he handed Patrick and I five-pound bags of fresh blueberries for our mothers. 'Tell your mothers their boys are good workers,' he said. That wasn't much consolation for the humiliation we'd suffered."

"Did you ever see him after that?" asked Marjorie.

I smiled. "This story has quite an ending," I said.

•••

THE NEXT DAY, Patrick and I showed up at the hardware store at 8 AM, like always. It might have been a normal workday for everyone else, but our attitudes were anything but normal that morning. That was pure humble pie we'd been forced to eat up on that hill in Independence. Mr. O'Hagan sensed something was wrong, but didn't ask any questions.

Patrick and I finished up at noon, and headed for the door.

"Hold on," said Patrick's dad, "I have something for you boys." He reached under the cash register and pulled out two envelopes.

"What's this?" Patrick wanted to know.

His father smiled. "When I opened the store this morning, Mr. Jennings was my first customer. He left these for you two."

I tore my envelope open. A folded piece of paper held a worn dollar bill and two quarters. Patrick's was the same. One dollar and fifty cents each—two bits more than the going day rate for a grown farm hand.

My envelope also contained a note, addressed to us both. In a rough scrawl, Mr. Jennings wrote:

> You boys gave me the best day's entertainment I've had since the circus came through these parts in '32. You are good boys, and fine workers. Any man who does a good day's work and keeps his word is always welcome around my place.
>
> Your friend,
> Silas Jennings

I looked at Patrick, and shook my head. I felt like an idiot for the way

I had stomped around all day yesterday after we'd lost the contest, and for the way I treated him. I didn't know if I wanted to laugh or cry.

Mr. O'Hagan solved my dilemma: "Boys," he said. "Here's seventy-five cents. How about you head across to the drugstore and get the three of us some hamburgers and fries. I've got a story of my own about Mr. Jennings—happened when I was just about your age, too."

•••

"MR. JENNINGS WAS QUITE the character," said Connie. "Didn't he end up donating his land for a school?"

"He did," I said. "When he died in the late '50s he gave it to the county, along with enough money to build a farm school for troubled kids. It's still in operation. I don't know how many young people have learned the value of a good day's work because of his generosity."

Eric shook his head. "I must pass that place twice a month," he said. "I always see the sign, but I've never stopped, and I never knew the story."

"You should pay them a visit, son," I said. "They're always looking for folks here in the community to get involved with the kids. You might enjoy it. And when you go, look a couple hundred yards due south of the administration building. You'll see a low hill topped with a stand of young oak trees. Mr. Jennings planted them about fifty years ago to replace the ones he cut down in '39. That's where Patrick and I got whipped by the one-armed wonder."

Peter and Marjorie stood as a nurse's aide wheeled my lunch in. She left it on the tray, but I didn't bother to uncover it.

"You said earlier that you learned all kinds of lessons that day," said Peter after the aide left the room. "What were they?"

"You tell me," I replied. "If the story's worth telling, it should speak for itself."

Connie led off: "Fair enough. How about, don't judge a book by its cover."

"And what about listen to your elders," said Eric. "If you had followed Patrick's father's instructions and not tried to negotiate, you would have saved yourself a lot of pain."

"But lost out on a great story," laughed Peter. "I was thinking that you and Patrick learned a little something about humility, too, and about the importance of keeping your word."

"Not to mention the value of sticking to the job even when everything around you crumbles into dust," added Marjorie. She squeezed Peter's arm and added, "You also learned the truth of the old adage that says wisdom and experience will beat youth and muscle every time."

"I think you saw the fundamental goodness that is inside most people," said my wife. "Mr. Jennings didn't have to drive into town to pay you boys, and he certainly didn't have to give you more than the going rate." She looked at me. "So what about you, Martin?" she asked. "We pretty much cover it? What did you learn that day?"

I thought for a moment. "I learned that work is the most extraordinary and meaningful activity that humans undertake. I think that's because when we work, we have the opportunity to experience and be tested on every one of the values we hold dear. Work is honest, and it's revealing. It creates a bond with others that is unlike any other relationship, too. If you want to know what you're made of—or what others are made of—work at a job with all your heart and soul and spirit. You'll discover more about yourself than you can imagine."

I had to pause to take a breath and have a sip of water before I could finish my thought. "The biggest thing I learned about work up on that hill is something that took a lot of years to figure out: I discovered that we are made stronger when we realize that the only helping hand we need—the one that we should depend upon first and last and always—is right there at the end of our own arm."

No one talked for a moment.

Then Eric laughed and said, "Even if you only have one arm to begin with!"

We sat there, Peter and Marjorie, Connie and Eric and I, joking and reminiscing together throughout the afternoon. It was so enjoyable, I almost forgot where we were. Almost.

They left me before my dinner was brought in.

I needed to eat up and rest up. Tomorrow would be a big day. Eric and Rachel were due back in, and they were bringing Jimmy and Gwen.

The nurses and doctors had been telling me to take it easy. Tonight I would listen.

COURAGE

I was starting to nod off after breakfast when Gwen skipped into my hospital room and clambered up onto my bed. Jimmy was right behind her, and in a flash my six-year-old granddaughter was cuddled against my left shoulder while her five-year-old brother crawled beneath the web of tubes and monitor wires to nestle against my right flank.

"I surrender," I said. "If you don't tickle me I promise I'll even eat my broccoli."

"Scout's honor?" said Jimmy. "That's a big promise."

I hugged him and pushed the control to raise the back of the bed to an upright position.

"Scout's honor," I answered. "Now, what are you two doing here in a stuffy old hospital when you should be at the park, and where are your parents?"

Gwen wrinkled her brow and took hold of my hand. "You're pretty silly, Grampa, if you don't know why we're here. Mommy said the doctors and nurses don't have the kind of cheer-up medicine that Jimmy and I make. So we brought you some."

"We brought you a lot," added Jimmy.

"I'll bet you did, Jimmy. Now, where are Mom and Dad? Do they think you've run away to join the circus?"

"No, no, no," sang Gwen, bobbing her head in time to the blips on the heart monitor behind my bed. "They're having lunch in the cafeteria. Dad said he thought you might like some time just with us."

How about another twenty years, I thought.

"Well good, then," I replied. "What shall we do, chase some pirates, or maybe catch a couple of wild ponies and break out of this joint?"

"We can't do that Granddad," said Gwen. "Mom says you have to stay right here in this bed until it's time for you to go to heaven."

"Gwen!" Jimmy shot his sister a withering glance.

Gwen scooted closer. "Well, she did, Granddad, that's exactly what she said."

"And she was right, Gwen. But I think Jimmy would rather not talk about that—it can sound kind of scary."

Jimmy tugged at the sleeve of his baseball shirt and turned his head away. "So, do you really have to go away forever?" he asked.

He looked up at me expectantly. I knew what he wanted to hear—what they both wanted to hear. That Granddad was going to get better and be able to take them to the park. That I'd be able to team up with them once again in the time-honored coalition of grandparents and grandchildren united against their common foe, the parents.

I stretched my arms out as far as the IV needles in my forearms permitted, and pulled my grandchildren close. In the corridor outside my room, the hustle and bustle of a busy hospital went on ceaselessly. Inside Room 512 though, the world had stopped spinning, if only for a moment.

"Forever is an awfully long time, Jimmy. No one lives that long, but no one is alone that long either, especially not in heaven. Heaven is where you get to be surrounded by the people you love, where you never have to be apart from them again."

Just then, Nurse Marsden bustled into the room. She was all business. She sized up the situation, planted herself in the middle of the room, and put her hands on her hips. She narrowed her eyes, glaring at each of the children, and then me, before smiling and asking, "So, what will it be for your roommates: hot cocoa or fruit smoothies?"

I nudged my fellow conspirators, and they hopped off the bed to follow the nurse down the hall. When they returned a few minutes later with their drinks, the nurse pulled two chairs alongside my bed. Gwen and Jimmy plopped down, and promptly put their feet up on the bed rail.

"What shall we talk about?" I asked. "How about school?"

"No, not today," said Gwen. "How about a story?"

"I'd love to hear a story," I said. "What kind would you like to tell me?"

"No, not her," said Jimmy. "You tell a story. Right, Gwen?"

"Mom said maybe you would like to tell us a story like the kinds you always tell at Christmas, the ones about your family back in the olden days," said Gwen.

"Well, we do have cocoa," said Jimmy, "so that sorta makes it like Christmas."

"You okay with that plan, Gwen? The story I'd like to tell you is about my grandmother, Elizabeth when she was just about your age."

Gwen sat up. "Was she like me, Granddad?"

"You mean was she brave and funny and smart? She was, very much like you. In fact, your great-great-grandmother had more courage than anyone I have ever known."

Jimmy looked a bit uncertain. He pulled an electronic game out of his pocket and turned it slowly around in his hand. Backup, I supposed, in case my story didn't contain the right ingredients, which for him usually meant rodeo cowboys or expeditions into uncharted jungle territory.

I pushed the button to change the angle of my bed a bit, and took a final drink of my protein shake. The activity in the corridor outside my room softened to a low murmur. Jimmy and Gwen shifted around in their chairs, anxious for the tale to begin. I closed my eyes for a moment, recalling memories of Grandmother Elizabeth. She had been a frontier rancher, teacher and homemaker. Quick to laugh, and always in motion, that was Elizabeth. My earliest memories of visiting her home weren't so much of activities as they were of smells—of yeast and molasses and fresh baked bread, of peppermint and maple syrup and apple pies cooling on the windowsill.

I cleared my throat. "I wonder how I should begin."

"With once upon a time in the olden days," giggled Gwen.

"With once upon a time in the olden cowboy days," added Jimmy.

"Well, you know, that's exactly where Elizabeth's story begins. Once upon a time in the olden cowboy days…"

•••

HER PARENTS JOINED THE GREAT MIGRATION west in the years after the Civil War. They filled their Conestoga wagon with everything they owned and made the perilous journey from Ohio to the Montana territory. They carved out a homestead in a great valley filled with tall forests and wide, grassy meadows. Their land was bounded on three sides by a trout-filled stream and on the fourth by a stand of lodgepole pines that swept right up to the base of the Bitterroot Mountains.

Elizabeth's father built a log cabin close by the stream. It was a tight, warm house with real glass windows, an enormous rock fireplace and a hardwood floor. He lined the porch rails with wooden planters for seed flowers and herbs, and behind the house he built a shed for the horses and their milk cow. His wife put two cane rockers on the porch, where they could sit and look across the creek, over the sweet grass meadows and up into the snow-tipped mountains.

In the summer of 1876, when Elizabeth was only a few months old, a grizzled old trader arrived at the cabin. His wagon was the horse-drawn supermarket of the frontier, with an assortment of pots and pans, bolts of cloth, sacks of sugar and coffee and beans, small bags of striped candy and even a few books.

Elizabeth's parents welcomed the old man into their home for the night. The next morning, in thanks for a homemade supper and a soft bed, he dug a tiny sapling tree out of his wagon and gave it to Elizabeth's mother. The willowy tree was not from these parts, he said. In fact, it had come all the way from Africa and was said to blossom just once in its lifetime, producing great bunches of scented flowers from which the most expensive perfumes in the world were distilled.

Her parents thanked the trader and he headed off to the next ranch. Even though they chuckled at the idea that this was a magic tree, her father planted it in a patch of wildflowers down near the creek.

That summer they added a second room to the cabin, and cleared trees from the fields to plant wheat and corn. Her father started a small blacksmith business, and her mother helped him work the fields and care for the livestock. It was hard work, from first light of day until well after dark, but it was satisfying for the young couple to see their dreams come alive and to watch the small town where they attended Sunday service begin to grow and prosper.

And then, not long after Elizabeth's third birthday, her mother fell ill.

The doctor did all he could to help, but he was unable to control her fever. As the first autumn winds swept down the Bitterroot and into the valley, Elizabeth's mother passed away.

The child was too young to understand the gathering of people around the grave a few days later, or the pain that was etched on her father's face as he planted a small white cross to mark her mother's final resting place.

•••

GWEN SHIFTED IN HER CHAIR. "Granddad, I don't think I like this story. It's pretty sad."

I smiled. "Some of the best stories start that way, don't they? Sad things happen in life, and they teach us about the things that really matter. But even though Elizabeth lost her mother, her story was just beginning."

"Did she still have a lot more to learn?" asked Jimmy.

"She did," I said. "A lot more to learn about happiness, and sadness, and about why living a full life takes a lot of courage."

"Okay, tell us some more, Granddad."

•••

AFTER HIS WIFE'S DEATH, Elizabeth's father poured himself into his work, returning home to his daughter and housekeeper long after sunset. Each night he read to Elizabeth in front of the fireplace until she fell asleep in his arms. His only purpose in life now was to care for her, to build a future for her that would be happier than his own.

A long, dark winter followed that terrible autumn. But when the spring thaw came, Elizabeth's tree burst forth in clusters of bright green leaves for the first time. No flowers bloomed, but its leafy canopy created a refuge from the blistering summer sun that grew thicker and fuller with each passing year.

In the summertime, her father knew he would find Elizabeth playing under the outstretched branches of her special tree each evening when he rode in from the fields. And on Sundays after church they picnicked on the grassy carpet that spread around its base.

One lazy afternoon, as they watched clouds drift high overhead, Elizabeth asked her father how far away heaven was, and if it was so far above them that humans could not see it. He pointed across the horizon to a V-shaped notch that had been carved by weather into the granite between two mountain peaks.

"Do you see the pool of light nestled in that rocky cleft, just where the snowline begins," he asked?

Elizabeth nodded. She had seen the last of the evening light settle in that place before. It was as if the wick in a golden lantern was slowly fading.

"That is no ordinary light," he said. "It's kind of like a rainbow, a promise of God's love for us. When you see a promise like that, you know that heaven is close by, so close that you can see it. It doesn't matter where you are, or what is happening in your life. The promise is always close by, especially when times are difficult."

It was a promise Elizabeth would never forget.

On Christmas Eve that year, a full moon settled over the snow-draped valley. Elizabeth's father carried a small burlap bag out into the still, cold night and spread its contents around the base of her tree. There were green, red and gold glass ornaments, a ball of scarlet ribbon, and dozens of small candles.

He hung the ornaments on the tree's ice-coated branches, and wound the ribbon around its trunk and limbs. Then he wedged the candles into the hollows of the branches, and lit them. The effect was magical. Candlelight bounced off of the ornaments, spraying ribbons of color across the snow, and the tree's reflection sparkled like a basket of precious jewels on the surface of the creek.

He returned to the cabin and pulled a sleeping Elizabeth from her bed, wrapping her in a warm comforter. He carried her down to the creek bank, and laid her gently on a thick, warm buffalo robe on the snow directly beneath her tree. Then he stepped back so that when she awoke the tree would be the only thing she saw.

It only took a moment. Elizabeth stirred in the chill night air, her eyes opened, and she looked around. She was uncertain at first, and for an instant she looked as though she might be afraid. Then she saw the illuminated tree, and her father standing close by, and her eyes widened in astonishment.

Oh, but I must still be dreaming, she thought!

The icy branches glittered with the reflection of the candles bouncing off of the glass ornaments. She clapped her hands in delight at the streamers of color that splashed across the snow as the ornaments twirled slowly in the night breeze.

Elizabeth sat up and watched the light from her tree spill down the creek bank, pour into the water and float off in the direction of the towering mountains. Could her mother see the tree and its glittering lights from heaven, she wondered?

She looked over at her father and saw that he was smiling for the first time since they'd lost her mother. He was looking across the valley, high up into the mountain pass where light from the full moon was beginning to pool. Elizabeth knew he was wondering the same thing.

Her father stood watch until Elizabeth fell happily asleep on the snowy mattress beneath her tree. The only sound for miles when he scooped her up and walked back to the cabin was the crunch of snow beneath his boots. He put her in her bed, stoked the fire, and pulled his chair near the window. Outside, the candles in her tree flung a golden curtain across the blue-white snow. Droplets of colored light from the ornaments dotted the snowscape. High above, gleaming like a crystal shower, the winter stars twinkled their approval.

•••

"OKAY, I LIKE THAT PART a lot better," said Gwen.

"Yeah, that would be a really cool Christmas tree," Jimmy added.

Before I could respond, a lab tech entered the room. It was time for my blood draw. But the ever-vigilant Nurse Marsden had seen him turning into my room, and she whisked in right behind him to ask if he could return in a while.

"But don't get your hopes up, Mr. Forrestal," she said as she left. "You and your teammates have to break this party up in thirty minutes."

"Boy, she's just like Mom," said Jimmy. "She sees everything."

"Jimmy, that's not the half of it," I replied. "I don't even think she sleeps."

"What happened then to Great-Great-Grandmother Elizabeth?" asked Gwen. "Did she sleep under her tree every night after that?"

"Not exactly," I said. "But that tree wasn't done with its magic, that's for sure."

•••

ELIZABETH WAS GROWING UP, and so was the valley around her. Settlers from the east poured in during the 1880s in search of cheap land and opportunity, and their small town became the county seat. Elizabeth went to school and church and made many new friends. When she turned twelve, she told her father that she was ready to take over the housekeeping chores.

Her father continued to work tirelessly at building up the ranch. He purchased an adjoining homestead, raised a herd of cattle and grew his blacksmith business into a prosperous enterprise.

Elizabeth's tree was growing as quickly as she was. Each spring it sprouted patches of shiny green leaves; each fall they turned orange and brown and fell to the ground without flowering. She read books, wrote poems, and day dreamed about the future on the soft grass beneath its outstretched arms whenever the weather permitted. And she and her father decorated it every Christmas. On Christmas Eve they would bundle up with warm coats and hot chocolate and sit beneath its ice-coated branches to watch the light dance across the snow and shimmer on the surface of the creek.

Elizabeth could have lived this way forever. But, as she would say when she was telling the story to my brother and I many years later, the fates don't often take the dreams of humans into account when balancing their books.

And so it was that when Elizabeth was fourteen, her father was badly injured in a rockslide on the slopes of Willow Mountain, where he'd gone in search of a stray calf. A neighbor found him bloodied and nearly frozen on a rocky trail just above the snow line. He had a broken shoulder, broken ribs and a busted leg, but he had managed to crawl through the thick brush and snow for several miles in a heroic effort to get back to his daughter.

The neighbor laid him over the back of his packhorse, and brought him to the cabin. The doctor set her father's broken bones as best he could, then helped Elizabeth wrap him in heavy blankets on a cot by the fire.

"Your father has internal bleeding," the doctor explained, "and probably other injuries—it's difficult to determine."

Only time would tell if he would survive.

The doctor and the pastor looked in on them for the first few days, but when the weather progressed from a light snowfall to an Arctic blizzard, the road from town became impassable. Caring for her father was Elizabeth's job now. There would be no one to help her until the storm cleared.

She stayed by his side day and night for three weeks, leaving only to feed the animals or bring in firewood. She read to him from the same books that he had read to her when she was a child. When he was chilled she fed him warm soup, and when he was racked with fever she kept a cool cloth on his forehead.

Elizabeth barely slept. Each time her father stirred or coughed in pain, she wakened and did all she could to soothe him. She had no medicine, no dressings or bandages, and no training in how to care for someone so badly injured. There was no one to help her, to comfort her, no one for her to even visit with.

When he slept, she sat by the fire, remembering all of the special times they had shared and all of the plans they had made for the future. She recalled the story of how her tree had come to be planted on the bank of the creek and about the legend the old trader told her parents about the tree's magical origins on the far side of the world. Each autumn she and her father had watched its withered leaves fall to the ground. Never once did the tree bring forth a flower, and the very idea that it could produce a crop of rare, perfumed blossoms made them laugh.

Day after long day, as the winds howled around them and ice and snow battered the walls of their little cabin, Elizabeth's father fought valiantly for his life.

On December twenty-third, the great blizzard began to subside. As the last of the storm swept out of the valley and onto the vast prairie beyond the mountains, her father gave up his struggle, and died peacefully in the arms of his beloved daughter.

The next day was Christmas Eve. Elizabeth's friends and neighbors huddled against a biting wind on the bank of the creek near the cabin. A fresh grave had been scraped out of the frozen dirt beneath snow next to her mother's resting place. It was marked with a simple white cross. The ceremony was brief, as befit the humility of the man and the severity of the weather. Her father had been a good neighbor, a respected businessman, and a friend who could always be counted on to help anyone in need.

Elizabeth politely declined the many invitations to join friends for Christmas celebrations. As each group climbed into their buckboard wagon and pulled their lap robes tight, Elizabeth handed them a jug of hot, spiced apple-cider.

She stayed outside on the porch until the last wagon disappeared around the red cedars at the bend in the road. Her heart ached with a sorrow and loneliness as deep as the bitter cold, but it wasn't until the sun dipped below the mountain crest that Elizabeth returned to the warmth of the empty cabin.

•••

That night, the valley rested peacefully under a blanket of powdery snow. A full yellow moon sat high above the granite peaks, and the smoke from Elizabeth's chimney curled lazily into the winter sky. She sat in her father's chair by the kitchen window, gazing past her tree, across the frozen meadow and up into the towering purple mountains. She was searching for the exact places where their craggy peaks made contact with heaven.

As the moon settled above the cabin, she pulled a heavy quilt around her shoulders and went outside. A carpet of stars swept across the sky, and the air was perfectly still, as if the earth was holding its breath. Elizabeth turned away from the warm cabin and its memories of happier times and dropped to her knees on the soft snow beneath her tree. She began to cry, and her tears melted tiny holes in the snow.

Her pain and loneliness at last gave way to exhaustion, and she fell asleep beneath the tree.

Dawn spilled softly into the valley the next morning, pouring over the mountain peaks and across the valley floor. The sun woke Elizabeth with a gentle caress. Her eyes opened to a bright and glorious Christmas landscape. A clump of snow fell to the ground from a tree across the creek, the Bitterroot Mountains glowed rose and violet, and a wisp of smoke drifted from the cabin chimney.

Elizabeth stretched and pulled the quilt tight around her shoulders. The warm sun felt good, and for a moment she forgot the hurt of the last few days. Then, a ray of light glanced off of the white cross that marked her father's grave. Pain flooded her heart, and she began to cry. She felt so alone. It would be unbearable, so difficult to go on.

She wiped at her tears and turned her head in the direction of the cabin. The milk cow was waiting for her, the hens needed to be turned out and given their scratch corn, and the horses would need a ration of oats and molasses. Life went on, and so did the chores.

Elizabeth leaned her head back to shake a dusting of snow from the quilt. As she did, something caught her eye. Something remarkable.

But, it couldn't be, she thought. Not here, not now, and certainly not after the worst blizzard in a quarter century.

She felt the morning chill on her face. Her feet were aching with cold, and she could smell smoke from the chimney—this wasn't a dream.

Elizabeth threw off her quilt and stood up. A feeling of joy washed over her, her tears stopped, and her heart swelled with happiness.

She stepped back, and looked up through the branches of the ice-coated tree. What she saw was nothing less than a miracle.

In the dead of winter, on the sun-drenched bank of a frozen Montana creek, a promise had been fulfilled. The tree that her father planted fourteen years ago was no longer just an icy skeleton. Elizabeth was astonished to see that one limb was now covered in a mass of gossamer white flowers, stretching from the trunk of the tree to the tip of the branch. The rest of the tree was as bare and icy as the day before, wrapped tightly in its coat of winter frost. Just one branch, arcing high above all the others, had burst into bloom.

Each one of the thousands of tiny flowers on the remarkable limb had a splash of deep red color in its center. A fragrance of rose and lavender and jasmine filled the air. It was the most wonderful perfume Elizabeth could imagine. The old trader's promise had come true. The tree he gave to Elizabeth's parents had blossomed just as he said it would. And on Christmas day!

Elizabeth took a few steps back so that she could take in the entire tree. It was then that she noticed something else about the tree's lone, flower-covered branch: it was positioned exactly so that it arched protectively over the two wooden crosses that marked her parents' final resting place.

Elizabeth returned to the cabin. She heated a mug of cider, went out on the porch, and settled into her mother's rocker. Across the creek, beyond the snowdrifts and above the cedar forests, the great mountains maintained their silent vigil. Elizabeth was certain of one thing: when the mountain snows melted next spring, a new pool of light would be visible high up in the cleft of the mountain pass, right next to the one her father pointed out that summer evening when she asked him if heaven was close by.

Her tree stood loving guard over the two snowy graves. As Elizabeth watched, two white petals fell from the branch and were carried in the arms of a gentle breeze toward the waiting mountains.

•••

GWEN AND JIMMY WERE LEANING forward in their chairs as I finished the story. I set my water glass down. "Grandmother Elizabeth told us that story every Christmas," I said. "And each time she told it, it was like the first time I ever heard it."

"She was so brave," said Gwen. "She took care of her daddy all by herself."

"And she had to take care of the animals and chop wood with a big axe, too," said Jimmy.

I was pleased to see that Jimmy's electronic game hadn't been switched on.

"Yes she did, and in fact, she worked that ranch by herself for a whole year until her aunt and uncle came west the next year and settled in with her."

"Did her tree ever grow flowers on it again at Christmastime?" Gwen asked.

"Not at Christmas or any other time. Her miracle came when she needed it most. That's the way that most real miracles happen."

A crowd appeared at the doorway to my room: Eric, Rachel, Peter, Marjorie and Connie. They squeezed inside.

"Come one, come all, there's room for you here. We'll have ourselves a proper shindig."

"How were the kids?" Eric asked.

"Oh, they were a treat," I said.

We chatted for half an hour, until Gwen and Jimmy reached the end of their respective five- and six-year-old attention spans. It was time for them to go. Hugs and kisses and goodbyes were exchanged. Peter, Marjorie and Connie were going to walk Eric and Rachel and the kids out to their car, and then come back up to spend more time with me.

As the group departed, Gwen asked her mother if she could ask me a question in private. Rachel looked at me, and then told Gwen to be quick. The rest of the group left me alone with my granddaughter.

"Granddad, that was the best Christmas story you ever told us. Even though it isn't even Christmas."

"Thank you honey. I hope you will share it with your own family for ever and ever."

Gwen laid a hand on my shoulder. "Granddad, I have a question. Since Elizabeth got to have a miracle happen after her parents went to heaven, does that mean that I get to have a miracle after you go to heaven?"

I blinked back a tear, and took her hand. "Gwen, the truth is that we all get to have miracles in our lives. The secret is to keep your eyes and heart open so you'll know when your miracles happen."

She leaned over and kissed me on the cheek. "Okay, Granddad, I'll watch really careful." She paused, and looked in my eyes. "When you do go to heaven, I promise I'll be brave and help everybody for you, just like Elizabeth did."

Then she turned and walked out. Gwen's footsteps echoed down the hall. For a moment, the only sound in my room was the blip of the heart monitor and the soft tap of a tree branch against the window. I was very tired, I realized in the stillness, and I closed my eyes.

FAITH

I WOKE BEFORE DAWN. I watched the light begin to stir the world outside my window, and reflected upon the fact that I have spent most of my life outdoors. My office ceiling was woven with clouds and sky instead of sheetrock and fluorescent tubes. The opportunity to observe the natural world on its terms has been one of the great joys of my life.

I look forward to the changes in weather, light and color as each season in turn relinquishes its control of the elements. Summer light is harsh and piercing. In the fall the light is all golden and shadowy around the edges. Winter light is weak and short-lived. But in the spring, light is reborn. It flexes its muscles and pulls the crocus and daffodils out of the hard winter dirt. It is soft and inviting and infused with energy. If you are patient, you can watch the spring light along the river caress the cottonwoods and alders to life, like a mother warming her newborn after a bath.

I have watched the light of spring renew the world right in front of me for over eighty years. I consider that a privilege, a great gift from God. And all I had to do was open my eyes.

•••

EACH MORNING MY NURSES wrote the date and the projected temperature on the dry erase board across from my bed. Today it said May 2, seventy-one degrees.

Connie was driving Peter and Marjorie to the airport for their flight back to Montana. My brother wanted to stay a few more days, but he did not argue when I turned down his request. Dying people are on that very short list of folks—brides on their wedding day, presidents at their inauguration—who are denied nothing at their special times.

It was, nonetheless, a difficult parting. Connie ushered a tearful Marjorie down to the lobby last night after her goodbye, while Peter stood vigil awhile longer.

"You don't think about days like this when you're a kid, do you?" he said softly.

"No, you sure don't," I replied. "Invulnerable, that's what you are when you're young. Nobody can hold you back, nothing can stand in your way, and certainly no chance of death getting his bony fingers around you. I think that God injects the young with so much life-force that it takes fifty or sixty years for that energy to wind down to a place where a man begins to acknowledge that the end of the road is actually just over the next rise."

"Do you talk to Him much—God I mean?" he asked.

"Do you mean am I talking to Him more now that the expiration date on this old carcass is about up?"

Peter smiled, and laid his hand on mine.

"Yes, I am. In part because I'm alone much of the time here, and in part because He and I have a lot of unfinished business to take care of."

Peter's voice was strained. "Are you afraid, Martin?"

"You're the second person to ask me that question this week. The first was Gwen. Funny how you two are the only ones who've asked."

"What did you tell her?"

"That I was no more afraid to die than I was to be born."

My brother laughed. "That wasn't altogether fair, was it?"

"Maybe not. But it is true. When you're standing at the doorstep of eternity, faith moves out of the realm of the theoretical, I can tell you that."

"Are you at peace with it?"

"As much as a man can be, I guess. The fact that I know my death is inevitable doesn't mean I'm folding my cards and giving up, though. I have plenty of reasons to keep fighting, and I will, right up until the end."

A nurse's aide came in to clean up my breakfast dishes. When she left, Peter drew a chair close to my bed.

"There's something I want to tell you," he said. "Do you remember that

Christmas a couple of years after the war, when Dad's appendix burst, and he almost died?"

"Sure I do. He was in the hospital for three weeks—he came home Christmas Eve."

"And you were falling timber up around Tillamook, six or seven hours away."

"I remember. It was the coldest, wettest, most miserable job site I ever worked."

"You came to visit Dad a couple of times, but we knew you wouldn't be there for Christmas because the weather was so bad, and the radio said the mountain pass was closed to traffic."

"It was a bear," I said.

"I was nine," Peter said. "And I had dropped about a million hints to Mom and Dad about what I wanted for Christmas—a Joe DiMaggio signature baseball glove and bat. I'd stand in center field on the baseball diamond at school and just dream of that glove and bat. I knew if I had them, I could hit in fifty-six consecutive games." He chuckled.

"But Dad was in the hospital," he continued, "and Mom was running the lumberyard by herself, and you were up on that mountain ramrodding a logging crew. When they brought Dad home Christmas Eve, we didn't even have a tree in the living room. Oh, I was thrilled he was home and on the mend, but I remember going to sleep that night, listening to the rain on the roof turn to snow, looking at that photo of Joe and the Yankees on my bedroom wall, and feeling pretty sorry for myself."

Peter sighed and shook his head. "When I woke up Christmas morning and headed outside to split kindling, I saw a package wrapped in Christmas colors on the kitchen table. Even without opening it, I knew what it was. My heart was in my throat. But, it was chores first, even on Christmas. Mom and Dad weren't up yet, so I got a fire going and got the coffee started. A few minutes later Mom helped Dad down the stairs."

Peter had a curious, wistful look on his face as he spoke. "When Dad told me how sorry he was that we missed Christmas, and that they'd make it up to me next week with a tree and presents, I was mystified. I told them to hold on a minute, and I ran into the kitchen and got the big package off the table. Mom looked surprised, and Dad didn't have a clue. I tore that paper off in a flash, and there they were, a beautiful oiled leather centerfielder's glove and that genuine hickory bat with DiMaggio's signature burned onto the shaft. Mom and Dad had no idea where they came from, or who snuck them into the house. But if it wasn't from them, and you were a hundred miles away on top of a mountain, who was playing Santa Claus?"

I pushed the elevation button on my bed and raised myself as straight as I could.

"We came to the conclusion that some friend of Mom or Dad's bought the glove and bat," said Peter. "Dad said they probably wanted to remain anonymous."

My brother squeezed my hand. "But it wasn't a stranger who did it, was it? You plowed off that mountain on Christmas Eve and drove through the worst storm in ten years so that your little brother wouldn't be disappointed on Christmas morning. And all these years you kept quiet. You let me think that some mysterious stranger brought those gifts."

I tried to hold back my tears, but I wasn't successful. It took both of us a minute to regain our composures. I had no idea that that Christmas had been so important to him.

"A few days ago you apologized to me for not being a better big brother," said Peter. "You were wrong. You were the best big brother a boy could ever have."

He took a deep breath.

"Martin, I have faith in God. I have faith in my wife and my country, and in my children. I have always had faith in you, big brother. You showed me what it takes to be a good man."

Peter took his jacket from a peg on the wall, and picked up a book I had given to him. Then he came over to me, held my hand, and bowed his head in quiet for a moment. His eyes welled up again. "Tell you what," he said through his tears. "I'll bring that glove and bat along when I see you next time. We'll hit a few balls, and maybe this time I'll belt one farther than you."

"I bet you will," I said.

And then he was gone.

•••

DESPITE THE EMOTIONAL FAREWELL with my brother, I was feeling better than I had in several days. My back pain had subsided, my appetite was pretty good, and I had no dizziness or nausea.

When Doctor McGuire had stopped by this morning he pronounced me fit enough to spend an hour outdoors. Connie wouldn't be back from the airport for several hours, so I decided to undertake the adventure while the sky was blue and the coast was clear.

Rachel solved the transportation problem when she dropped by with some books and magazines. "Sure you don't want to wait for Mom so you can have some company?" my daughter-in-law asked. "I can take you down to the park, but then I have to leave to get Jimmy to the dentist."

"The hospital will have someone come get me," I assured her. "I may not feel this good tomorrow, so if it's all the same to you, I'd like to go now."

Rachel waited in the hall while Nurse Marsden helped me dress. She insisted I wear a light jacket, and she slipped a pager into my pocket when she helped me into the wheelchair. "I know you're only fifty yards from the front door," she said, "but if you need help push the button and someone will be there in a flash. We'll get you in exactly one hour."

Rachel wheeled me into the elevator and we rode down to the lobby. I breathed deeply as we exited through the main doors. Several people were sitting on the low wall surrounding the fountain just outside, and as we passed by a cool mist sprayed my face. It felt wonderful. Across the drive sat Salem's crown jewel park. A stream meandered across the one hundred-acre site, its banks ablaze with brilliant rhododendrons and early azaleas. And there were Connie's favorite wood hyacinths, wrapping their violet flowers around the bases of the park's old growth oaks.

I asked Rachel to wheel me along the gravel path to a wrought iron and wood bench about a hundred yards from the hospital. The bench sat high on the creek bank, sheltered from the breeze by a weeping willow whose branches dipped down to the creek's surface. To the west I could see a grove of cherry trees in full blossom. Across the creek a hill topped with a line of flowering maples blocked the view of anything that looked like civilization.

As long as I didn't turn back toward the hospital, I could imagine I was in the country, miles from city noise and clutter. It's just what I wanted.

"They won't be happy about you coming way over here," said Rachel. "But I don't blame you. It's beautiful. Are you sure you'll be okay?"

I got out of the wheelchair, and hugged her. "You go on now, and take care of Jimmy's tooth," I said. I plopped myself down on the bench. "This is just right."

"Then I'll be on my way," said Rachel. She gave me a kiss, and left.

For the first time in over a month, I was alone.

There were no sounds of people or cars or anything to distract me—just the breeze through the willow, and the water tumbling over rocks in the stream. The May sky was soft blue. I slipped off my sandals and felt the cool grass beneath my feet. It was a magnificent feeling, and it set my mind in motion.

Connie and I have attended the same church for over forty years, and as buildings of stone and wood and glass go, it is a fine construction. It serves its purpose of sheltering the congregation against the elements, and providing a place for people to gather to worship and celebrate and remember—but that building is not a place where I have ever felt a particular connection to God. For that I prefer a canopy of cedar branches under a starry sky instead of a vaulted masonry roof, a carpet of wildflowers in place of polished wood and rugs.

Nature is my cathedral.

A perfect example of that is just an hour's drive from where I sat. It is located on six hundred forty acres of timber out near Kings Valley that I bought and logged in the early '60s. It's in its second growth now, with towering fir, cedar, and hemlock, but it will never be logged again. We're giving it to a conservation group with instructions that it be left as it is, a place of solitude for hikers to discover and enjoy on their own.

I first saw what was to become my outdoor chapel one summer day, many years ago, when I was looking for a good spot to rig choker cable lines to haul out the trees we fell and bucked. I walked over a rise, and looked down into a miniature valley, about seventy-five yards long and thirty yards wide. The ground was carpeted with meadow grass, red huckleberry and wild rose, and bounded on all four sides by a slope that rose gently about fifteen feet from the valley floor. My first thought on seeing the shape of the place was that Paul Bunyan himself had grabbed a giant shovel and dug an outdoor swimming pool.

Ever since then I have gone there several times each year. I have seen it thick with flowering crocus in February, and alive with forest iris and foxglove in May. At the south end of the vale sits the charred stump of a massive oak tree that was split by lightning. Wildflowers take root in the hollow of the stump every spring. It is the perfect altar for this pristine place.

There is no end of church history, doctrine and verse with which I am unfamiliar. When I am out on the land, though, surrounded by the simple glories of nature under a welcoming sky, all such theological and intellectual affectation withers away. I have yet to see the building that can compare to a red rock canyon, the snowy crest of a granite mountain, or my humble country meadow. And where is there a stained glass window that can rival a beam of sunlight glistening through a drop of morning dew?

My hat is off to the artists and architects and stone masons who have struggled over the centuries to match the genius of the Creator, but in this arena of endeavor, mankind's best efforts are but a shadow of what nature unfolds for us around each bend in the road.

I am content to attend church, visit with friends and worship as part of a community on Sundays. My life is richer for it. But it is in the outdoors that the man-made barriers fall, and the politics of religion fade and the unfiltered, direct honesty of God's Word shines through so clearly that even a simple man like myself cannot mistake its meaning.

My last trip out to our land was in October. Connie drove the four-wheel drive pickup as far off the gravel road as she could, and we hiked in the last quarter mile. The afternoon light was pale and gold as we made our way to the open-air chapel. Oak leaves covered the ground and crackled under our boots, and the crisp air around the old pioneer orchards smelled of wet earth and overripe apples.

The rim of the amphitheater was dotted with stands of lush green fern and tangles of orange-leafed viney maple. There was more than a smattering of poison oak about, too. That plant had been my nemesis in the woods for most of my life. I called a truce for just one day though, and left my machete in its scabbard. That day even the red berries and three-leaf clusters of my old enemy found favor in my eyes.

If in the years to come even one person experiences the peace and spiritual contentment that I found in my chapel garden, that would be just fine.

•••

THE SOUND OF LAUGHTER interrupted my reflections. A mother and two children were chasing a puppy along the creek bank. As they whisked past, the little boy waved at me. I checked the time on Nurse Marsden's pager.

In fifteen minutes a nurse's aide was going to come to collect me at the rendezvous point. If I wasn't there at the appointed second, the escape alert would be sounded.

I slid from the bench and eased into my wheelchair. The distance back to the hospital was about the length of a football field. How hard could it be to wheel there by myself? I released the footbrake, and tried to push forward. The chair moved a little, but the wheels had settled into the gravel path, and I couldn't get enough traction to launch. I pushed again. No luck. The third time I tried, a searing pain ripped across my back and took my breath away. I coughed, trying to get my breath back, only to feel my eyes blur, and a wave of nausea pour over me.

I struggled to catch my breath. I inhaled deeply, fighting the urge to vomit, or worse, to pass out. The nausea subsided as quickly as it came on, and I shook my head in an attempt to clear my vision. It helped.

Well, this was a fine pickle. I was only a hundred yards away from the hospital, but it might as well have been a hundred miles. The fact that I'd have to be rescued while sitting in the middle of a public park on a perfectly fine spring day didn't help my attitude much.

Then I heard a rushing sound and the crunch of gravel. A boy of about twelve made a racing turn on his bike and slid in beside the bench, scattering gravel as he braked. He was followed in close order by another boy on a bike.

"Hey, mister, you okay?" asked the first boy.

I looked up and saw a face full of freckles beneath a Yankees baseball cap.

"Well, to tell you the truth son, I'm having a little trouble with my giddyup here. Maybe you could give me a push to help get me started."

The boy hopped off his bike and set the kickstand.

"Sure, I can do that," he said.

He stepped behind my wheelchair, and just as easy as that, pushed me out of the gravel sand trap. I nodded thanks, and started to push forward while I still had some momentum. I made it all of five or six feet before I bogged down again. This time, I wasn't going to strain. I couldn't chance having another episode.

I settled back in the chair and resigned myself to waiting for the search and rescue party that would be fanning out from the hospital in about seven minutes. As bad as the lecture I'd get from Nurse Marsden would be, the shellacking from Connie would be far worse.

My freckled friend had his own plan, though. He came up around my wheelchair and laid his bike on the grass next to the path.

"So, where are you going?" he asked.

I pointed to the hospital. "I'm vacationing over there," I answered. "They'll be sending somebody to fetch me here before too long."

"If you want to go back now, I can push you," said the boy. "It'll only take a couple minutes."

"You know what," I said, "that would be perfect."

The boy asked his friend to follow with the bikes. Then he began to push me along the path toward the hospital.

"What brings you out here today?" I asked.

"Baseball practice. Tryouts are next week, and I'm hoping to make the team. I'm a pitcher."

We talked about baseball as he wheeled me across the park and right up to the entrance doors of the hospital. He parked me near the fountain. According to the timer, I'd made it back with three minutes to spare.

"Could you wait a few minutes?" I asked him. "When they take me back to my room, I'd like to send down some money for you and your friend to have lunch on me."

He smiled, and adjusted his cap. "Nah, you don't have to do that, but thanks just the same. Maybe I'll see you in the park some other time."

"Maybe you will. Thanks again."

The boys whisked off on their bikes, and a moment later, right on time, an attendant in green hospital scrubs came through the doors to fetch me. Before he wheeled me into the lobby I asked him to turn my wheelchair back toward the park. A breeze came up, ruffling the leaves on the great oaks and scattering white cherry blossoms in every direction. I heard the sounds of families playing, and I could just make out my young friend and his pal riding off to the practice filed. The sun was warm on my face.

"I'm ready," I said.

•••

CONNIE ARRIVED LATE IN THE AFTERNOON, just after I was wheeled back from my final radiological treatment. After today, the care I received would be purely palliative. A cure was out of the question, and there was no reason to expect that the cancer blazing through my body like a wildfire would halt its course and go into a natural remission. No, from here on, my "progress" would be measured only in terms of the absence of physical pain. Based on my experience in the park earlier today, that didn't sound like a bad plan.

Connie visited until after dinner. As she sat reading by the window this afternoon, I was reminded of a poem we read in high school. It was by John Milton, and was titled, "On His Blindness." In it, Milton expressed his belief that even though he had lost his sight he still had a role to play and a duty to perform in God's world. The last line of that poem made me think about Connie, and about all those who can only wait as terrible events swirl around them: "They also serve who only stand and wait."

How my dear Constance has served. And how I look forward to her wait being over.

●●●

I'M NOT SURE WHAT AWAKENED ME. They say that some people can't sleep when it is too quiet. That is usually not a problem in a busy hospital, but as my eyes opened I was struck by how unusually quiet it was in the corridor outside my room. I looked at the nightstand clock. It was exactly 3 AM. I pushed the button to elevate the back of my bed so that I could get some water. That's when I saw him.

You would think that it would be a startling—even frightening—experience to wake up at three in the morning to find a stranger standing at the foot of your bed. That's only true if you've never spent time in a hospital. The parade of doctors, nurses, technicians, therapists, housekeepers and assorted other interested parties is unending. You are as likely to be wakened at 3 AM as you are at 2 PM. So the fact that a stranger was standing at the foot of my bed in the middle of the night reading something on a clipboard was not at all unusual. What was unusual was the stranger himself.

He was of average height and build, with short dark hair, a little grey at the temple. He wore a dark sport coat over a dark polo shirt, and khakis. His skin was deeply browned from a lifetime in the sun, and when he raised his head from the clipboard to look at me, I saw that his eyes were a deep emerald green.

"Good evening," he said, in an accented voice whose origins I couldn't quite place. Eastern Europe?

"Good evening to you," I replied. "Pretty late to be making rounds, isn't it?"

"Ah, but there is no such thing as 'late' in our business, is there?" he said. "But in the interest of full disclosure, I am not a physician."

Not a doctor, I thought? Who else would be here at three in the morning? Judging from his clothing he wasn't a nurse or a therapist. He lifted the papers he had been reading. That's when I saw that it was a yellow legal pad he was holding, not a clipboard. In fact, it was my legal pad, covered with my notes on the values I had been focused on.

"I hope you don't mind me taking a look at your work," he said. "You are something of the talk of the town around here, you know. No one on staff can remember a patient doing anything remotely like what you have undertaken, especially under these circumstances."

Reading my work? Not a doctor? Then it struck me: I had heard that the hospital chaplain kept offbeat hours. If that was it, his timing was certainly good. I had been struggling all day to put into words my feelings about the value of faith, and its role in my life.

"I don't know about being the talk of anything, but I can tell you that 'these circumstances' are the only reason I'm giving this project a go. All things considered, I'd really rather just go fishing."

The stranger smiled. "I'm sure you would." He dropped the legal pad on the foot of my bed. "What interests me, Martin Forrestal, is why a dying man would not simply accept his sentence and fade away. You have done your share. You fought a war, had a great marriage, raised a son, built a business and did much good work in your community. You have earned the right to rest now." He pointed to the notepad. "So, why this? Why now?"

I was taken aback by his directness. He had cut right to the heart of issues that my own family had hardly broached. And he had done it all in less than a minute.

"Would you care to sit?" I asked.

He came around the bed, and pulled up a chair. "Thank you, yes," he said.

That accent. I still couldn't place it. And from the formal tone of his expression, I was certain that English was not his birth language. He also seemed to know a lot about me, so he must have spent time with Connie.

The ceiling lights were off. The lamp beside my bed provided the only illumination in the room, leaving the stranger half in shadow. He sat straight, legs crossed, waiting for me to speak. His eyes would have shone even in a completely dark room, I thought.

"'Why this?'" I said. "'Why now?' It's funny, but when I thought about the fact that all I was leaving behind was a little money, some property and a bunch of photographs of an old bird that no one will be able to identify in twenty or thirty years, I actually got a little angry at myself. What kind of legacy is that?"

"The kind most people leave, I'm afraid," said the man. "Seeking a position of immortality in the minds and hearts of those we leave behind has pretty much been the historical prerogative of pharaohs and poets, not lumbermen like yourself."

He flipped the pages of my legal pad to my notes from this afternoon. A smile creased his face. "And now you are talking about faith," he said. "A subject few people attempt to tackle."

"I nearly left it off my list," I conceded.

"You mean it wasn't a significant enough value in your life for you to want to share it with your descendants?"

I chuckled. "No, quite the opposite. Faith is so important to me that I was afraid I could never do it justice. I'm no theologian. I don't know doctrine from donut holes." I shifted in bed. "I just know that I believe. And I know what belief has meant in my life."

I heard a noise and saw Nurse Leticia step into the room. She looked in my direction, but did not come over to the bed, or make eye contact with me. She left as quickly as she had popped in, as if the room was empty. Odd, I thought.

"So, if I understand correctly," he continued, "you were intimidated by the thought of trying to share what faith has meant to you in your life, but only because you were afraid you wouldn't be able to translate it adequately into words?"

"Something like that, yes. But there's more to it."

"Tell me," said the man. "I'd like to know."

"It's something I haven't shared with anyone, not even my wife or pastor," I said. "But at the end of the day—and that's pretty much now in my case—it comes down to the simple fact that I don't know if I have lived my life in a way that—let me think of the right word here—a way that truly honored the faith I have tried to follow."

"And, whose faith is that?" he asked. He leaned forward and rested one hand on the rail of my bed. "Are you talking about the faith of your parents, the doctrine of your church, the interpretations of your Sunday school teacher, the books you have read about faith, your own interpretations of scripture? Whose ideal of faith do you feel you have not measured up to?"

For the second time in a couple minutes this stranger had baffled me. Had I lived a faithful life?

I suddenly felt very tired. I had done my best since the day Doc McGuire pronounced my sentence to avoid going down this path. When I began this project, I decided to focus on the stories from my life that would be instructive to my family. I was also determined not to fall prey to any temptation to get absorbed in too much soul-searching or self-reflection. The time for a course in Self-Knowledge 101 was long past. After all, one would think that by the time he reached eighty-two a man would have a handle on all of the big questions. That thought made me smile.

The stranger saw the look of bemusement cross my face.

"Did I ask a funny question?"

"Not at all," I said. "I was just thinking about something one of those Beat Generation writers said back in the '50s. It was something along the lines of, 'when it comes to the great road trip of life, the truth is that we're all bozos on this bus.'"

"Yes, there is plenty of comedy in life," said the man. "Intentional as well as accidental. And the less grounded a person is in his or her faith, the more their life seems to take on all of the trappings of a full-blown comic opera. I see that often."

He put his hand on my shoulder. For some reason, it comforted me. "But I see no aspect of that in your life, my friend. I see a good man who is soon to throw off all mortal cares. I see a deeply caring man who wonders what difference he has made in this world, and if his passage through life has truly mattered. And I see a man who is asking a natural question about the way he has lived his faith. The road he traveled on his faith journey was somewhat of his own making. He did not follow the precise model provided to him by other people or religious institutions. Now he wants to know if his choice will merit the approval of the God whom he hopes to stand before one day very soon. Does that sound about right?"

I stared at my hands in my lap, and at the IV needles in the back of my wrists. Who was this man? How was he able to cut through a lifetime of questioning and self-reflection with such precise aim? And why, from among the dozens of patients on my floor, and the hundreds of patients sleeping in the hospital tonight, had he sought me out?

I heard myself simply answering, "Yes, that's about it."

My visitor finished scanning the notes I had made about faith.

"You have been dedicating so much time to sharing your stories. May I take the time to share a story about a man from my country whose faith, like yours, took a path all its own?"

"I would like that."

He pulled his chair a little nearer the head of my bed, and began to tell his story.

●●●

THERE WAS A FARMER in our province, my visitor began, who was much admired for the purity of the olive oil he produced and for the perfect sweetness of his grapes. He was also much envied by the people in the neighboring town, as over the years he purchased more and more land, and planted hundreds of new trees and vines. At harvest time his warehouse bulged with the fruit of his labor, and each October a stream of trucks loaded high with his products would pass through the town square on the way to the capitol city.

The townspeople admired the farmer's success, but he was also the object of much gossip and jealousy. He had never taken a wife, he did not join the other men for wine and conversation at the inn, nor did he take part in town business or festivals. Worst of all, townspeople would say, the farmer was never seen in church.

He first came to our town when he was about twenty. He purchased a small plot of land on which sat an old stone cottage. Shortly after he settled in and began to work his land, the parish priest made the two-mile walk from town to invite the farmer to attend church.

"I thank you," said the young farmer. "But I cannot do that. I must care for my trees and tend to my vines. And I must do that every day, Sundays included."

For the next sixty years, a succession of priests made the occasional visit to invite the farmer to join in the faith life of the town. They were always made welcome in his home. Each would be invited to stay for a fine meal. When the priest had dined, he would be sent back to town carrying a basket filled with the farmer's finest olive oil and most splendid wine.

It is probably true that the farmer's hospitality was at least part of the reason that each priest in turn was happy to make his acquaintance. Oh, they would have been equally pleased had the farmer taken them up on their invitation to attend church and become a respected part of the life of faith in the town, but that was not to be. In fact, it became part of the ritual of transfer of authority from the old priest to his replacement that along with the keys to the silver cabinet and a review of the account books, the story of the farmer would be conveyed.

The first priest to visit the farmer had assumed, as did all those who followed him, that the farmer simply meant that he could not and would not leave his work, even for something as important as attending church service. And so, across the decades, and through dozens of visits, each priest in turn heard exactly the same words when they invited the farmer to come to church: "I must care for my trees. I must tend to my vines."

One summer afternoon, the year before the war began, a boy raced across the town square and into the tavern of the inn. "A big black car just pulled up to the mayor's office," the boy announced breathlessly. "A man in a dark suit with a briefcase got out, followed by a younger man dressed in workman's clothing. The two of them were joined by the village priest, and together the three men walked up the steps and into the mayor's office."

Now, remember that these events occurred many years ago, in a poor town, where most people still walked or rode in horse-drawn carts. For someone in an automobile to come to their town, especially in the dark days leading up to war, well, that was big news, indeed.

The men in the tavern left their board games and wine, and went out into the square. They were soon joined by more of their curious, idle and concerned fellow citizens. In short order, most of the people of the town were assembled at the foot of the wide steps leading up to the mayor's office.

That's when the first rumor swept through the crowd: had they heard? The reclusive old farmer died yesterday! After more than sixty years in their midst, the rich proprietor of one of the most successful farms in the province was gone.

"How did he die," one person asked?

"Who cares how he died," another said. "Who gets his land and his money? That's what I want to know!"

"Of course, his land and money," said others as they joined in the chorus of speculation.

One merchant spoke up loudly, suggesting that since the farmer had no family or heirs, perhaps the best thing to do would be to divide the vineyards, orchards and acreage among the people of the town: "All of us could share in the riches the old miser selfishly amassed for himself!"

"Why not?" said another.

"Yes, that makes perfect sense," chimed in voice after voice.

"After all, did the rich man share his success with us while he was alive?"

"Did he support our businesses, hire our fathers and brothers, or pay his tithe to the church? Did he assume any responsibility for the privilege of growing wealthy in our community?"

Indeed, the crowd agreed as one, no one has a right to the money as much as we do.

Just as the chatter about the disposition of the farmer's worldly goods was reaching a frenzied pitch, the door to the mayor's office opened. The crowd became quiet.

The townspeople watched as the priest shook the hand of the man in the dark suit. Then the man set his briefcase on the stoop, and embraced the simply dressed young man who had arrived in the car with him. The businessman retrieved his briefcase, made his way through the crowd on the steps, got into his car, and sped away.

The people of the town watched as the priest took a weathered old Bible out of his bag and handed it to the young man. Then the priest pointed to the road leading out of the south end of the square and into the countryside beyond. The young man shook the priest's hand, slipped the Bible under his arm, and walked down the steps, ignoring the inquisitive stares of the people gathered around him. He turned at the bottom of the steps, waved once to the priest, and walked away.

"Father, who was the man in the car?" a member of the crowd called out. "Is he from the city? Is there news of the war?"

Several other townspeople shouted questions of their own at the priest. Then the wife of the town's leading merchant yelled, "And what of the old farmer who died yesterday? What is to become of his land and his money?"

Many in the crowd echoed the question.

The priest thought for a moment. In a small town like this, there were few secrets and fewer mysteries. Gossip and idle speculation were more than just hobbies here; they were a way of life. Better to get the story out in the open now, than have it fester and mushroom in the days to come, he concluded. He looked down upon the anxious crowd. Then he raised his hands to ask for them to be silent. When the last murmurs died away, the priest spoke.

"My friends," he said, "these are troubled times. We have suffered many years of economic hardship, and now a war is coming. I am afraid that even more hardship lies before us. We will be tested. In our time of trial we must have faith that there will be a resolution of these conflicts, and that peace and prosperity will return to our town. Today, I have been witness to the conclusion of a great story of faith. I share it with you now because I believe it may help each of you in the troubles to come. To answer your question, yes, the old farmer did indeed die yesterday."

A voice from the crowd yelled, "And his land and money? What of them?"

Another voice joined in, "Yes, how will they be distributed? We think that his estate should be divided between all of us, even you, Priest. We should all benefit after so many years of his arrogance and indifference to our town. He did nothing for us in life. Let him do something for us now in death!"

There was much cheering at that little speech. But the priest did not reply right away. He simply stood at the top of the stairs, waiting for the crowd to calm. Then he spoke to them in the same authoritative tone he used from the pulpit each Sunday.

"The man who left here a few minutes ago is a lawyer from the capitol. He came to the mayor's office today to see to the disposition of the farmer's estate. And with the mayor's signature on the documents, that allocation is complete. Furthermore, I cannot think of anyone who deserves more than each of you to know exactly what is going to happen with all of the farmer's money and property. After all, over a sixty-year period that old man earned a fortune from the sale of his olive oil and grapes."

A fortune! Excitement rippled through the crowd. A fortune—and the priest said that each of them deserved to know about the money.

A hundred sets of ears fixed greedily upon the priest's next words.

"I will tell you about the events of the past days just as they happened," said the priest. "Yesterday, the old man's foreman came to the rectory with the news that his employer had died peacefully in his sleep. He knew the end was coming, for he left a note upon the kitchen table with instructions his foreman should follow. That note was in an envelope on top of the Bible you saw me hand to that young man a few minutes ago."

"A Bible?" a woman's voice cried out. "That old devil never attended church a day in his life. What use did he have for a Bible?"

"As to what use he had for it, I cannot tell you," replied the priest. "I have no power to see into a man's heart. But as to the issue of its use, that I can speak to. The spine on the farmer's Bible was completely broken down from being opened and closed so many times. The pages were thumbed and threadbare. The margins were filled with notes, some in the firm, clear hand of a young man, and others from much later, in the shaky scrawl of an elderly gentlemen bending close to the page. I have never, in all my years as a priest, seen a Bible so thoroughly used or so reverently cared for."

A man at the front of the crowd said, "Well of course he had time to read, he never once made the walk to town to attend church service, not in sixty years! And with all due respect, Father, your sermons are pretty long. Seems to me that if a man traded time in your church for time with his Bible, that book *would* be pretty ragged by now."

The crowd roared their approval.

"Get on with it now," yelled an impatient voice. "We want to know what is to become of the old man's money. It's not his library books we're interested in!"

"Very well," said the priest. "As it happens, this is a case where the tale of the money and the story of the faith are one in the same. The farmer was abandoned at birth by his mother. She left him on the doorstep of a poor convent in the capitol. The nuns cared for him and the other orphans as best they could, but their parish was poor, and they could not provide much in the way of good food, or medical care or education. As a teenager, he went to bed hungry many nights, giving his meager soup and bread to younger children who were sick or simply famished.

"He was never a brilliant student, but the nuns discovered that he had a remarkable talent for working the soil in the convent garden. By the time he came of age, the garden was producing enough vegetables to feed all of the children and nuns, with a little extra that could be sold at market. And before he left the orphanage, he taught the younger children how to tend the garden just as he had.

"On his eighteenth birthday he went out into the world to make his mark. As he walked through the convent gate for the last time, he committed his life to improving the lot of orphans like himself. He did not know what he would do, or how he would do it. He simply pledged before God that he would remain faithful to his task until he drew his last earthly breath.

"For two years, the young man took on the most dangerous jobs he could find, because they paid well. He lived frugally, and saved every penny. When at last he had earned enough money to buy the smallest plot of land that he believed could turn a profit, he traveled the province in search of the richest soil and most abundant water. He found our town, and settled here. That was almost sixty years ago. Many of you know at least part of the rest of the story. The young man worked tirelessly, month after month, year after year. He spent no real money on himself. He lived as simply as any man could.

"He turned a profit the third year he farmed here. Half of that money went to purchase adjoining lands, vines and olive trees, half he gave to his old orphanage in the capitol. He followed that pattern for over half a century. He built oil presses and a storehouse to hold the thousands of oak casks in which he fermented his wines. While he was building a warehouse, he was also building a school. When he was pressing olives, he was constructing a fully staffed medical clinic.

"Thousands of children have been raised in clean surroundings because of his faithful generosity. They receive good educations and the best medical care. Many have even earned scholarships to college. All because this one good man was faithful to the pledge he made before God."

No one said a word. The priest looked out over the crowd, and studied the faces of the people. He saw expressions of disbelief, and of surprise. He saw disappointment, too, and even some anger. Mostly, though, he saw pursed lips, and eyes turned downward in pensive contemplation.

The priest continued. "In his letter to me, the farmer included money for his burial. And, he even joked that I would at last have the pleasure of his company in church, if only for one service. He also left a message for all of you, which I will read."

Those words stirred the crowd. At last, some thought, now we will learn how much he has left to us! Anxious faces turned toward the priest. He pulled an envelope out of his pocket, unfolded the paper, and began to read the farmer's words.

"My friends," the farmer began, "I can only imagine your thoughts upon receiving word that I have died. Let me thank those of you who will remember me in their prayers tonight, as I have remembered you these past many years in mine.

"Ten years ago I traveled to the capitol to meet with the board of the institution which I founded to provide for the orphanages, the schools, and clinic—whose operation my lifetime of work has funded. My goal was to provide for the transition of my holdings following my death. I asked the board to begin a search for one young man who would be prepared to commit his life to caring for my trees and tending my vines. It took many years for them to find such a man. Only last week, I received a letter informing me that they had selected a candidate from within the orphanage, and would be sending him to meet me.

"Unfortunately, I fear that the time of my death is upon me, and that I will not live to meet my successor. I humbly ask that each of you welcome him and make him feel at home. If, like me, he should choose to exercise the practice of his faith by toiling in the vineyards and amongst the trees rather than joining you in Sunday services, I pray you will keep him in your thoughts and prayers, as I know you lifted me up over the years.

"And now, goodbye. I have new vines to tend, and new trees to care for. God bless."

The priest folded the letter, and returned it to his pocket. Conversations began to break out in the crowd. Some were loud and animated, others were hushed.

They have much to think about, said the priest to himself. As he walked down the steps, the priest looked off to the south. In the distance, at the crown of a hill where the road disappeared from view, he could make out the form of a young man striding purposefully in the direction of the vineyards and olive trees in the valley beyond. And there he will tend to his vines and care for his trees, thought the priest. As should we all.

•••

THE STRANGER FELL SILENT. I shifted in my bed, and straightened one of my IV lines. That's when I noticed that the first streaks of dawn were beginning to pierce the blackness outside my room. We had talked all night. I felt exhilarated and exhausted at the same time, the way I did on the third or fourth day of a vacation when I actually let myself start to unwind.

"Thank you so much," I said. "That was a wonderful story."

He stood up, and returned my notes to the nightstand.

"You are very welcome, my friend," he said. "I thought you would have a special appreciation for it. But now, I must go."

"Of course," I said. "I'm sorry, I've monopolized your time, and kept you up all night. There must be so many others you need to visit."

"This was my only destination tonight."

"Then I am even more grateful to you. This conversation has meant a lot to me. I think it has even given me the strength to complete the task I set for myself." I indicated the yellow notepad with a nod of my head.

The man smiled. I don't know how it was possible, but his eyes looked even greener in the emerging light of dawn. He took my left hand in both of his. They were calloused and rough—a workman's hands.

"Some say that faith begins where the will of God is known," he said softly. "The farmer in my town discovered God's will for his life, just as you discovered His will for yours. Your faith has been a testament to that discovery. You have earned your rest, Martin Forrestal. Fear nothing."

Suddenly, I couldn't keep my eyes open. I wanted to say goodbye, and to thank him again. But sleep overpowered me.

•••

WHEN I WOKE AND SAW that it was well past noon, I figured that I wasn't the only one who had fallen asleep at the wheel; in the course of a typical morning I would have been poked, pinched, measured and turned at least four or five times. But not today.

A few minutes after I came to, Nurse Marsden bustled into the room with a fresh IV tray and drip bag. It looked like I had only been given a brief reprieve from the day's ministrations, not a full presidential pardon. A moment later Connie arrived, coffee and newspaper in hand.

My wife kissed me from the right side of the bed while Nurse Marsden attended to her duties on the left side.

"Well good afternoon Mr. Van Winkle," said Connie. "We were beginning to wonder if you were going to sleep all day."

"Remind me not to stay up all night visiting," I replied. "Or at least to have my visitors come at a more decent hour."

Connie sat down beside me. "You had a late-night visitor? Some old pal who doesn't like being seen out in public during the day?"

"Nothing like that at all. It was the hospital chaplain, and for some reason he was making his rounds at 3 AM. He stayed until almost 5:30 this morning. It was quite a visit, I'll say that."

The nurse set down the IV line she had been preparing.

"Did you say it was the chaplain? At 3 AM?"

"Please don't give him any grief over the hour," I said. "In fact, I wanted to thank him again but I fell asleep as soon as he finished sharing a story with me."

Nurse Marsden look puzzled. "Mr. Forrestal, what did this chaplain look like?"

"What did he look like? You know, medium height, nicely dressed. If I were a woman I suppose I'd say he was pretty handsome. Dark hair, outdoor complexion, big smile—and the darndest green eyes I have ever seen on a person. He had an accent I couldn't quite place—Greece? Maybe Yugoslavia?"

"I'm almost sorry I wasn't here," said Connie. "A chaplain who is also a dish." She turned to the nurse. "Be sure and send him my way if I'm ever in for an appendectomy, would you?"

Nurse Marsden finished setting my IV line. Then she removed a syringe from her pocket, and injected the contents into the plug. In an instant I felt a soothing warmth flow through my body. In a minute, I knew I'd be asleep again. As I began to drift off, I heard my nurse say, "I would be happy to do that, Mrs. Forrestal. Problem is, we have only one chaplain here. And she works pretty much nine to five. We have a part-timer on the weekends, but that chaplain also happens to be a woman."

The two of them shared a concerned glance. I struggled to talk, but the song of Orpheus was too powerful, and once again I found myself slipping into dreamland.

PHILANTHROPY

I AWOKE WITH A FEELING of complete dislocation. I didn't know where I was, and I felt a momentary sense of panic when I realized that my wrists were bound to the rails of an unfamiliar bed. Why was my body crisscrossed with plastic tubes and wires? I heard what sounded like the intake valve of some kind of pump, and a chorus of clicks and beeps from a bank of dimly lit monitors beside my bed. I couldn't see anyone, but I could hear voices, low and whispery, somewhere close by.

I strained to speak, but I could not form any words. I shook my head in an attempt to clear the thick cloud blocking my memory. It didn't work. Then a face materialized above me, and I heard Connie's voice, soft and reassuring.

"Martin. It's alright. Honey, you're in the hospital. I'm here. Eric and Rachel are, too. You've been sleeping all day, it's late afternoon. Can you hear me, darling?"

My eyes and my ears were starting to work again. I tried to glance around the room. Bits and pieces came back to me. Yesterday Doctor McGuire ordered the insertion of a urinary catheter. Shortly after, a technician wheeled in another IV tower to join the forest of stainless steel that ringed my bed. That's when Nurse Marsden administered the chemical cocktail du jour that had knocked me for such a loop.

I was unable to eat solid food last night, and this morning's oatmeal and dry toast was still on my tray. Sometime during the night the duty nurse wrote several phone numbers on the dry erase board in my room: my wife's, my son's, and my pastor's. Apparently they wanted to be ready to contact the important people in my life in a hurry.

"Could you get me a little ice water?"

Connie held the straw to my lips and I took a couple of sips. My mouth was parched. Eric and Rachel appeared on the other side of my bed. Rachel was holding a piece of paper with a big red crayon heart in the center. My sweet Gwen.

"Can you raise my bed?" I asked Connie. "It's hard to see you all when I'm flat on my back."

Eric answered for her. "We can't do that right now, Dad. They're giving you a medication that requires you to lie down for a while. They'll raise you up when they can."

I nodded in reply. My head was clearing. I no longer felt like I was half asleep. But I also didn't have an urge for a cup of coffee, and that seemed almost as strange as the effects of the drugs on my mental faculties. For the better part of sixty years my first waking thoughts have always included coffee. The only urge I felt at that moment was a desire to go back to sleep.

But that was something I had no intention of doing.

Eric and Rachel left to get the children at the babysitters. They'd be back later in the evening. An unfamiliar nurse came in and removed the restraints that held my hands down. Connie settled into the armchair next to my bed. I didn't like being left flat on my back, partly because I couldn't see the trees or the sky outside my window. I determined to do whatever I had to do to make enough progress to have the back of my bed raised up. If my body would just cooperate, I would sit up once more. The thought of such a tiny miracle made me smile. It also reminded me what a lucky cuss I was. The fact that I was even here to tell my story was proof of that. By all rights, I should have met my end a dozen times or more by the time I was diagnosed with cancer. The doctor nearly wrote me off during my battle with pneumonia when I was nine.

When I was twenty-five, I was working as a high climber—a tree topper—on a logging site outside Sweet Home. My job was to scout out a tall tree in the landing area of the logging site. Then I'd scramble up the tree using iron climbing hooks and rope. As I climbed onto the next higher limb, I chopped off the one below me with a razor-sharp felling axe. When I had worked my way up a hundred feet or more, I would cut off the top of the tree, and attach pulleys and rigging so the tree could be used as a spar pole to skid the logs we fell up onto the landing so they could be loaded onto trucks and hauled to the mill. That done, I'd throw a rope around the tree, grab it with both hands, and shimmy back down to the ground.

I was half way up a big Douglas fir one morning, and was leaning out above a ten-inch limb. I hit it once with my axe. Faster than a rattlesnake can say howdy, the limb splintered. A three-foot piece slashed upwards and tore deep into my belly. I dropped my axe, and fell back against the rigging line. I didn't remember passing out.

When I came to in the hospital, the timber faller who raced up the tree to get me said that I had somehow managed to tie myself to the tree with my rope before I blacked out. I didn't remember doing that, and to this day I can't figure out how I was able to. In those days, spar poles were known as widow-makers. Connie likes to say that it's a good thing I was single at the time.

When you add up my logging accident, assorted childhood diseases, car wrecks—including one where my '54 Willys Jeep slid off a dirt road and tumbled down to the floor of a flooded canyon—and the mountain avalanche, it's a wonder I was here to tell the tale at all.

I came to the conclusion not long after I was admitted to the hospital two weeks ago that when it comes right down to it, there are only two ways that our tickets can get punched when the ride is over. We either go out with a short, spectacular bang, or via the long route, along a slow, downward-spiraling path. Martin Forrestal had been tapped for the slow boat out. I'd known plenty of folks who had been handed a ticket on the express elevator.

I was at peace with the idea that my exit plan was just right for the tasks I wanted to complete before my ride coasted to a complete stop. I didn't think any man could ask for more.

•••

I CLEARED MY THROAT. "Connie, I feel like I just ran a marathon with a fifty-pound pack on my back. I'm not sure I can even sit up. And I can't seem to feel anything below my waist."

Connie squeezed my hand. Her eyes brimmed with tears she was fighting to hold back.

"The cancer has spread around your spine, my darling. It's been there for a while. It's a miracle that you've been able to be up and around as long as you have."

I stared at the ceiling. That I was dying had been a forgone conclusion for weeks. There had been plenty of time to digest that news. But anyone who tells you that hearing the news about an upcoming experience will prepare you emotionally to actually live the experience is about as wrong as a person can be. There are different degrees of understanding, different degrees of acceptance. That I was dying was true; now it had become truth.

I had always been physically strong. It was a part of my character. I fished, hunted, logged, milled timber and hiked rugged terrain for more than seventy years. I built my house and my sawmill with my own two hands. I played ball and roughhoused with my son and his pals, and on rare occasion I was even known to dance until dawn with my wife.

Heck, I was still chopping firewood the week that Doctor McGuire booked my stay here. And now this. As true as innocence.

"Is it nice outside?" I asked my wife.

She didn't answer. Her lips pursed, her shoulders tensed. Then she sighed. It was one of the saddest sounds I have ever heard.

Finally she said, "Oh, Martin."

I pulled my hand from hers, and, ignoring the Doctor's instructions to lay flat, depressed the button to raise the head of my bed. When it was up as far as it would go, I summoned all my strength, leaned over the rail, and gathered my wife in my arms. I felt her go limp, and a moment later she began to cry into my shoulder.

•••

OUR PASTOR ARRIVED a little later to visit and to take Connie down to the hospital cafeteria. I was determined to use the time alone. Before Connie left, I asked her to set up the digital recorder for me. It was hard for me to work the thing, so she wedged the small device between the rail of the bed and the edge of my pillow and turned on the automatic voice activation feature. Anytime I began speaking, the recorder would switch on.

I didn't know how much I was going to be able to accomplish, but I needed to get back to my list of values. And today's topic, philanthropy, was important.

Like most children, I became familiar first with philanthropy's sister value, charity. When the collection basket was passed at Sunday school, I knew that the nickel or dime I carefully dropped in was going to help out people here at home, and also in far away lands. Years later I still did charity through force of habit. From the Sunday school collection plate to the Salvation Army Kettle, from checks sent to the Red Cross for disaster relief to our small monthly donation to support orphaned children in Haiti, my charitable activities operated pretty much on autopilot.

My involvement with philanthropy was something altogether different, and far more edifying. Once I figured out that charity meant giving for purposes that were determined and administered by others, while philanthropy meant discerning a human need myself and taking the initiative to do something about it, well, I was hooked. My participation in philanthropy has lead to some of the most meaningful experiences of my life—like the work Connie and I were able to do with Lois and The Academy over the years.

It all started when I was a boy, with something that came to be called the SS&P. My mother and Patrick's mom were the first models I had for what philanthropy looked like in practice. By the fall of 1933, the Depression had taken a heavy toll on the farms and businesses around the Willamette Valley. In fact, in the three short weeks we were gone to see my Grandfather Jake in Montana, two more businesses in downtown Salem had boarded up their doors. Patrick's father was hanging on at the hardware store, and my dad somehow managed to keep the lumberyard open and a half-dozen men employed, but only by virtue of the exercise of sheer will twelve hour days and a pioneer work ethic that didn't know the meaning of the words, "I give."

My mother used to say that we may not have had much, but we always had sufficient. That wasn't true of many of our neighbors. Some of my friends' fathers jumped the rails, heading to Canada and Alaska where folks said there were still jobs laying railroad track, fishing, and mining. Others went on the dole, and lined up every week outside the National Guard

Armory where boxed food, clothing and blankets were distributed to those who registered. And some families just disappeared.

I remember getting up one morning and seeing my friend Ralph's family carrying all of their belongings from the house and packing them into and onto an old jalopy. They piled mattresses, dressers, lamps, clothing, chicken coops and even the proverbial kitchen sink onto that truck, and lashed them down with rope and baling wire. Ralph's dad had even welded a small porch-like attachment on the back of the truck, where they squeezed on a couple of rabbit cages and a dog kennel.

My mom and dad and I went across the street to say goodbye. Mom carried a hamper packed with sandwiches and fruit. Dad had a jerry can of gas and a couple quarts of oil. My dad asked Ralph's father where they were bound.

"I don't rightly know," he told my dad. "I expect we'll just keep moving along until we find something better, or until this ol' truck gives up the ghost. Whichever comes first. It ain't my decision to make no more."

I was eight. That was the first time I ever heard someone just flat give it all up. Not to God, not to a boss or to some faceless government official, but to fate. To chance. I didn't like what I heard that morning. I like it even less today.

My mom didn't like what she heard, either. But mom was a doer, not a worrier or a complainer. She marched right over to Patrick's house with me in tow, and told Patrick's mom that it was about time the two of them did something to make a difference. Ralph's father might be right that a lot of things are outside our control right now, my mother inveighed, "but there are things we can do to help other folks, even if they're little things."

Patrick's mother agreed. By the time they finished their second cup of coffee, the basic business plan for Salem Soup & Pie was sketched out on the back of a wrinkled envelope. Thus the SS&P was born.

That afternoon the ladies descended upon O'Hagan's Hardware Store like an F5 tornado. First, Patrick's mother informed her husband that she was commandeering the storeroom at the south end of the building. It was dark and dusty, with only a sink, a crumbling fireplace and a wood burning cook-stove to keep the spiders company. But the storeroom had a door and a window opening into the alley behind the store, which made it perfect for the ladies' purpose.

Patrick and I helped, but mostly watched in awe as our mothers whipped that fifteen-foot wide by thirty-foot long storeroom into shape in just two days. Word of what the ladies were up to got around town, and by the end of the second day, a half dozen of their friends signed onto the cause. Together they cleaned and painted the room, built shelves, stacked dishes, gathered pots and pans, and somehow scrounged up a couple of battered commercial iceboxes.

On the third day the ladies fanned out across town to visit every business, church and charitably inclined adult they could corner. By day's end the converted storeroom was packed with canned goods, fresh vegetables, sacks of flour and baskets of fruit.

At first light on the fourth day, the ladies of SS&P donned their aprons, picked up their knives, rolling pins and ladles, and set about baking pies and preparing huge pots of chicken and dumpling soup. Patrick and I raced around town on our bikes plastering telephone poles, the sides of buildings and pretty much anything else that didn't move with handbills that told folks to show up at the window in the alley behind O'Hagan's at 2 PM for free soup and pie.

Word travels fast when times are tough. By noon, a line began to form in the alley behind O'Hagan's. By 2 PM when the window opened and the ladies began dishing up meals, the line snaked down the alley, out onto the main street and around the block. The ladies had expected a few dozen people at best to turn out. They were not prepared for the avalanche of men, women and hungry children who poured into the alley in search of a meal that day. By 3 PM the soup was gone, and ten minutes later the last slice of pie had been handed out. My mom asked Patrick and I to go outside and see how many people were still waiting in line. We raced down the line and counted more than a hundred people, many of them children, still waiting to eat. The ladies had no choice but to offer an apology to those still waiting when the food ran out, and slide the serving window closed. None of the people still waiting to be fed got angry. No one hurled insults. They simply melted away into the hot afternoon sun, hands in their pockets, heads low. These were people who knew disappointment on a first-name basis.

•••

MY MOTHER AND THE OTHER LADIES convened around the pickle barrel
in the hardware store when the clean up was done. They agreed that the
day had been a disaster. They were glad to have been able to try to do
something to make a difference, but it was pretty clear that running a soup
kitchen was not as easy as it looked from the outside. They were about
to wrap up their conversation and head home when an old man came
through the front door of the store and walked over to them.

Mr. Napier was a black gentleman who did deliveries and odd jobs for
Patrick's father. When he was a teenager working in an Alabama rock
quarry, a rock powder explosion left him blind in one eye, and fused
together three fingers on his left hand. Some genius had improperly mixed
the dynamite, which was supposed to be sixty percent purity for shooting
rock. The batch that morning was composed of eighty percent nitro.
A chunk blew up in Napier's face when he picked up the shot box for
delivery to the quarry foreman. He showed up in our town about a year
ago, and had become a steadfast part-time worker for Patrick's father ever
since.

Mr. Napier doffed his cap. "I saw what you did for the folks today, ladies,"
he said. "That was mighty kind of y'all. Course, and I mean no disrespect,
I also saw you had yourselves a little bit of a management issue, food-wise,
that is. If you don't mind my making an observation, I think you might be
needing a little help in that department."

Patrick's mother spoke for the group. "We appreciate your offer, Mr.
Napier. But the truth is we don't have the money to hire anyone, and if we
did, I'm afraid we would have to hire someone with experience at this sort
of thing."

The other ladies nodded in agreement. Mr. Napier turned his cap around
in his hands.

"Oh, I expected that'd be the situation, Mrs. O'Hagan," he said. "But
here's the thing: you ladies have done a fine thing here, a good thing,
something this town needs. And y'all have taken this fine idea about as far
as you can. Now it sounds to me like you're maybe thinking of pulling the
plug, and giving it all up. I'm here to tell you ladies, that ain't your only
choice. There's a way to make your enterprise work, and to feed every last
man, woman and little one who comes to that window. All of 'em."

Napier had their attention. He had mine, too. I set down the strap-on
shoe skate I had been fiddling with and paid attention. What could this old

man do that my mom and Patrick's mom and all these others ladies hadn't figured out?

My mom was reading my mind. "And how, exactly, do you think we could keep it going, Mr. Napier?" she asked.

"Well you see, ma'am," replied Mr. Napier, "after me and the dynamite got into that tussle when I was a boy, there weren't much I could do as a laborer. I got me a job on the Southern Pacific Railroad, washing dishes in work camps. Not much of a job, and no future to it, but I had me a pretty good boss, and one day he's letting me peel potatoes, and the next day I'm cookin 'em, and pretty soon I was running the kitchen."

Napier paused. I had a feeling he wasn't used to doing this much talking. The ladies stood patiently as he collected his thoughts. By now, even Patrick's father had come out from behind the counter to listen to the story.

"The short of it is, ladies," he continued, "that ten years later I was in charge of eighteen work camp kitchens stretching across four states. I did the hiring and firing. I ordered supplies, decided what went on the menus, supervised inventory, created training programs and did the budgeting. I did that job for thirty-six years, until they retired me out about two years ago. Gold watch, pension, the works."

You could have heard a pin drop on the polished wood floor of O'Hagan's Hardware at that minute. The good ladies of the SS&P had known Mr. Napier only in his role as an errand man who carted packages around town for Patrick's father at two bits a delivery.

Patrick's father grinned. "So, what the devil are you doing working for tips and hamburgers?" he asked.

"Man's got to work to keep his dignity," said Mr. Napier. "I moved out here to Oregon to go fishing and plant a little garden. I bought me a nice little house outside town, and I planted the prettiest garden you ever seen, but it ain't the same as working."

Then Napier addressed the ladies. "Now, here's what I propose to do, and you ladies can take some time to think on it, and let me know later if you want to go for it. I'll help you with this here enterprise. I'll do it without pay, same as y'all. I'll get you in railroad shape, and I'll line out a plan for the kitchen that'll cover you from getting the best deal on supplies to estimating how much food you need to prepare to meet the daily demand. You all can focus on rustling up supplies, and making your soup and those tasty fruit pies. That and serving the people."

He paused for a moment, then continued, "Before you decide about me coming on board, I need to tell you that there is a condition attached to my taking this on. It's something simple, but it needs to be said. It's about our creed, if you don't mind me using that word. What I'm saying is that every person who comes up to the window for a meal must be treated just like it was our own family coming for Sunday dinner. They ain't beggars; they are our guests. The poor fella without shoes will be treated the same as the laid-off banker in a three-piece suit. The scoundrel the same as the little child." Mr. Napier surveyed the group before him and added, "And the black folk the same as the white folk. Everybody in the soup line will be special, just the way God intended. That's my offer."

Napier put his cap on. "I'll be around for your answer." No one said a word as the old man walked to the doors leading out to the sidewalk.

Then my mother spoke: "Mr. Napier."

He turned. My mother walked over to him, reached into her apron pocket and produced a door key. She handed it to Mr. Napier and said, "That is the key to the kitchen. What time would you like us ladies to be here in the morning?"

Mr. Napier smiled. He slipped the key into his pocket. "How about we all meet here at 8 AM," he said. Then he nodded in my direction. "And bring Mr. Martin and Mr. Patrick along with you. Plenty for them to do, too."

It took Mr. Napier a week to re-organize the SS&P. When the window to the alley slid open for the first time under his supervision every man, woman and child waiting in line received a steaming bowl of vegetable beef stew, a quarter loaf of fresh bread and a big slice of apple pie. No one was turned away. Each person was treated with respect and courtesy. Patrick and I were in charge of handing out and collecting plates, bowls and utensils. Mr. Napier also taught us how to wash dishes restaurant-style in the three-tub stainless steel sink.

The SS&P soon became a fixture in downtown Salem. Mr. Napier never missed a day of work. Our moms built a volunteer network through every church and service club in the area that kept the kitchen fully staffed and supplied seven days a week.

•••

When Mr. Napier died suddenly in the fall of 1943, my mother guessed that he must have been at least eighty years old. You would have never known from the way he routinely slung hundred-pound flour sacks over his shoulder, or played stickball in the alley with children waiting to be fed. He left instructions that the proceeds from the sale of his house and possessions should go the creation of an expanded kitchen operation.

My mother and the other ladies used those funds to renovate and equip the spacious basement of a local church into a complete commercial kitchen and cafeteria-style seating area. It is still in operation today, providing a big mid-day meal to all who are hungry. On the side of the building next to the steps leading down into the cafeteria there is a weathered brass plaque. The inscription reads: "With grateful appreciation to Mr. Napier and the ladies of the SS&P. February, 1944."

I had the privilege of watching my mother, the other ladies, and Mr. Napier work diligently for years in the service of a cause greater than themselves. I learned how important it is to treat every person you meet with respect and dignity, including those who, for whatever reason, may find themselves in line in an alley waiting for a window to open and a bowl of soup to appear.

My mother contributed her time and energy to that kitchen for the rest of her life. About a year ago, Connie and I took little Gwen and Jimmy there for lunch. We got into line with everyone else. We each were handed a plastic tray on which volunteer servers placed a bowl of hot soup, a piece of warm cornbread slathered with honey-butter, a carton of milk and a slice of fresh blueberry pie.

As we ate, I told the children the story of their great-grandmother and the Salem Soup and Pie kitchen. When the meal was over, we cleared our table. Then, I took two ten-dollar bills from my wallet, and slid one each across the table to Gwen and Jimmy.

"Is that to pay for our lunches, Poppa Martin?" asked Gwen.

"No, honey," said Connie. "Our lunches were paid for by some very nice people who help to make sure that no one ever has to go hungry."

"Like Great-Grandma in the story?" said Jimmy.

"That's right," said Connie. "That is what our family does. We help people."

Gwen held up her ten-dollar bill.

"Can I help people, too?"

"You sure can," I said.

Jimmy waved his money. "Me too?"

"Do you see the lady over by the door, the one who greeted us when we came in?"

The children nodded.

"Let's go talk to her and see what you two can do."

•••

I ASKED CONNIE TO SWITCH THE RECORDER OFF. While I couldn't see out the window, I could tell by the softening light inside the room that it would soon be dark outside. Time for Connie to go home.

My wife anticipated my next sentence. "I'll be out of your hair soon," she said. "First though, let's talk about tomorrow. Janine and Teresa are driving up tonight. Teresa's grandson, Mark, is coming too. They're going to be here tomorrow, assuming you're still up for seeing them."

I smiled. "Is that a question?" I was definitely looking forward to seeing Janine, regardless of how I was feeling. I turned my head to look over at Connie. The long days and sleepless nights were taking their toll. Her sweater was rumpled, her eyes were rimmed with red, and, even from a man's less than competent perspective, it looked like she hadn't been to the hairdresser in a while.

"I think I'll manage to be awake for their visit. But do something for me, would you?" I asked.

She smiled. "I don't know about that—you've been racking up the favors pretty steadily these past couple of weeks. What did you have in mind?"

Connie had never been a vain woman, her natural beauty was just part of who she was. Even now at seventy-three she still turned heads. Especially mine. I knew she would consider my request to be a little on the frivolous side, but it was for her sake, not mine, that I was making it. One way or another I was going to get her out of this place for a few hours, and her mind off my situation.

"You know that summer dress you bought a couple of years ago, the white one with the pastel apple design?"

"They're peaches, and the dress is at least ten years old," she answered.

"Peaches, apples, no matter. You looked stunning in that dress. If it's not too chilly tomorrow, would you mind wearing it?"

"Honey, I can do that, it is a pretty dress, but my hair, my gosh I haven't done it in weeks, and I just feel a mess."

"Is that so hard to remedy?" I asked. "Can't you get into the hairdresser in the morning? Maybe have your nails done while you're at it?"

"Martin, what am I going to do with you? You want me to do my hair and put on a summer party dress now, with—" she hesitated, "—with everything that's going on?"

I pulled the bed sheet up around my neck. I had been getting chilled all day. "My darling," I said, "I can't think of anything that would make me happier. Besides, a man never gets tired of showing off his best girl."

That remark earned me a kiss. "We'll see," Connie said, but I noticed that her cheeks had a little more color in them than I had seen in days.

"Shall I read a little before I go?" she asked. I could see that she was holding a book of poems by Robert Service. Nate Holden gave me the book when I was fourteen, not long after we returned from our ill-fated trip into the Cascades. Service was not on the list of flowery world-class poets preferred by most English teachers, but his rough-hewn celebrations of adventurous prospectors in the frozen north were pretty exciting to a youngster who had barely survived his own adventure in the snow and ice. I don't think I had picked the book up in thirty years.

There was one poem, though, that came into my mind. I only remembered the opening line, and Connie had to search the book's index of first lines to find it.

She reached over the bed rail, took my left hand in hers, and began to read:

"And when I come to the dim trail-end,
I who have been Life's rover,
This is all I would ask, my friend,
Over and over and over:
A little space on a pleasant hill,
With you someday beside me,
Sky o' the North that's vast and still,
With a single star to cheer me…"

Connie's voice trailed off to a whisper. She didn't cry—I took care of that for the both of us. We sat in silence, in the truth, holding hands.

SACRIFICE

AFTER CONNIE WENT HOME for the evening, I received instruction from a respiratory therapist on how to exhale into a plastic bottle contraption. I was to do this exercise three times a day now.

Doctor McGuire had ratcheted down the pain medication as I had asked, enough so that I wasn't in a perpetual haze, but I was paying the price for my desire to remain as alert as possible. Sharp, stabbing pains shot through my abdomen, and radiated up my chest with each breath. If I hadn't known better, I would have diagnosed the pain as broken ribs. A lot of them.

Connie placed my notepad on my lap when she left. Every one of the legal-sized pages was filled, front and back. Scribbled notes filled the margins, and some words were circled with arrows that pointed to other text, or referred to other pages. While I had been following the original order in which I had first listed my values, I realized going into this project that time wasn't exactly on my side. So, while my energy level permitted in the first four or five days, I had recorded bits and pieces of stories related to the values that were closer to the end of my list. The values near the bottom of my list weren't any less important to me than the ones at the top of the page. That's just how they spilled out of me when I decided to take on this project. One whole page of my notes told Connie where to find the out of sequence stories in the digital recordings, and asked her to do her best to add those bits and pieces to the stories I added for each of those values later on. If there was a later on, of course.

I had known exhaustion in my life, the kind of weary-to-the-bone tired you experience when you do hard manual labor for twelve or thirteen unrelenting hours, or when you go for weeks without a decent night's sleep. I know tired. But what I was experiencing now was something different. Any time I ran my body ragged with work or worry, I knew that my batteries would get replenished. I knew I would heal from my wounds, recover from aching muscles, and be able to drop onto my bed and sleep as long as it took for my body to regroup. There had always been a pool of vitality into which I could plunge when I was drained.

What I had been experiencing these past few days was something different. I wasn't getting tired. I was being drained. Even my skin felt different, and it had taken on a loose and almost translucent appearance. My body was marshaling its diminishing resources for this one last battle, and focusing what life force I still had on keeping the critical components of my system in some kind of functioning order.

It was quiet in the hospital corridor. I turned my head and I could see Nurse Letitica at her small table, writing chart notes and orders for the day nurse who would be here in a few hours. I smiled inwardly at the realization that I had become so familiar with the hospital routine. It was ironic that I would be leaving so shortly after becoming acquainted.

•••

WARM LIGHT FLOODED MY ROOM. I looked beyond the cherry trees, and saw that the sky was clear and bright. According to the dry erase board, it was going to be balmy again today. I wished I could go outside to enjoy it.

The hum of a busy hospital rolled in from the corridor. I knew Nurse Marsden would be in the process of reviewing the patient charts prepared by the night duty staff. It was another routine day for them. Bones to mend, wounds to heal, surgeries to conduct, spirits to encourage. I had my own routine, as well. A physical therapist came each morning to help me to loosen muscles that tightened during prolonged bed rest. Then the first blood-draw of the day, followed by my respiratory exercises. A quick check-up from the nurse, and then the clickety-clack of metal wheels announcing the arrival of the dietician's cart with its promise of another great adventure in gourmet dining.

There was a knock at the door. It was Dr. McGuire, not breakfast. He was reading from a clipboard as he came in. I raised the back of my bed.

"This a business call?" I asked.

"Hello, Martin. Yes, I suppose you could call it that."

"How's it behaving—my heart, I mean."

"You've been experiencing some arrhythmia."

"The fluttering feeling I get in my chest?"

McGuire nodded and made a note on the clipboard. "Martin," he said, "we can probably manage the arrhythmia with medication. Under different circumstances we might look at more tests and possibly surgical intervention, but…"

He didn't have to go on.

"Don't worry about it, Mac," I said gently. "Something's going to shut me down pretty soon, and it might as well be my heart as anything else."

Dr. McGuire smiled and shook his head. "Alright Martin, then let's get down to cases. How is your pain?"

"It's getting to be a bear. But so far, I don't feel like I need to ask for more pain medication."

"I don't believe you, my friend, but I'm going to respect your wishes—at least for now." He got up. "Just remember, when Connie comes to me and says she doesn't want to see you in this kind of discomfort, I'm coming back with the cavalry, and we're going to give you whatever it takes to comfort her—not you—her. Understood?"

I felt myself grin. I could not have asked for a better physician, or better friend, than Mac.

"In your best professional opinion, how much time do I have?"

He gathered his thoughts. I'd seen Mac put on his fully professional face any number of times over the years, usually when he had to share some less than pleasant news. I expected to see that face now, but he surprised me: he put his hand on mine, and I noticed that his eyes were a little misty.

"I could give you numbers and guesstimates, Martin. But that's all they'd be. The truth is, your body is just plain worn out. It's run its race." He squeezed my hand. "Your time is very near, old friend, very near. It's a blessing that you are still able to visit with your family." He picked up my digital recorder, and put it in my hand. "Whatever you have left to say, Martin, this is the time."

•••

AFTER DR. MCGUIRE LEFT, I was bolstered somewhat by the recollection that I would be seeing Janine, Patrick's widow, today. I thought about the last time I had seen her. It must have been fifteen or twenty years ago, at her home in Mt. Shasta. I was on my way then to Eureka to purchase a cutting head for my sawmill. And before that? I think we'd visited just a handful of times since I got back from the war. I thought back to a picnic she and Patrick and I had had when we were seventeen. I could hear the effortless lilt of her laughter in my mind, and I smiled at the prospects of being able to hear that laugh again soon.

The door opened, and a shaft of light spilled into my room. The brightness made me blink. The aroma of lavender and mimosa announced my wife's arrival. Then she was standing at my side. Without saying a word, Connie did a slow spin. She wore the sleeveless white summer dress imprinted with pastel peaches, banded with a pale green belt. She'd had her hair done, and she wore the kind of makeup normally reserved for a special night out on the town.

Her modeling turn completed, she said, "Approve?"

I felt a great big goofy grin spread across my face. "Are you kidding? How about we spring me from this joint and go dancing. Dinner first— grilled salmon, I think. Then dancing."

Connie bent and kissed me, and then pulled a chair alongside my bed. "That's exactly the response this outfit should get from a fella," she said. "Catch me up on your day so far. Did I miss anything exciting?"

"You mean other than your arrival?"

In between sips of ice water, I brought her up to speed on my morning. The subject eventually turned to Janine—and to Patrick. This was the visit I was most looking forward to. The ring of Connie's phone interrupted our conversation.

"They're just parking now," Connie said after she hung up. "I'm going downstairs to greet them. We'll be right back up."

A few minutes later, I heard a chorus of singsong voices and that unmistakable laugh echoing up the hall. I smiled broadly as the crowd entered. Connie led the way as Janine, her daughter Teresa, and Teresa's grandson, Mark, entered my room.

Janine used a cane to walk. Her knee had been replaced, I remembered, since I last saw her. She had gained some weight, and the years had etched their passage on her face, but her eyes were as shining and bright as the day I stood up beside she and Patrick at their hurried wedding in San Diego in the fall of 1943.

Teresa was a spitting image of Patrick—all freckles and smiles and flame red hair. All I knew about Mark was that he had recently moved in with Teresa when life with his own parents had become more battle zone than family home.

Janine came straight up to me and kissed me on the cheek. "Oh, Marty," she said, "dear, dear, Marty."

Mark pulled chairs close to my bed, and everybody settled in.

"It's so good to see you," I said.

We fell right into the comfortable conversation of great friends who had a lot of ground to cover. We touched upon a wide range of subjects in short order.

"It's been too long," Janine said when we came to a pause. She held my eyes for a moment. She seemed to remember something, and she smiled. "I brought something I think you'll appreciate."

She rifled through her oversized purse, and pulled out a framed photo. "What do you think of this?" she said. "For years I thought it had been lost. Teresa found it in the attic just a month ago."

"I call it Mom's traveling antique store," said Teresa. "Wherever she moves, forty or fifty huge cartons stuffed with who knows what go with her."

"You'll find out soon enough, dear," said Janine. "They'll all be yours someday."

"And on that day I'll be hiring a backhoe and a crew to plant them with you, Mom," laughed Teresa. "Mother, you save balls of string, for heaven's sake!"

Janine tapped her cane heavily on the ground. "Don't make me remind you what it was like growing up during the Depression, young lady," she warned. "Martin, what do we do with our children?"

"I just try to get out of their way," I said. "Let me see the photo." It was difficult for me to reach for it through the tangle of cords, so Teresa took it from Janine and held it before my eyes.

The eight by ten black and white print was faded around the edges.

Staring out at me were three impossibly young faces. Two well-scrubbed Marine PFCs had their arms around a stunning young woman with long dark hair. An orchid was pinned to her dress, and she was holding her hand up to the camera to show off her wedding band.

"Oh my gosh."

"Mighty pretty trio, weren't we?" said Janine. "It was the day before you and Patrick shipped out. Look at the grin on Patrick's face."

"What wasn't to grin about? He'd just married himself the prettiest Irish colleen this side of Dublin," I said. "And then you two had what, an eight hour honeymoon before we had to report at the dock? Not much time."

Janine put her hand on Teresa's shoulder. "It was time enough, Marty, plenty time enough. The proof is sitting here beside me." Janine chuckled and then looked quickly away. When her head turned back, her eyes were glistening.

"I'm sorry, Martin. I promised myself I wasn't going to do that…oh, my makeup. I know that we're both at that age where driving past a cemetery feels like apartment hunting—"

"Mom!" Teresa said.

"Don't 'Mom' me. You'll be here soon enough. But I'm not worried about it." She looked back over at me. "Tell you the truth, it gives me a little comfort to know what lies ahead. No more worries, no aches and pains, and all of our family there to greet us."

We reminisced about past glories, old friends and family. We told the kinds of stories—big and small—by which we mortals try to come to grips with our brief personal journeys through a sliver of eternity. We joked, we whispered, and some tears were shed.

At one point when Connie was engaged in a side conversation with Janine and Teresa, I reached out to Mark, who had been spending most of his time silently watching us older folks chattering away. "So how'd you get roped into this?" I asked.

"They needed a chauffeur, and I offered," he said. "I didn't think it would be right for them to make the six-hour drive on their own. Plus, I've got the time at the moment."

He explained that after graduating high school in January, he had been working a couple of part time jobs. He was figuring out what to do with himself. He planned on going to community college in the fall. In the meantime he was lending a hand at Janine's place, painting her kitchen, staining her deck, cleaning out the attic. He seemed like a good-natured guy with a decent head on his shoulders. He was pleasant to converse with.

After some time the women stood up and prepared to depart for lunch.

Mark picked up the framed photo of Patrick, Janine and I, and said, "Mr. Forrestal, would you mind if I stayed behind with you?"

Teresa looked at Connie, then at me. I nodded to Teresa.

"I'd like it very much if you'd stay, though you'll be missing out on a better lunch with them. That photo is making me think. It brings back a lot of memories about your great-grandfather and great-grandmother." I turned my head to the bedside table and gestured at the digital recorder. "You think you could help me run that thing? I've been needing to record this."

"I think I could figure it out," he said.

After the women departed, Mark and I talked for a while about his family, and things he wanted to see and do in the years to come. I told him about my values project. I had Mark turn on the digital recorder, and I asked him what he knew about his great-grandfather, Patrick.

"Not much, really. Wasn't he killed in World War II before Grandma Teresa was born?"

"He did die before she was born, yes, but he wasn't killed. It wasn't like that at all. He gave up his life willingly. He sacrificed himself to save his buddies—including me. That's different than being killed. You end up just as dead either way, but it's different when you choose the time and the place and the way you're going to die—and why you're going to die."

"So, he was a hero?" Mark asked.

"He wouldn't agree with that title, but yes, he absolutely was. He'd say he was just doing his job. The Marine Corps called him a hero. They presented your great-grandmother and his parents with the Silver Star, one of the highest honors a Marine can receive. The other fellas in the rifle platoon whose lives he saved, they'd call him a hero, too."

"So this photo—" he pointed at the framed picture.

"There's a story behind it."

•••

THE PHOTO TOOK ME BACK, over sixty years, to when Patrick and I had our final two-day leave from Camp Pendleton, before we shipped out.

We were awaiting orders for parts unknown, waiting with the rest of
Rifle Platoon 787, with whom we had completed basic Marine infantry
training at Camp Lejeune in North Carolina. Eight weeks of grueling
training were behind us, days that began at 0400 and didn't end until lights
out at 2200. From close-order drill, to bayonet course, to instruction in the
full range of armaments used by combat Marines, it was the hardest work I
have ever done.

On boot camp graduation day, when I dressed in my service greens and
was handed three bronze Marine Corps globe-and-anchor emblems, I felt
stronger, more confident, and more certain of myself than I have ever been
in my life—even to this day. I was seventeen.

It hadn't been easy for my parents—or Patrick's—to approve our
enlistments. We still had a year of high school to complete. My dad relied
on my help at the wood lot, and Mom, like all moms, could not bear the
thought of her boy going off to war.

In the summer of 1943, America was struggling against implacable foes
in Europe and the Pacific, and the war only seemed to be ramping up.
Like millions of other parents who made that long drive to the bus station
or induction center to say goodbye, our folks knew that we were the best
ones to get the job done. They knew we had to get the job done. Many
of our buddies had joined up already. We knew what we were facing:
every week at our high school football and basketball games, the names of
classmates who had died in battle were read at halftime over the PA system.

Patrick and I hatched the plan to join up one day after school. We were
trudging along the train tracks, gathering scrap metal for the war effort.
We found a couple of old car bumpers, and were making the trek with
our wheelbarrows to the collection center out by the state prison. It
was drizzling, and there was a cold wind blowing down out of Santiam
Canyon.

"You know, Marty," Patrick said, "this war's not going to last forever."

"I hope not."

"So are we going to get into it, or is this all we're going to contribute—
hauling scrap metal along railroad tracks while there's a shooting war going
on? We're old enough to sign up."

I didn't respond for a minute. "How long have you been thinking about
this?" I asked.

"Only since Pearl Harbor, that's all."

"Me too. You think our folks will go for it?"

"You don't think your dad—or my dad—wouldn't be thinking the same thing if they were in our shoes?"

"I guess you're right."

"You know I'm right. Question is, Mr. Scrap Metal Picker, what are we going to do about it?"

A few months later, there we were with C Company, 1st Battalion, 2nd Marines, lined up on a dock at San Diego Harbor preparing to board a converted luxury liner for the journey across the Pacific Ocean. We had had two days of freedom, and it proved to be enough. Janine traveled down from Oregon for the whirlwind wedding and honeymoon. As we headed up the gangplank with full transport packs, bedroll, M1 carbine and helmet, she waved goodbye from a fenced area a hundred yards away.

•••

WE HAD NO IDEA when we boarded the dull-grey ocean liner that we were the spearhead of the invasion that would hop island to island across the Pacific toward the Japanese mainland for the next year and a half. The ship was crowded, and we had to double bunk outside on the upper deck, but the weather was clear and the seas were calm as we steamed to Pearl Harbor for refueling and provisions. The poker skills Patrick had honed playing against old-timers around the wood stove at his family's hardware store were put to good use.

On our third night out of San Diego, I was watching from the fantail as a school of dolphin crisscrossed over our wake. There was a full moon, huge and bright, lighting the ocean horizon for hundreds of miles. Patrick appeared out of nowhere. "Shame you're not prettier, Martin—I'd have to give you a kiss, what with that moon and all."

I slapped my friend upside the head. "Where were you at chow?"

"Chow? Why would I want food when I can have this?" He dug into his jacket pockets, and pulled out a wad of cash. "Six hundred bucks!" he said. "Six hundred. You know what that'll get me?"

"I don't know, six or eight months in the brig?"

He shoved the money back into his jacket. "That, my moon-watching friend, is enough for a down payment on a house for Janine and I. That's almost half a year's pay back home."

"So why'd you quit? Why not parlay that little nest egg into something even bigger—buy the house outright?"

Patrick grew uncharacteristically somber. "Martin, you know we won't all be coming home from this little party the Japs are throwing for us. If my number gets called, I want to make sure Janine has this money to help her get started. The chaplain will hold it for me. But if something happens to me, you make sure it gets to her."

In all the years I had known Patrick, I had never seen him so serious. I could only nod.

"Oh, hell, Martin, don't get all teary-eyed on me," he said. "Boy, I tell you, this moonlight is sure wasted on a guy like you. What do you say we saunter up to the foredeck and catch up on the skinny—I hear we're headed for Australia."

In fact, after Pearl Harbor we steamed for New Zealand, where we spent the next two months training for amphibious landings in LVT Alligator landing craft and the Navy's new rubber attack boats. The Corps did plenty of things well, like keeping us busy ten to twelve hours a day with exercises designed to make us better at our jobs. We conducted amphibious landing exercises day and night, and we cross-trained with every weapon in the Marine arsenal.

It was on New Zealand's western shore that I first came face to face with the currency of war. During a nighttime landing exercise on a rocky beach, nine Marines were drowned when their landing craft got tangled in the rocks and was subsequently swamped by a freak wave. I knew them all.

I would see death in its most grisly form hundreds of times in the months to come. To this day I see them in my dreams, my dead and wounded and dying buddies. It is those nine young men, though, I think about most often. Nine boys who would never know the embrace of a loving wife, the laughter of their babies, boys who would never build a house, work a farm, start a business or watch their children grow and begin lives and families of their own.

Whatever romantic notions I had about the glory of war were snuffed out when that wave crashed over my friends and carried their bodies out to sea. The morning after the accident, I looked at my reflection in a shaving mirror. An old man looked back at me—not exactly the face I expected to see on my eighteenth birthday. From that day onward, I no longer thought of myself as young.

•••

ON THE TENTH OF NOVEMBER, the 2nd Marines boarded the task force flotilla and headed north toward Fiji and the New Hebrides. Our destination was the sixteen atolls along the equator known as the Gilbert Islands. The war had pretty much bypassed the Gilberts, but both Imperial Japan and the United States knew the strategic importance of these tiny coral islands for use as air bases. The Japanese had already constructed an airfield on Betio Island in the Tarawa atoll. That was my unit's destination. A flat, featureless mound of coral rising barely above the ocean's surface, this tiny island was not quite two miles long, and only seven hundred yards across at its widest point.

Its size, however, was disproportionate to the impact that the three-day battle known simply as Tarawa would have on the war in the Pacific, and in the annals of warfare. It lasted only seventy-six hours. But when the smoke cleared, and the battle was over, more than thirty-three hundred of my fellow Marines were dead or wounded. In return, we killed all but seventeen of the island's forty-four hundred Japanese defenders.

On November twentieth, the first assault teams assembled before dawn on the sea-sprayed deck of the USS Zeilin. There was a light cloud cover, and even though I could already feel the tropical heat beginning to build, I was shivering. Patrick had wrangled a couple of chocolate bars from somebody, and we munched in silence as we waited for the order to climb over the side rails and down the rope nets to the LVTs bobbing up and down in a light swell alongside the ship.

Suddenly, a wave of carrier-based planes flew overhead. We cheered as they swooped toward the island to bomb and strafe the entrenched Japanese positions. A few minutes later the huge naval guns opened up, firing salvo after salvo toward the island. I didn't think anyone, or anything, could survive the massive bombardment.

There was a pause in the shelling, and we were ordered over the side. Patrick crammed half of his chocolate bar under a rubber band around his helmet, and slipped over the railing. The Zeilin rose and fell in the light chop, and the heavy netting swung back and forth against the sides of the ship. Below us, the waves swept the LVTs ten or fifteen feet up and down and against the hull. I had fifty pounds of gear on my back, and each time the net swung out from the side of the ship and then back against the hull, the weight slammed me against the steel without mercy.

When I was halfway down the rope netting, I heard a shout. A medic lost his handhold on the wet rope, and plunged fifty feet into the choppy ocean. I watched as he went headfirst into the water, and as a fully loaded LVT smashed his body against the side of the ship. My hands froze on the netting. Sweat poured from under my helmet and stung my eyes. I couldn't move.

"Marty! Marty, hey—listen! Get moving, boy." It was Patrick. He'd made it to the bottom of the net and into the LVT. His hands were cupped and he was shouting at the top of his lungs. "Forrestal, get your ass down here or I'm coming up after you!"

I don't know why I laughed, but Patrick's taunt got me moving. I climbed hand over fist to the bottom of the net, and as the next swell raised the stern of the LVT up toward me, I simply dropped into the bottom of the boat.

"I'm sure glad you decided to join us," Patrick said.

Our commanding officer, Lieutenant Rattan, talked us through a gear check as we shoved off from the Zeilin to form up with dozens of other LVTs preparing for the six thousand yard run to the shore and the battle ahead. We had to cross a shallow reef as we neared the island, and then transit a wide lagoon, probably under heavy fire from Japanese gun emplacements, before we could make it to our designated landing area. The line of boats stretched as far as I could see, north and south.

We were the first wave—fifteen hundred men storming the beach. There would be two more landing forces behind us. Patrick and I were crammed into the middle of the thin-walled boat, and as we bobbed in the rising swells, another ferocious bombardment cut loose from the warships behind us. What little we could see of the island was obliterated in a massive wall of smoke and dust.

All around me, Marines were getting seasick. Each time the Alligator rose and fell in the race to the shore, another guy would upchuck. The roar of the air bombardment, sweet sea spray, vomit, pale faces, whispered conversations and noxious, swirling black smoke all blurred together like some ungodly symphony. I checked and re-checked my gear, and I prayed.

"What do you think Mr. Holden would say if he was here?" I called out to Patrick.

"I think he'd tell us to get those umbrellas up, that's what I think."

We felt grinding beneath our LVT.

"We're crossing the reef boys," shouted the Lieutenant. "Hang on!"

Our LVT hit the coral reef, shuddered a minute, and then slipped over into the shallow lagoon. We were now just two hundred yards from our objective: the freight pier at Red Beach Two.

As we raced toward the beach, I felt comforted by the massed line of combat power that was about to spring out of the LVTs that stretched the entire length of the island. Then, as suddenly as it had started, the air bombardment came to a halt. There was only the sound of our engines and the clanging of our gear against the thin hull.

Lieutenant Rattan crouched down beside the .50 caliber bow gun and whistled for our attention. "We'll be there in a couple minutes, men. Water's shallow at the approach, knee deep. We've got a five foot seawall to breach, and according to the owner's manual, this Alligator taxi of ours should be able to knock through it."

"Where are the Japs?" somebody shouted. "They're not shooting—think the bombs took them out?"

"Don't count on it," replied the lieutenant. "They've got 70s pointed at us right now, machine guns too. You'll meet them soon enough, that's for sure."

We were close enough to the beach now that smoke from the bombardment was rolling out over us. Patrick leaned close to me as we neared the jump off point: "Stay close, Martin."

PFC Calder Thomas, our radio operator, stood up next to me on the side rail between the two forward machine-gun stations to get a view of the beach. The instant he popped his head up, he flew backwards on top of me. I rolled him off, and looked down to see a bullet hole in the middle of his forehead. Before I could react, Sgt. Guererro yelled for us to get ready to debark. Patrick pulled me away from Calder's body.

When we were about one hundred yards from the beach our driver opened the throttle wide. I could just make out the manmade seawall near the pier, shrouded in thick smoke. Our gunner unleashed with the bow-mounted .50 caliber, sweeping the landing area. At the same instant, the Japanese defenders, who had been quiet until now, let loose with everything they had on the dozens of landing craft streaming across the lagoon and up to the beach.

The LVT to our immediate left took a hit amidships from a Jap 75 mm. Our boat was showered with metal fragments, loose gear and body parts. Whatever master plan our commanders had for this assault, it was chaos along the waterline.

The Alligator engine cut out, and Lieutenant Rattan ordered us out of the boat—fifty yards from the beach. I swung over the side, and into thigh deep water. The seawall was directly ahead, the pier off to my left. We raced to the seawall, thinking it would provide cover from Japanese fire. To my amazement, a Japanese officer popped up just a few yards ahead of us on the beach, waving a sword and screaming.

Before I could release my safety and open fire, a hail of bullets hit the sand in front of us, and we all went down against the seawall. Then, fire came toward us from the right. The Japs were hitting us from the side and the front, and we had no safe cover.

Lieutenant Rattan split us into three teams. Mine was going straight over the wall, Patrick's was going to the left around the wall, and Rattan was going right.

I slung my gear over the wall and pulled myself on top. Just as I was about to drop to the other side, I saw the lieutenant disappear in a spray of red mist, hit dead on with a shell from a Japanese 37 mm gun. Sgt. Guerrero and another PFC went down beside him, and were quickly picked off by machine gun fire from a concrete bunker.

Four of us made it to the other side of the seawall. I couldn't see Patrick's squad. Smoke from grenades and flamethrowers made visibility straight ahead impossible. Behind us was the ocean. To our right were machine gun nests. To our left, the Jap 37 mm that had killed the Lieutenant.

Lance Cpl. Starr made the call: "Straight on!" We unsheathed bayonets, and raced into the smoke. What we didn't know is that we were only about seventy-five yards from the main Japanese 88 mm gun position—the very gun that had been smoking our landing craft as they crossed the lagoon. From this position we were too close to be targeted by the big gun. The Japs must have figured this was some kind of planned attack on the gun emplacement. A dozen Japanese soldiers appeared through the swirling yellow-green smoke, running right at us.

We were so close that I only had time to get off one round before I literally ran into a Japanese soldier. He swung his rifle barrel at me as if to push me back—he had no bayonet. Instinct kicked in, and I dropped my right foot back in mid-stride, lowered my weapon, pulled it back and thrust my bayonet deep into his abdomen with everything I had. Just like in training.

I withdrew my bayonet, and faced the next attacker. There was no time to think. A bullet struck Cpl. Starr in the throat, and he fell hard against my side, knocking me to the ground. Out of the corner of my eye I saw Antoinelli go down. Instantly, three Japanese soldiers were over his prostate body, slashing and hacking with bayonets. That left just three of us—Jeffers, Creedmore and me. We bunched together, firing point-blank in a sweeping pattern in front of us.

A grenade exploded, and my right leg felt like it had been hit with a blowtorch. Two Japs rushed me, shouting and swinging wildly with their bayonets. I backed up, trying hard to avoid tripping on bodies.

I didn't want to die, not now, not on this dirty little atoll, not in this blistering heat, not at the hands of these bastards, not like this. I fought for my life, thrusting, blocking, shouting back. The soldier nearest me nicked my face with his blade, and I reflexively snapped my head back. That was the opening the other Jap was looking for—his bayonet flashed toward my gut, and I knew I was going to die.

A shotgun blast rang out, and the Jap nearest me toppled over, cut nearly in half. Where'd that come from? Another blast, and his partner lifted off his feet and flew several feet backwards into a palm tree stump. I staggered forward and slid down into a crater. I came up to one knee, and swung my carbine into firing position as another Japanese soldier materialized through the smoke. The 12-guage roared again, and the body of the Jap flew into the crater beside me, his back torn apart by the point-blank shot. I sank back on both knees to catch my breath. Hot, greasy smoke billowed around me like a small tornado. The staccato chatter of rifles and the fusillade of grenades and mortar shells were deafening. But there was something else, a voice, the sweetest darn sound I'd heard in my short life.

"Martin, you sorry son-of-an-excuse for an honest-to-God Marine, didn't I tell you to stay close?" Patrick appeared from out of the wall of smoke. His helmet was gone. His face was black with soot and grime. He held his shotgun at the ready, and smiled brightly.

"Where on earth did you get that thing?" I asked, pointing at the shotgun.

"It seemed like the right tool for this donnybrook," he said, grinning.

I couldn't argue. Patrick leapt down into the sandy crater beside me.

"Creedmore, Jeffers," Patrick yelled. "Hustle over." Jeffers and Creedmore raced out of the smoke, and took up defensive positions next to us.

"We're not out of this one yet," said Patrick. "They're gonna figure out pretty snappy that the four of us are all that's here, and they're going to come back for the rest of the party."

"You mean you're it?" I asked. Seventeen Marines had plunged into the lagoon and up Red Beach 2, no more than ten minutes ago.

"We're it, Marty. Four Marines and a couple hundred Japs. Looks like the Corps expects us to earn our pay this morning."

Patrick looked over at me and noticed my leg. "Let's take a gander at that," he said. I was bleeding from five or six shrapnel wounds that ran from the top of my boot up to my thigh. He pulled out a field dressing, tore it in pieces, and taped it to the worst of the wounds. "You won't go dancing tonight," he said, "but you're not going to lose that leg either."

A plane swept low through the haze and the fires, blasting its cannons into the gun emplacement. It circled, and made one more strafing pass before flying back out to sea.

"Jeffers, what can you see?" yelled Patrick.

"Our guys are trying to push off the beach, but they're taking some major fire down there," said Jeffers.

The smoke was beginning to thin, and the sound of small arms fire slowed a bit. It was only 1000 hours, but the tropical sun was high and burning hot. The Japanese 88 mm crew opened up again, sending shells out into the lagoon, blowing landing craft filled with Marines out of the water.

"Jeffers, you're the demo guy—what have you got we can use against that gun?" Patrick asked. In the absence of a CO, Patrick just took charge.

"Two packs coming down," answered Jeffers.

We quickly assembled charges out of dynamite and fuses.

"Jeffers, Creedmore," Patrick said, "I want you and Martin to lay down some cover fire for me while I drop off these party favors."

I crawled up to the rim of the crater. The firing from the gun emplacement was steady. The massive 88 mm gun was positioned behind a concrete wall. There was no way to tell how many Japanese were in the compound with it.

"I'm coming with you Patrick," I said.

My friend clapped one hand behind my neck and leaned his head against mine.

"Not today, Marty. I need you here with these guys—with luck, the three of you will be able to make enough noise to force those SOBs to keep their heads down."

He popped up, and took off, racing toward the backside of the big gun emplacement with the explosives. We opened up with two M1s and a Browning, peppering the wall in front of the massive gun mount with everything we had. Patrick sprinted sixty yards across broken coral, downed brush and the bodies of Japanese and American dead, and took cover before the gun emplacement. We kept firing while Patrick lit the fuses, and lobbed the satchels one by one over the wall.

The gun crew saw the charges coming in. They opened fire on Patrick as he turned to run back to the safety of the bomb crater. At the same instant the first satchel exploded in a ball of fire. Patrick was hit in the side and the leg. He spun to the ground, rolled once, and then got back up to his feet.

I dropped my M1 and raced up to him, just as the other three charges went off in quick succession. The force of the explosions blew me off my feet. Pieces of metal and concrete flew through the air, and I dug my face into the gritty coral sand as deep as I could. Debris rained down for several seconds.

When I looked up the gun emplacement was a smoking pile of rubble. I moved as fast as I could to Patrick and pulled him to his feet. He was stunned from the force of the explosion, and blood was seeping through the side of his shirt, but he was able to stumble back to the crater under his own power.

I pushed Patrick down, and pulled his shirt up above his waist. The bullet had gone through his side, tore him open. I sprinkled the wound with sulfa and applied a field dressing. I used my Ka-bar to slit his trouser leg so I could get at his leg wound. It looked like the bullet was still in his calf.

"Can't do much about that one, Patrick," I said. "I'll tape it, but the medics are going to have to dig it out later."

Patrick rubbed his forearm across his face, and winked at me through his pain. "Looks like we might both be taking a little vacation from this war, Marty boy."

Jeffers climbed to the rim of the crater for a look-see. "Couple dozen Alligators on the beach, boys," he shouted. "Lots of our men moving up to the seawall. Looks like we'll have company in a—" a burst of machine gun fire caught him in the head and chest. He rolled back down to us, dead.

Creedmore carefully edged his head up to the rim of the crater, and then shared the bad news. "Fifteen or sixteen of 'em, fanned out, coming up on us…fifty yards to the south…looks like one light machine gun—there's an officer with them. Jesus, the guy's carrying a sword!"

Patrick and I bellied up beside him.

"No easy way out of this one, boys," said Patrick. We rested our M1s on the coral sand on the edge of the crater and sighted in. "Good shooting," Patrick said.

As I squeezed off my first shot, I noted how beautiful the sky looked through the clearing smoke. Pure, tropical, opalescent blue. I fired and aimed and fired and aimed, fast, steady and straight. The sun broiled my back, sweat and blood fogged my vision. The Japs didn't stop or take up defensive positions. They just kept trotting toward us, a slow charge, exhorted on by the manic shouts of the sword-wielding officer. I aimed at the bastard, and missed, shot again and missed again. The third time I fired I hit him dead center in his chest. He dropped his sword, fell to his knees, and toppled slowly to the ground. We were dropping them, but eight or nine kept coming for us, straight and steady, firing and screaming all the way. They were not panicked, and we were not panicked. They would kill us, or we would kill them. It was that simple. Every man there understood that.

Patrick dropped his M1 and un-slung his 12-guage. The clip on my rifle ejected—I grabbed my last one. The Japs were only about twenty yards from us now, firing in steady bursts. We fired back. Out of the corner of my eye I saw Creedmore go down. I stopped firing and checked him. He had been hit in the face. Creedmore was gone.

Patrick and I kept shooting, Japs kept falling, and the rest of them kept coming. I fired my last round, and reached over Patrick to grab Creedmore's weapon. I fired once—another Jap went down. Twice more— and my clip ejected. No more bullets.

Something massive slammed into my shoulder. It hurt like hell and knocked me back. I looked down and saw blood streaming down my chest. For some reason, it made me feel silly. Patrick was hunched up against me, firing steadily at the advancing soldiers. He paused to load shells into the shotgun, and turned to me. He cocked his head to the side, and flashed that big Irish grin. He sat up. I knew what he was going to do.

"No need to be a cowboy," I said.

"Who said anything about cowboys? I'm going hunting," he said.

Then he stood, and leapt out of the crater. He charged the five remaining Japs, pumping his 12-gauge. One went down, then another. They fired on him, hitting him in the leg, shoulder and in the abdomen. Patrick fell to one knee, but kept firing. Three Japs were left.

I pushed myself out of the crater, and wriggled over to Jeffers' body. I rolled him on his side, and pulled his M1 from his grip. I fired and hit one of the Japs. Patrick got another. The last soldier rushed forward, firing wildly. Patrick was hit again—I couldn't tell where. He dropped like a stone. I moved forward, firing the M1 point blank until I emptied the whole clip in the Jap's body. He collapsed in a heap next to Patrick.

I bent down beside my friend. His torso was drenched in blood, but his eyes were open, and he was breathing. I put my arm under his stomach and started to lift him.

"Don't get funny with me, Martin," he said. "I can get up."

"Like hell you can." I pulled him to his feet. He clutched his shotgun in one hand, and put his other arm around my shoulder.

As we took fire, we staggered back to the crater, where I hoped we'd be able to wait until reinforcements could make it up from the beach. I poked my head out of the hole. The three remaining Japs were coming in quick. They fired at us as they closed in. I crouched down beneath the rim of the crater and tried to cover Patrick. I was dizzy, it was hard to breathe, and my vision was blurred by smoke and blood. I was out of ammo.

Suddenly, Patrick pulled at me. He grabbed the front of my shirt with both of his hands, and shoved me ass over elbow down into the crater. I struggled to get back up to my knees, but my shattered leg wouldn't support my weight, and I collapsed onto the hot sand.

"Stay down!" Patrick shouted to me as he somehow popped back up and out of the hole. Japanese rifles fired close by, and then I heard the pump slide of Patrick's 12-guage as he fired, once, twice, and then stopped. I summoned up my last ounce of strength, and pulled myself back up to the top of the crater. Two Japs lay dead a few feet away.

Patrick was kneeling above the third, trying to wrestle a pistol from the soldier's hand. The gun fired, and Patrick was thrown back, clutching at his stomach. The Jap sat up and tried to level his gun on Patrick, but before he could shoot again, Patrick bounced back and stuck him in the chest with his Ka-bar knife. The Jap gasped, and Patrick collapsed on top of the dying man.

I pulled myself out of the crater and crawled to my friend. He pushed himself off the dead Jap, somehow got to his knees, and crawled in my direction. I pushed myself up on my knees, wrapped my arms around him, and held him tightly.

"Damn you, O'Hagan, you stupid Irish farmer, what did you think you were doing?"

All around us, for a hundred yards or more, the ground was littered with the bodies of Japanese and American soldiers who had died on this crappy little mound of coral and dirt. Planes flew overhead looking for Jap positions to strafe, while behind us more Marines were fighting to move off of the kill zone on the beach.

Patrick wiped blood and dirt from his face with his forearm. He was breathing heavy. "What am I doing?" he whispered in a hoarse voice. "I'm looking out for you, Marty."

A howitzer shell exploded close by, showering us with gritty sand and dirt. I didn't have the strength to stand, to run, to move, let alone to lift Patrick. We stayed on our knees, face to face, bleeding into the sand. Patrick rested his head on my shoulder. Finally, he raised his head. He struggled to open his eyes.

"You remember that creek in the mountain pass, Martin?" he said in a soft, faraway voice. "Those fat fish we caught? And the sky, the sky that day in the snow after the avalanche, that white snow, did you ever in your life see anything as blue as that Oregon sky above that snow?"

His head dropped to my shoulder. He coughed once, then went still. I looked up into the vast blue tropical sky, and held my friend in my arms.

•••

CAPTAIN WILLIAM EMBRY, the commander of the company that fought its way up to our position an hour later, described the scene in a letter to his wife, which she sent to me some years later. He wrote:

> We had no idea any of the first wave Marines had made it this far off the beach.
>
> We expected to be assaulting a Jap gun emplacement.

Instead, we found a scene right out of an old Knights of the Round Table story. The gun emplacement had been blown by a squad of four Marines.

Scattered around an area about fifty yards in radius were the bodies of twenty-six Japanese soldiers, including a colonel. Two Marines lay dead in a shell crater near the gun emplacement.

But the most remarkable thing, something that haunts me to this day, was the sight of two Marines at the exact center of that circle of death. They were on their knees, face to face under that smoky, sweltering sky. Their helmets were gone, their bodies were soaked in blood, their weapons lay beside them, and as we approached, they were absolutely still. It was like a sculpture, or a classical painting. One of the men's arms hung limp at his side. The other Marine's arms were wrapped around his buddy. The bodies of six Jap soldiers were within five feet of where those two Marines were frozen in place. That fight must have been intense.

My men came to a halt, transfixed. I've seen a lot of fighting, and a lot of terrible, remarkable sights in battle, but never anything more powerful than these two men on Tarawa. I came up close, and saw that only one was dead. The other was badly wounded, his eyes were swollen nearly shut, his lips and cheeks were blistered raw by the sun and the fires. He was bleeding from wounds in his legs and upper body, but he wouldn't let go of his friend. I called the corpsman forward, and we radioed for a stretcher. But that Marine did not want to let go of his buddy.

I don't know where he found the strength to stay upright—let alone hold the body of his friend up—with injuries like his, in that heat, on that battlefield. I finally put my arm around him and said, "It's all right, son, you let us take care of your friend now. Let go…you've done your job." The corpsman eased the body of the dead Marine down onto the sand, and started to cover him with a blanket. His wounded friend stopped the corpsman's hand. He leaned close to his dead friend, and put his hand on the young man's head. He said, "Patrick, I'll see you at the creek." Then he pulled the blanket over his friend's face, and let us evacuate him to the hospital ship.

•••

AFTER HE FINISHED READING the letter out loud, Mark fell silent. His eyes scanned the yellowed typewritten page again. He finally folded the letter, and carefully slipped it back into its envelope.

"I think you can turn off the recorder," I said. "Would you mind getting me some water?"

He set the recorder back on the side table. He placed the envelope back with the other papers in the folder that held my notes. Then he helped me drink. I realized that telling the story had taken a lot out of me. I was exhausted, and the water felt refreshing.

Mark cleared his throat, and then spoke softly: "I've never heard a story like that. I mean, I studied the war in school, and I've seen movies and stuff, but I've never actually talked to anybody who was there."

"There aren't too many of us left to do the talking," I said. "About a thousand vets die every day, so I'm told. An awful lot of stories are never going to get passed along. Thank you for helping me share mine."

"You were a hero, Mr. Forrestal."

"You're wrong about that, Mark. I was doing my job. A couple million boys my age were out there in the Pacific and in Europe with me. We weren't heroes. Not those of us who made it home, anyway. That's not how we think of ourselves."

"It's just crazy. You were younger than I am now."

"I think you need to get outside more," I said. "There are heroes all around you. You sure as heck don't need to carry a weapon to be heroic in my eyes, though there are plenty of young men and women standing watch for you and me in some pretty scary places around the world right now who fit the bill. But they're not the only heroes. Somewhere out there right now there is a person doing the right thing even though no one is looking, or speaking up in order to prevent a wrong. That person is a hero. There are teachers out there doing thankless work, getting paid next to nothing, just because they genuinely care for their kids, and are willing to take some responsibility for building a better tomorrow. They're heroes. My wife volunteers a few hours a week at a soup kitchen, and my doctor volunteers every year at a children's clinic so far out in the bush in Mexico that there isn't a paved highway for a hundred miles. There are plenty of heroes, Mark. Just look around, son. They're on every corner."

Mark thought for a minute. "Was it worth it?" he finally asked.

"That's a good question. Would you mind getting me one of those pillows?"

Mark put another pillow behind my back.

"There was a pretty strong argument in favor of fighting: our way of life, everything we believed in, was at risk. We were attacked at Pearl Harbor. Hitler was bent on turning the lights out in Europe. By the time we got into the scrap, millions had already died. Was it worth it? The loss of my friend, and millions like him all over the world? Sometimes the stakes are so high, and the consequences of not fighting are so complete, that to not fight would be, well, immoral. All these great freedoms we enjoy every day are not free. The plain fact is freedom is the most expensive commodity in the world, because it's so scarce. I don't know that we'll ever get caught up with the payments, either. The bill just keeps coming due."

I saw that Mark was looking over at the picture of his great-grandparents and I.

"I miss Patrick every day. I miss him when I hear a good joke, and every time I see a face full of freckles. And when I vote, or write a letter to the editor or call my Congressman to give him hell about one darned thing or another, tell you the truth, I say a prayer in my heart for him. He knew exactly what he was doing that day on Tarawa. He knew when he pushed me down in that bomb crater and took those last soldiers on by himself that he wouldn't live. And that was just fine by him. He sacrificed every tomorrow he would ever have so that I could have at least one more for myself. I can't ever pay him back for what he gave to me, and gave to you, for that matter. All I can do is remember, and honor him, and make damn sure his story doesn't fade away."

Mark nodded.

"When I was a boy I had a Scout leader who said that when you were really up against it, in the middle of the most terrible situation imaginable, you would deal with it as best you could with what was already deep inside you. Heroes don't suddenly learn to be brave when the bullets start to fly—they already have it within them."

•••

CONNIE ARRIVED THE FOLLOWING MORNING with Janine, Teresa and Mark in tow. We chatted for a little over an hour.

Then it was time for them to leave. Janine insisted I keep the photo of she and Patrick and I. I didn't object. Janine fidgeted and fussed around for a minute before she could say her last goodbye.

"I have to tell you, Martin, the worst part of living this long is seeing so many of those you love go away." She laid her hand against my cheek. Her eyes filled with tears. Her voice was barely a whisper. "It won't be long, will it? I mean, for you and me and Patrick to all be together again?"

It took a lot of strength, but I was able to take hold of her hand and kiss it. "No, my dear. Not long. We'll spread a picnic on the creek bank, just like we used to. Just past the bridge, remember, where the berries are thick right down to the water's edge—"

"—and the wild irises grow, and crawdads nip at your toes, and when you lay down to watch the clouds drift past, the grass is softer than any down comforter," Janine finished.

She leaned down and kissed me on the lips. "Tell Patrick I sent that along," she said. "Godspeed." She stepped out into the hall with Connie.

Teresa and I talked about her family for a minute, and then I bid her farewell. "Thank you for taking the time to talk with Mark," she said. "I think you made quite an impression on him."

She turned to go, and Mark held back a moment.

"Thanks for the story," he said. "Sure wish I'd known you."

"Likewise, Mark. Good luck to you."

He shook my hand and looked me in the eye. "It was the 2nd Marine Division you joined?"

I smiled. "They're in the phone book."

Forgiveness

I WAS MOST COMFORTABLE NOW with the bed completely flat. But, if there was anything that rattled my spirits, it was having to lie there staring straight up at the ceiling tiles. My right hand found the bed control, and I raised the back to a forty-five degree angle. The movement, gentle and slow as it was, sent a spasm of pain radiating up my spine that found an unwelcome home in my neck. For a moment it was hard to breathe. I put my thumb on the button that would summon the nurse, and then thought better of it. If my pain medication was increased, I'd either fall asleep or be too groggy to do something as simple as visit with my wife or talk into the digital recorder. And I had plenty of reasons to do both.

Connie was due back shortly. Eric would bring the children by this evening after dinner. I loved seeing them, but I was going to suggest to Eric that he bring them in for just a minute tonight. I could only imagine how difficult—or at the very least how complicated—it was for Gwen and Jimmy to see their grandfather fading away before their eyes. How much of this did they truly understand?

I swung my arm over and felt for the digital recorder in the jumble of wires and tubes that covered my body like a spider's web. My fingers had memorized the location of the controls on the tiny device. I played back some of the files I had recorded over the past couple of days.

I put the gizmo back down and found myself listening to the clicks and whirs and hums of the equipment arranged around my bed. It occurred to me that there were only two empty folders left on the recorder, and I still had three values left to address. A few days ago I wouldn't have thought that a problem: Rachel would simply download the files, as she had been dutifully doing all along, and then I would plunge ahead with my stories, right up until the end.

The end.

Those words had taken on a definite significance. The end of my stories, the end of my life. There was a time at the start of this process where some of what was occurring registered as surreal. Now it was all very real.

I reflected on the three remaining values from the original list of fifteen that I had scribbled down on my second night in the hospital: forgiveness, patience, love. And at that moment, I experienced a foreign feeling. I hadn't felt it at the height of the Depression, on the beach at Tarawa, when my business was in ruins, not even when Doc McGuire delivered the news that I was dying. I realized that for the first time in my life, I had undertaken a job that I was not going to finish. Call it pride, hardheaded stubbornness, or a simple man's just-get-it-done philosophy of life—the realization clobbered me with its stark finality. I blinked back a tear.

I looked around the room, and focused on the cherry tree outside. Was it time to give up, and let the doctors medicate me so heavily that I would not feel the icy fingers of disease squeezing the life from my body?

I closed my eyes and I was eight again. My father was standing in front of me under the wide Montana sky. He was handsome in his blue shirt and leather vest, his cowboy hat cocked back just so. He held the reins of his horse in one hand as he placed his other hand on my shoulder. "I hope you never have to fight, son," he said. "But if you do, make sure that what you are fighting for is worth the price you will have to pay." He swung up onto his horse. He smiled at me and tipped his hat to my mother, who I knew was standing right behind me, even though I couldn't see her. Then he wheeled his horse around and galloped off across the vast prairie.

I had been fighting this cancer for over a year.

The hospital setting for the last round of that fight was preordained, and of course, the fix had been in from the start. My opponent didn't lose many fights. He was patient. He was methodical. He had tenacity and skill to spare. I could muster up my remaining strength and land a few more jabs here or there, but even my seventeen-year-old self in combat fighting-shape couldn't hold off this adversary for the full fifteen rounds. I wasn't ready to throw in the towel, that's for sure. I would fight on, even with the chips stacked against me, and an adversary who—unlike me—was growing stronger with each round. I had plenty of reasons and each was worth whatever price I'd have to pay. I'd be riding out to join my father soon enough. But not today.

•••

CONNIE HAD SOMETHING ON HER MIND. We had been sitting quietly together for a while. She finally spoke up and told me that I was going to have one more visitor before Eric brought the grandchildren to see me.

"Honey," she said softly, "Louis Drury arrived in town today."

For twenty-five years the mere mention of that name would raise my blood pressure to the boiling point, and the idea of having to spend time in the same room with Drury would have turned my stomach. But now I didn't feel any of that.

"Are you sure you want to go through with this?" asked Connie.

"He's come a long way to see me," I said.

My wife's cheeks flushed: "And I'm of half a mind to turn him right around and send him straight back to the hole he came from, whether he sees you or not."

"Which would defeat the whole point, Connie."

"He almost destroyed us," she said.

"But he didn't, did he? He stole from the business, stole our peace of mind, smashed some dreams, but he couldn't destroy us. I don't need to hold onto that anger anymore. It ate me alive for years," I said.

"You could have had him arrested for fraud, Martin. You could have pursued him across the country. He never spent a day in jail. He never had to repay a penny of what he took from us. You didn't go after him. Isn't freedom forgiveness enough?"

"Do you really think he's free?" I asked.

I reached for my wife's hand. She had opposed my plan to find Drury and ask him to come to Oregon. But she honored my request, and Eric tracked him down by phone to a squalid boarding house in Phoenix.

I'm sure that she had to bite her tongue when she told Drury the purpose of her call. Discovering that he was flat broke and that she would have to buy a plane ticket for the man who had literally robbed us blind rubbed salt into what was, clearly, still an open wound for her.

"Why do I get the sense that all these years later you are more hurt by it than I am?"

"Probably because I am," she said.

"Well with all due respect and consideration, my love, I can't help you with that." I looked at her softly. We were quiet for a minute.

"I only have control over so much," I continued. "I choose not to take any anger with me to my grave. I have no use for it. Yes, Louis escaped punishment. Though based on what I've heard about his circumstances theses days, I'm not sure he has escaped justice. You know, those two don't always go hand in hand. But I don't want to see him to exact revenge, Connie. I wanted that for a long time. How long did it take us to rebuild? Five, six years?"

Connie held my hand, but she was looking off into space. She knew all too well how long it had taken to recover from Louis Drury's treachery, which had come at the worst possible time. Connie and I had done everything we could think of to avoid taking on a partner. Our business had grown at a slow but steady pace, and we were debt-free. But then the national economy went into a tailspin. The combination of high interest rates, new logging regulations, a weak lumber market, and competition from cheap foreign timber nearly knocked us out of the game.

Drury appeared out of nowhere with a little cash and a lot of promises. He knew people, he had contacts, he'd made some pretty big deals happen. We had checked out his resume of course, and while we got the feeling he wasn't going to win any awards for humility or warmth, we couldn't deny that his wheeler-dealer ways had delivered the goods. We gave him twenty-five percent of the business against a promise of a substantial cash payment within ninety days, and his guarantee to bring us contracts for the delivery of dimension lumber to some of the big home builders he had worked with in the past.

Drury didn't waste time; he moved right into the office beside me and began a flurry of phone calls and trips around the Northwest. What we didn't know was that everywhere he went, he signed contracts that said we would deliver lumber at prices that were far below our actual cost of harvesting and milling. And each time he made a deal with a slightly incredulous—or shady—building contractor, Drury got a sizeable kickback. The deals he signed were twenty to thirty percent below what those contractors could get from anyone else, so they were happy to throw some cash his way. Later, when we discovered what had gone on, and I personally confronted each of the contractors Louis had done business with, the story was the same: yes, the contractor would acknowledge, the deal had seemed too good to be true. But they all knew the reputation that Forrestal Lumber had built since my father started the business over forty years earlier. As far as they were concerned, Forrestal Lumber was cutting prices to the bone in order to stay competitive in a brutal economy. Why was our pricing policy any of their concern?

Drury traded on our good name for three months, racking up cash advances and kickbacks from contractors all over the region by selling lumber to them at a loss. About the time the first delivery orders for the contracts Drury signed began to show up in the mail, he disappeared. I realized we had been duped by the time the second order arrived. Delivery contracts dripped in for more than five months. I winced whenever the postman showed. It was an agonizing time for us.

Each time a new order arrived instructing us to deliver X amount of lumber to yet another building site for far less than it would cost us to produce, I'd put on my hat and visit the contractor. Some of them did the decent thing, and agreed to cancel or modify their orders and pay the fair going rate for lumber. Others said they couldn't cancel because they had ordered their lumber months before they broke ground; if they didn't get delivery on time, at the rate Drury quoted, it would cost them a fortune. And, I'm sorry to say, a few turned me down flat just because saving money in the short-term was more important to them than a relationship that had been built over two generations.

Connie and I sat up one sleepless night deciding what to do. We could close the business down and face a barrage of lawsuits. We could file for bankruptcy and take our chances on getting a reorganization plan that we could handle. Or, we could tough it out, raise all the money we could from the sale of excess equipment, mortgaging our home and cashing in our retirement savings, and honor the contracts that Drury had obligated us to fulfill. The next morning we called all fourteen of our employees into the lumberyard. It was gray and drizzling. Most of our employees had been with us for years and were like family to us.

We gave it to them straight: whatever choice we made would bring a heap of tough times upon us all. Our preference was to tough it out, to work harder than ever, and to do what we had to do to honor our commitments, keep everybody working, and maintain our reputation. It would mean longer hours, cuts in pay, and fewer vacations. What I didn't have to say was that I'd make it up to each of them eventually, and that Connie and I would be right there beside them every hour of every day— and then some.

I asked for a show of hands for each of our three options. Not a single hand was raised to vote to shut down, or to file bankruptcy. When I asked if they would stand beside Connie and me and battle our way through, fourteen hands shot up. It was one of the proudest moments of my life.

I never could get my head wrapped around the notion that a man could consciously set out to ruin people as Drury had done. The hate I carried in my belly fueled a ferocious work pace for several years. I imagined catching up with him, and thrashing him to within an inch of his life. I lay awake at night for months, cursing the day I met him, and blaming myself for the decision to allow him to sign the Forrestal name on those contracts. As time went by, and my anger and resentment and desire for retribution grew, I came to realize something about myself that made me do some serious thinking about my own character: my hatred for Louis Drury was forging a stronger and stronger bond between us.

It was as if each angry thought about him forged a steel link in my soul. Day by day, month by month, that chain was growing longer and heavier. Anger was becoming the dominant emotion in my life—greater than my love for my wife and young son, greater than my commitment to my business, my community, and my church. Anger was overwhelming me.

The breaking point occurred one summer evening when I got into a silly argument with Connie about whether we should get a puppy for Eric. It was hardly a subject worthy of the steam that I felt shooting out of my ears—or the angry things I said to my wife. I stormed out the door, hopped into the pickup and made a beeline for the liquor store. I bought a fifth of bourbon, and pointed my truck toward Kings Valley. The moon was rising above the tree line when I parked along a dirt road, grabbed the bourbon, and hiked into the brush. I was headed for the outdoor chapel I had discovered a couple of years earlier. It was dark now, but the rising moon lit my path better than a flashlight. A few minutes later I was seated on the big stump at the south end of the clearing. The stars were beginning to pop, and an owl welcomed me with its mournful call. I could smell wild strawberry and ripe blackberries. I uncorked the bottle raised it to my lips, and then just as quickly set it down without taking a sip.

What was I becoming? I hadn't taken a drink of hard liquor since I was in the Marines. And shouting at my wife? Since when did I do that?

I poured the bourbon out on the ground, and contemplated the turn my life had taken since I met Louis Drury. What was becoming of that better husband, wiser father, and more generous employer that I had strived to be? I didn't have the answer to a lot of life's questions; but one thing I did know was that the hatred I felt for Drury was consuming me. Link by link, the chain that bound me to the man I had invited into my business, the man that had cheated me, was growing stronger.

The moon was full and bright, and I could make out most of the trees and flowers that ringed my little valley. I knew that I had to find it in my heart to forgive Drury, if for no other reason than to save myself. As I hiked back to my truck for the drive home, I also knew that there was someone whose forgiveness I needed to seek that night.

•••

THE ROOM WAS STILL. After more than a half-century together, Connie and I didn't always have to complete our conversations. We knew each other's hearts. We could say more with a glance than many people could say in an hour of chatter. This was one of those times.

When I finally spoke, it had nothing to do with Drury. "You look beautiful, Connie. Wish I could drive you up the canyon for dinner at the Riverhouse."

My wife leaned over and kissed me on the lips. "Oh, I'm not done with you by a long shot, mister…"

Just then, the door opened, and my son entered. He gave Connie a hug, and then told me that he had just returned from the airport. Louis Drury was outside my room. Was I ready to see him?

I looked up at Connie. She squeezed my hand. I raised my bed as far as it would go, and reached for a comb on the nightstand. Connie took it and combed back the hair from my forehead. Then she dipped a cloth in my water glass and wiped my face. There were tears in her eyes. She kissed me again, and then walked over to the window and turned her back to the room. She would stay with me.

I took a deep breath. "Alright, son." I said. Eric left the room. A moment later the door opened, and Louis Drury was standing at the foot of my bed.

•••

So many times I envisioned the scene in which I finally confronted the monster that had nearly destroyed everything that mattered most to me. For a long time, those scenes were filled with violence. That brand of fiery passion and fury had dissipated years ago. But the memory of the wrong he had done to my family, my business, and my employees was as fresh as ever. As I took my first look at Louis Drury in over thirty years, I heard the voice of my pastor in my head: "To forgive is to set a prisoner free and to discover that the prisoner was you."

The monster, for his part, had lost his menace. Drury seemed shrunken. It was obvious that he had traveled some hard roads. His loose, rumpled clothing gave him the appearance of a scarecrow that needed another bale of straw to fill him out. He had gone bald, and wore the ruddy complexion we used to call a drinker's tan when we were kids. He curled his fingers around the top of the bedframe, steadying himself. He opened his mouth, as if he was about to speak, and I saw that his false teeth looked a size or two too big. In that moment of hesitation, I saw a little fear in his bleary eyes.

"Sorry you're up against it, Martin," Drury said. "Guess neither of us is getting any younger."

The sound of his voice opened a floodgate of emotion. I grit my teeth, and focused on remaining calm. "Louis," was all I could say.

"Your wife," Drury nodded toward Connie's back, "said you wanted to see me. Funny a guy would want to see me in the hospital, though, don't you think?"

"I hope you can appreciate that it was very difficult for my wife to call you, Louis. As difficult as it is for me to see you here tonight."

Drury took his hands off the bed rail. "So that's why you asked me to come here Forrestal? So you could tell me you didn't want to see me?"

Connie turned, and for a moment I thought she was going to say something. She thought better of it, and sat down in the window seat, facing us this time. I was almost surprised at how calm my voice was when I answered Drury. "No, Louis. I asked you to come partly because it was so difficult—difficult for me, difficult for Connie, and difficult for you, too, I'm sure. I appreciate the fact that you came all this way."

I cleared my throat, and looked right at him. "I asked you here because I need to give you something. I believe that it's a gift; you may think it is simply the last ditch attempt of a dying man to pave his way into heaven. You can choose to regard it however you like."

His face was a mask of puzzlement. He looked around the room, as if he wasn't sure if it was a cop or a brightly wrapped present that he should be looking for.

"Well, I'm here, Martin," he said. "After all these years, with no contact between us, no letters, no phone calls, you wanted me to fly a thousand miles to see you when you're—" he thought about how he was going to continue "—when you're on your way out. Well, you got my curiosity up. What is it? I'm listening."

I gathered myself. I ran my tongue around the inside of my mouth, and at last felt like I could speak. I made eye contact with him and held his gaze. "It's pretty simple, Louis. I asked you here so that I could tell you that I forgive you. From the bottom of my heart, I forgive you."

It got so quiet you could hear a pin drop. Drury said nothing. His eyes dropped. Then he slowly shook his head, as if he wasn't sure he had just heard my words. He looked around the room. He looked at Connie. She turned her head away. Then Drury looked at me. Beneath the gray stubble, his face twitched. His eyes darted around, and then came back to me. It wasn't quite sadness, or embarrassment, or shame that was revealed in that look; it appeared to me to be more a matter of weight—or the sudden absence of it, to be precise. It was hard to read, but it seemed clear that, whatever battles had been fought in his mind, whatever tortured questions of integrity, worth, and responsibility had been explored—this was not something he had considered. The look on Drury's face was resolving from the unsettled, hardened cynicism he carried when he first stepped into the room, to what bordered on composure. When he finally spoke, his tone of voice revealed his amazement and maybe a tinge of gratitude.

The simple words that came out of his mouth were not a question but a statement: "To forgive me." He closed his eyes and ran his hand over his bald head. He took a deep breath. "So what now?" he asked.

"Now you go home," I said.

"That's it?"

"That's it."

•••

ERIC DROVE DRURY back to his airport hotel. It felt good to close out that chapter. Connie and I were left alone again. She came and sat beside me. She took my hand and kissed it.

For several minutes we sat there, accompanied only by the soft whir of the various machines to which I was connected. At some point during the meeting with Drury, something had shifted in Connie. She had been very still ever since he left. I glanced at her and saw tears on her cheeks.

"Thank you," she said.

"For what?"

"For showing me that people can move on…that I can do better. For being my man. For being a husband and a father. For getting up at dawn for all those years and doing whatever needed to be done." She choked up.

"I'm sorry," she said.

I squeezed her hand.

"Please forgive me," she said. "Forgive me for every time I didn't believe."

"Connie…"

"I mean it. You have to forgive me."

"My dear, there is nothing to forgive."

"That man—if I can call him that—did everything he could have done to ruin us short of killing us. Martin Forrestal, if you can forgive him, I hope you can forgive me."

"I forgive you," I said, "truly and completely, without reservation." I paused. "But you're not the one who needs to be asking forgiveness." I was about to continue, but a searing wave of pain rolled up my back, rendering me breathless. I grimaced and pinched my eyes shut. Connie stroked my arm, and sat through it with me.

After a minute, I could speak again. "Connie, forgive me."

"I forgive you."

"Forgive me for every time I doubted…"

"But you never doubted," she said.

"Yes I did." I could tell immediately that this came out of my mouth with more force than I had intended. The soft whir of the hospital machines again filled in the space around us.

But it was true. I sure had doubted. And that was just the tip of the proverbial iceberg. I had done my fair share—in many departments. In thought, in word, in deed—I had wronged her and wronged others. I had done a lot in my time that I wasn't proud of. I had earned the right to feel justified in seeking forgiveness.

When I looked over at her she was smiling gently at me. "From the bottom of my heart, I forgive you for any and all transgressions, real or imagined, that you may have committed against me."

"Thank you," I whispered.

"Your welcome. But don't get ahead of yourself; my forgiveness is conditional."

"Is that so?"

She nodded. "I forgive you—so long as you promise to forgive yourself."

I tried that on for size.

"I promise," I told her.

"Good," Connie said, "because, 'with all due respect and consideration, my love, I can't help you with that.'"

•••

I WAS ASLEEP WHEN ERIC AND RACHEL came by with Gwen and Jimmy. My eyes opened later to a nearly pitch black room. The door was closed, and the only illumination came from the soft green and blue lights of the equipment surrounding my bed, and from the digital clock on the nightstand. It said 4:15 AM. I could not reach my ice water, so I pressed the call button on the bed rail. A moment later Nurse Letitica bustled into the room. She held the straw to my lips and I drank deeply. Then she adjusted my pillows, straightened the light coverlet, and checked my pulse and temperature. Before she left the room she rested her hand on my cheek for a long moment, and closed her eyes. She smiled lovingly at me, but didn't say a word.

•••

M<small>Y MOTHER'S FAMILY CAME FROM</small> I<small>RELAND</small>, and she had an Irish expression for almost every event and occasion in life. Most of those sayings were at least slightly humorous. But there was one expression that she reserved for only the most serious occurrences. When she uttered the words "unfinished business," you knew there was a tale worth the telling about to be shared over a proper cup of tea. It might be about a romance interrupted by war, a father and son alienated for decades, too proud or too afraid to acknowledge their part in the original dust-up, or about some hurt done by one person to another that lay festering for years before some combination of fate or determination brought them and their business to a conclusion. It was with that kind of unfinished business in mind that I had asked Louis Drury to visit me. I think my mother would have understood. I have always found it satisfying to put that sort of business to bed.

When I was fourteen, I became part of the story of my mother's own unfinished business. My mother's sister Nora and her husband Phil moved to Oregon the year after we did. I loved visiting them and my cousin Charlie on their small dairy farm outside of Philomath. Charlie and I were the same age, and we shared the same taste in comics, radio shows, baseball teams and adventure novels. In the summer we'd swim or laze on the grassy bank of the Little Luckiamute River reading tales from the Arabian Nights and the legends of King Arthur's court. On chilly fall Saturdays we'd sit on hay bales in the barn and munch fresh apples while catching up on what was happening in our respective classrooms.

Charlie was quick and clever and fast to laugh. He had a wicked sense of humor, and took delight in orchestrating the most elaborate practical jokes, none of which, unfortunately, ever came off quite as intended. But he never gave up, and his spirit never flagged in the quest for the perfect joke. Charlie, everyone agreed, was going to be a famous research scientist one day.

His mother Nora was a singer who once had dreams of a professional career. She was the strong one in the family, the anchor that kept it all together. She had to be. Her husband, my uncle, Phil, was a drunk. He wasn't the surly, nasty, fall-down kind of drunk who inhabited back alleys and harbor-side taverns. In fact, Uncle Phil was cheerful, witty, easy-going and good-natured, drunk or sober. He bought the dairy farm sight unseen, and without a clue as to the twenty-four-hour-a-day obligation he was taking on. But he worked hard to make a go of it; everybody gave him credit for that.

When he set down the milking can he picked up the bottle—any bottle, as long as there was alcohol in it. I don't recall seeing him without a bottle of beer or a jug of whiskey in his hand. And once he'd started he didn't stop, not for a minute. He drank long, hard and fast. And the more he drank, the mellower he became. No cursing or fistfights, no sad tales of gloom and woe. He just grew quieter and chuckled to himself a lot.

At the end of any given bout of drinking—and that was most nights—he'd steer himself out to the barn and collapse on a pile of hay. But, drunk or not, he never missed the 4 AM milking.

Uncle Phil's drinking was a family secret, and in those days secrets were kept. My mother made no secret of her disapproval of him, however. He and Nora and Charlie were only invited to our house for the big holidays, and when they'd pull up in their old Packard for Thanksgiving or Christmas meals, Mom would meet them at the curb and give Uncle Phil her best not-in-my-house-mister look. I was impressed with how little my mom's personal prohibition on alcohol seemed to upset him; at least, I was impressed until one Easter Sunday when I went out to the garage to fetch a vacuum tube for the radio and found him leaning on the hood of Dad's car taking a long pull from a hip flask. Phil simply winked at me, took another swallow, slipped the flask in his back pocket and whistled his way back into the house. I didn't tell my mother. Uncle Phil took Charlie and I fishing whenever we asked, he showed us how to tinker with engines, repair dairy equipment, and even how to braid genuine cowboy-style leather whips. I figured he'd earned the right to expect that I'd keep his hip flask a secret.

• • •

No SECRET CAN BE KEPT FOREVER, of course. One muggy July night when I was in the ninth grade, my dad rousted me out of bed about 2 AM.

"Get out to the car," he yelled.

I tossed on my trousers and a shirt, and slipped on my shoes as I ran out the door and down the stairs. My mother and Peter were in the back seat; the engine was running. I hopped in the front, and an instant later my dad jumped in behind the wheel. His face was grim. My mother was sobbing quietly. Dad jetted out of the driveway, and floored the accelerator. He blasted through three stop signs without so much as a sidelong glance, sped south on Commerical Street and turned west onto River Road, a narrow two lane gravel highway that wound along the banks of the Willamette for about ten miles to the old pioneer town of Independence. My dad was so focused on navigating the twists and turns of the old pack train road in the pitch black night at high speed that I thought better of asking him what was going on. I turned to my mother, who was huddled in the back seat with Peter.

"Mom, where are we going?" I asked.

She answered in a soft, teary whisper. "To my sister's…" Her voice trailed off, and she began to cry.

I had a bad feeling.

Then we were at the bridge that spanned the river. We flew across, wheeled south, and began a series of shortcut loops and turns through farm country. My dad knew how to get from point A to point B without a map pretty much anywhere. Tonight he did it at high speed in total darkness. The drive from our house to Philomath normally took an hour. That night it took just thirty-five minutes. When we were about a mile from Aunt Nora's farm, my father finally spoke.

"There's been a fire, Marty. Nora and Phil's house is gone. Doesn't look like they got out in time."

I grasped for words as our car hurtled the last few hundred yards along the country lane to the dairy farm. There was a long line of fire rigs, cars and pickup trucks on the semi-circle drive in front of the smoking ruins of Charlie's house.

As my dad pulled into the long drive, I asked softly, "Dad?"

My father pulled behind a pickup and shut off the engine. He didn't answer. He just looked at me. There was deep sadness in his eyes.

He turned to the back seat, where my brother was sleeping in my mother's arms. "Stay here until I get things sorted out," my father told her.

"Please find them, Chet! Oh, please find them and tell me they're alright!"

My father stretched over the seat and put his hand on my mother's cheek. "We'll be back soon," he said. He motioned for me to come with him.

We got out of the car and trotted up the drive toward a group of men assembled around a portable generator that was powering two floodlights pointing at the gutted farmhouse. Firemen were still pumping water onto the smoldering remains.

The chief recognized my father, and shook his hand. My dad wrapped one arm around my shoulder as we joined in the conversation.

"Glad you're here, Chet," said the chief. "Can't tell you how sorry I am."

My stomach churned, and I felt tears well up from a place deep inside me. It was true. Nora, Phil and Charlie had perished in the flames.

"The fire had probably been going for twenty minutes or more by the time we got the first call," said the chief. "An old place like that, and in this weather…" He didn't have to finish his sentence.

My father spoke slowly. "Have you been able to find them?" The chief nodded, and pointed over to the ambulance. Two gurneys sat outside its opened doors. Sheets covered the bodies. "I'll have to ask you to identify them, Chet," said the chief. "You can do it here, or you can come into town in the morning. You might like to wait till then." He paused. Then, in a gentle voice you wouldn't think could come from this burly mountain of a man, he added, "so they can be cleaned up first."

"You've only found two?" my father asked.

"A woman and a boy," replied the chief. "We're still looking in there for Phil. We'll find him, Chet."

My father told me to stay put. He walked over to the ambulance. When he reached the gurneys he turned his back to us to hide what must have been an awful sight. He slowly lifted one blanket, and then the other. The expression on his face as he walked back was a mix of pain, sadness and loss. Before he spoke to the chief, he told me to go back to the car and stay with my mother until he joined us. Just as he turned to the chief and said, "It's them," we heard a shout from the hay barn fifty yards from the house.

We turned toward the shouts, and someone swung one of the big floodlights in the direction of the barn. Two firefighters were walking toward us. We could see that they were half carrying, half dragging something—or someone—from the barn. When they got a few yards away, we saw what it was. I should have rejoiced. Instead, I felt like throwing up.

The firemen were holding up my Uncle Phil. He was shoeless and shirtless. When they got him up to the chief and my father, you could smell the liquor seeping out of his pores. He was dead, stinking drunk. He was also completely unharmed. Not a scratch or burn on his body. The firemen hauled him into the center of the circle. Phil was coming to, but it was clear that he had no idea what was going on, or why all of these people were at his place. He pushed away from the men who were holding him up, and looked around. That's when he saw the pile of charred wood that used to be his house. He reeled unsteadily on his feet. Then he turned, and recognized my father.

"Chet," he slurred. "What happened? Chet, what's going on? Where's Nora? Where's Charlie?"

The magnitude of what had gone on while he lay in a drunken stupor in the hay barn was just beginning to sink into Phil's consciousness. The dozen men around Phil regarded him with looks of anger, disgust and disbelief. I did not see so much as an iota of pity or sympathy in the eyes of those firemen or my father.

Phil dropped to his knees in front of my father. He placed his hands on his thighs, and began to rock back and forth. He began to sob. "Dear God, Chet, where are they? Please, man, tell me where my family is."

"Where your family is?" replied my father through clenched teeth. "I'll show you where your family is, you miserable bastard." My father grabbed a handful of Phil's hair, yanked him up, and dragged him across the gravel in the direction of the ambulance. The night air was steamy hot and acrid with smoke.

The firefighters watched in a kind of horrified fascination as my father pulled a screaming, crying Phil past the broken picket fence to the ambulance beyond. The heat, light and shadows reminded me of a tableau from Dante's Inferno. I had never seen my father consumed by this kind of sheer, primal anger.

Uncle Phil struggled to free himself, but my father only gripped his hair more tightly and yanked him along with greater force. When they reached the ambulance, my father pulled Phil to a standing position so quickly that I thought he was about to jerk out a clump of his hair. None of the men around me knew what my father was going to do. And at that moment, I wasn't even sure I knew who my father was.

"Where is your family?" hissed my father. "Right here, damn your eyes!"

With that my father flung the sheet from one gurney onto the ground, and then the other. The firefighters around me were hard men. They had all seen death too many times, and in ways too awful to imagine. But when my father threw back the blankets under the white floodlight and exposed what remained of the bodies of my Aunt Nora and cousin Charlie, I heard gasps and soft moans.

I sucked in my breath. It was the most horrifying thing I had ever seen. I wanted to look away, but I could not compel my eyes to move. Like the firefighters around me, I was transfixed as Chet Forrestal half-shoved Phil's face to within inches of the bodies of his dead wife and son. My father yelled and wrenched Phil around for what seemed like an eternity. Then, as easily as if he were tossing a log into the woodshed, my father threw Phil onto the muddy ground.

No one spoke. Phil lay there a moment, and then crawled up onto his feet. His face was frozen in an expression of absolute shock and horror. His eyes were wide, terrified, helpless. And he was sober.

We stood by the fire chief's pickup and watched him. A dozen pair of eyes convicted Phil and sentenced him on the spot. Before anyone could speak, Phil turned away and walked in the direction of the forest. In a moment he was outside the reach of the floodlights. No one went after him. There would be no mercy for Phil. Not tonight. Probably not ever.

•••

IT TOOK MONTHS FOR LIFE to cycle back to anything approaching normalcy. I stayed in my room for three days, numb with grief and stricken with shock at the loss of my cousin. My mother was inconsolable for weeks. But life has a way of pushing you forward no matter where you may be stuck emotionally, and in time we returned to school and work and Scouting and church and all of the other activities that carry families across troubled waters.

In the aftermath of the fire, an inquest determined that the blaze began at an electrical panel in a storage closet. The deaths of my aunt and cousin were ruled accidental. Somehow this fact did not appear to matter to most observers, including, it seemed, my parents.

The day after the fire, the Benton county sheriff had ordered a quick sale of Phil's dairy cows so that they would be properly cared for. The proceeds of the sale paid for Nora and Charlie's funeral and burial plots. Phil did not surface for the funeral.

About a month after the fire, my father got a call from a friend who said he'd seen Phil walking along the highway near his farm. According to Dad's friend, Phil had taken on the appearance of a wild man; he'd grown a shaggy beard, and smelled like he hadn't bathed in weeks. In the time that followed we got more reports; Phil had moved into the barn next to the house and was slowly beginning to clean up the property, but as far as anyone could tell, he wasn't trying to re-build the dairy. That was just as well, since no one in the community would have done business with him.

On the first Sunday after the fall term at school began, we drove out to Kings Valley for church. My mother had gone there several times with her sister, and after Nora's death Mom wanted to hang onto that connection. It meant a forty-five minute drive each way, but Dad was fine with it, and I had friends out there, so it worked out for all of us. As we rounded a tree-lined curve not far from the church that September morning, we saw an unkempt, bearded figure walking in our direction on the other side of the road. It was Phil.

My mother's face turned ashen. Phil recognized our car. As we passed him, he stood stock-still. He held his hand over his heart, and stared straight down at the ground. My father asked if she wanted to return home, but Mom was made of sterner stuff. On to church we went.

It was the beginning of a ritual that lasted a year. On the long drive out to Kings Valley each Sunday we would encounter Phil somewhere along the road. He cleaned up some as time went by, but he made no attempt to signal us or to say anything. When he saw our car he would simply bow his head, place his hand over his heart, and wait for us to pass.

No one at church knew anything about Phil's circumstances. The truth is, no one cared to go out to his place, even to satisfy the morbid curiosity of an entire community. The lack of compassion was comprehensive. Every man, woman, and child in the community knew that Phil had committed an unforgiveable sin. A freak accident had occurred…and he was responsible. It was as simple as that. To hear people talk about him, you would have thought he had strapped his wife and only son into twin electrical chairs and then flipped the switch. Why didn't the man do the decent thing and just pack up and leave? He was a pariah. When would he get the message that he wasn't wanted around here?

On the first anniversary of Nora and Charlie's deaths, Phil did something that changed the whole uneasy dynamic of his existence in our midst. When we drove to church that Sunday, we expected to see him alongside the road as usual. Peter and I used to make secret bets as to the exact spot where Uncle Phil would pop up. But that morning Phil was nowhere to be seen. As we walked up the steps leading into the small frame church, it seemed like a burden had been lifted from my mother's shoulders. Her relief, it turned out, was premature. Just as the choir finished the opening hymn, a murmur rippled through the congregation. Someone whispered in my mother's ear, and she whipped her head around toward the back of the church. I looked back, too. There, in the pew nearest the door, sitting by himself, was Phil.

I felt a chill descend upon the congregation. The pastor stepped up to the pulpit, and for a moment I was sure that he was going to address the situation. How could he ignore it? Whether the pastor would ask Phil to leave or if he would extend my uncle the hand of redemptive forgiveness, I wasn't sure. From the look on the pastor's face, it was clear that he was wondering the same thing. But when the pastor began speaking, it became apparent that he was going to take a third path: he said nothing to Phil or about him. He acted as if my uncle and over a hundred of his former friends and neighbors were not even in the same building.

My mother stood hesitantly when the service came to a close. She was mustering her strength for the walk to the back of the church, and a possible confrontation with the man she believed had robbed her of two of the dearest people in her life. Phil solved that issue for her, and for all of us, really. He was nowhere to be seen inside or outside of the church. He'd slipped out just before the end of the service.

Thus began the next chapter in Phil's story.

In the weeks and months that followed, the routine was set: a few minutes after the congregation was seated and the pastor began to speak, Phil would slip into the corner of the back pew. He acknowledged no one, and the congregation acted like he didn't exist. He did not stand for songs, join in ceremony or interact with anyone or anything that went on during the service, and he was scrupulous about leaving during last prayer so that he would have no contact with anyone.

From time to time I would steal a quick glance to the back of the church. I might as well have been looking at a statue in a museum: Phil stared at the floor, his arms crossed, his body perfectly still. Whatever the sermon topic, no matter the heat or cold, if babies were crying or folks were greeting one another with handshakes and hugs, Phil was silent, still and stone-faced. My mother caught me looking back at him once and rapped my hand with a church bulletin, but it didn't stop me. I was frankly bewildered by Phil's actions, and equally confused by the fact that neither my parents or anyone else I knew would entertain a conversation on the subject of Phil, let alone speculate on why he was disturbing the harmony of the community by showing up in the only place he knew he was welcome.

•••

THAT CHRISTMAS, we were running late for church.

The sleet and wind that battered the car on the drive to the valley didn't help us make up any lost time. We pulled into the gravel lot beside the church and raced up the steps just as the choir finished the last line of the final verse of "Silent Night."

Mom and Dad shook the rain off their coats, and hung them on the rack in the entry lobby. With Peter between them, they pushed open the double oak doors that led into the sanctuary and made their way up to their usual seats near the front of the church.

I hung my jacket, and started to follow them. But as I stepped through the doors and into the cozy church decorated with fresh evergreen boughs and candles, something made me stop in my tracks. I wish I could say that I had given a lot of thought to what I was about to do, but the truth is, I hadn't thought about it at all.

Even with the traditional overflow Christmas crowd, the two pews at the back of the church on either side of the main aisle were empty. Except for the last pew on my right. In the far corner, his arms crossed, his head down, sat my Uncle Phil.

I looked up to the stage behind the pastor, where the choir had just been singing. Two beautifully decorated Christmas trees graced the stage, one at each end. Suspended from the ceiling directly above the center of the altar was a life-size angel in a pristine white robe, with golden wings and trumpet, heralding the birth of Christ. Below the angel was a hand-built manger scene. A papier mâché Joseph knelt before Mary, who was standing with the baby in her arms. Joseph's head was bowed, and his arms were crossed upon his chest.

The pastor asked everyone to stand for the opening prayer. All did, except Phil. I waited until the prayer was concluded, fully intending to join my family for the rest of the Christmas service. But when the pastor motioned for everyone to be seated, I stayed right where I was.

I looked at the pastor, the angel and manger, and then at my parents. My mother turned her head, saw me standing there, and gave me a questioning look. She nudged my father, and he, too, turned and looked at me. The pastor also noticed me, and he saw that my parents were silently entreating me to come and join them. The pastor motioned for me to come and take my seat. As he did, a number of people turned around in their pews to see what was causing the hold up.

What I did next was as much a surprise to me as it was to the pastor, my parents and brother—in fact, to the entire congregation. I stepped to the right, shuffled down the narrow space between the rows of pews, and sat down right next to the community's number one undesirable.

I did not look at Phil, nor did he turn his head so much as an inch in my direction. I kept my gaze fixed directly at the pastor, shutting out the disapproving—and disbelieving—stares from all over the church. It was eerily quiet, so quiet that you could hear the freezing rain as it splashed off the metal gutters outside. The pastor looked right at me. He lowered his head a bit, and then raised his eyebrows, as if to say, do you know what you're doing, young man? I felt compelled to nod at him in return. The pastor looked down at his lectern and closed his eyes. A moment later he raised his head and flipped opened his Bible. But before he began speaking, he smiled at me.

I tried to listen to the sermon. But my heart was pounding so loudly in my ears that I couldn't make out a word. Every now and then someone in the church would turn and stare at me. There wasn't much Christmas spirit in those glances. Uncle Phil sat as he always did, arms crossed, head down. I wondered if I had offended him by breaking into what had been his private church. I felt painfully alone sitting there next to him.

Then the sermon was over, and the choir took to the stage to sing "Joy to the World." I was thinking about going up to sit with my parents for the music when Uncle Phil caught my attention. He uncrossed his arms and placed his hands palm down on his knees. Then, for the first time since he had come to church after the fire, he raised his head. I could see that he was looking straight up at the stage at the figure of Joseph on his knees before his wife and son.

Tears began to flow down my uncle's cheeks. He made no sound, he didn't move. He just stared at the papier mâché family on the stage. The choir finished their song, and the pastor shared a few final holiday thoughts. I heard my uncle breathe deeply, as if to staunch the tears that were rolling off his face and onto his lap. It didn't help.

I wanted to do something, to say something, but no words came to me. Then I lifted my right hand, and gently put it on top of my uncle's hand. He didn't look at me, but his tears began to subside. I didn't hear the pastor dismiss the congregation, but in a moment people began to stream past my pew on their way to the door. I felt a thousand eyes burn into me. I tried to stare straight ahead, but it wasn't a very effective strategy. I can't say for certain what was in the minds of the people passing by. I hoped that a few, at least, felt some small measure of empathy—especially on this Christmas morning.

I kept my hand on my uncle's as the congregation thinned to a few stragglers. My uncle never turned his gaze from the stage. When my parents came down the aisle and stood at the end of the pew, I looked up at my mother. Her eyes brimmed with tears. But they were not tears of anger or hatred. I only saw sadness and pity on her face. My father nodded at me, not so much in approval, I think, as in simple acknowledgement that I was a man now, and he respected the decision I had made, no matter what his feelings might have been. "It's time, son," he finally said. I raised my hand off of Phil's, and then thought better of it.

I put my hand back on top of his, and gave it a firm squeeze. Then I stood up and joined my family.

•••

THAT WAS THE LAST TIME that any of us saw Uncle Phil. We learned that he moved to Washington state, but no one back home ever heard from him again. Over time, Phil became a distant, if painful and perplexing memory for us. Many years later the new pastor at the church in Kings Valley contacted my mother.

Uncle Phil had died. He had been cremated, and in a brief letter forwarded from his church in Washington, he asked my mother's permission to have his remains buried alongside Nora and Charlie in the Philomath cemetery. The letter included money for the burial and for a separate headstone for Phil's plot.

My mother called Connie and I out to her house when she received the letter. She'd read it over and over. "Martin," she said, "why do you think that Phil moved away right after that Christmas service? Did it have something to do with you sitting next to him?"

"I've thought about that a lot over the years," I told my mother. "I think that Phil was seeking forgiveness. But he didn't believe that he had the right to ask for it. I also think that he believed that if forgiveness was granted, it didn't have to be some kind of big public affair. In fact, Mom, I don't think it even had to be you or me who offered it to him."

"I'm not sure I understand," she said.

"Phil was a drunk, Mom, but he didn't start that fire. We don't know if his being in the house when it started would have made any difference. In fact, if he had passed out in his rocker instead of in the barn, he'd probably have died in the fire with them. It's hard to fathom what that would be like. I can't imagine the pain and guilt and shame he lived with. He lost his wife and his only child, and everybody blamed him. But he never begged you or anyone else for mercy or understanding. If he had, and if you had given it under those circumstances, I don't think it would have calmed his heart one bit. Not if he had to beg for it."

I looked over at the letter my mother was holding tightly. "I think that what Phil hoped and prayed for was that just one, single, caring human soul would extend a hand to him, to acknowledge him. I guess even something as small as what I did when I took his hand at the end of the service was enough. Maybe, in his mind, someone finally stepped out of their own hurt, and offered to take some of his."

We were quiet for a minute.

My mother finally spoke. "There's no way I'd allow a separate headstone for Phil next to Nora and Charlie's marker. No way." She paused for a moment. "We'll have a brand new marker made that will look down on all three of them—they'll be there all together, side by side. As a family."

Connie leaned across the couch and hugged my mother. Both of them were teary-eyed. "Get my coat, would you Marty? Let's take a drive out to Kings Valley."

LOVE

I SLEPT EASILY and woke at 7 AM. The first thing I noticed was a complete absence of pain. I didn't know whether the cocktail of medications I was receiving had been adjusted to a perfect level, or the nerve endings and pain receptors in my body had shut down. Perhaps it was a little of both. In any event, I suppose it didn't matter—the end result was a welcomed reprieve.

The door to my room was closed, and the ceiling lights were off. Just enough light shone through the partially opened blinds that I could tell it was overcast. Perfect hiking weather. There was a still, deep pool on the Siletz River that I used to fish on mornings like this. The steelhead trout is a crafty bugger, and I'd usually go through a half dozen or more hand-tied flies before I landed one that Connie would pronounce fit for her famous lemon butter pan fry.

I turned to see today's messages on the dry erase board. It was Friday, rain was likely, and the temperature would top out at sixty-three degrees. That's when I realized I wasn't alone; Connie was seated on the window bench. I didn't say anything because I wanted to enjoy watching her. She sat with her back against the window frame, her knees pulled up and her head turned toward the green trees and bushes outside. A mug of tea and a book lay on the small table beside her.

"A penny for your thoughts," I finally said. She turned her head slowly, and graced me with a soft smile.

"And a nickel for yours," she replied. She swung her legs off the bench, came over beside me and kissed my forehead. Then she pulled the chair close to my bed and sat down. She rested her hand on my arm. "Would you like some water?"

Connie held the straw to my lips, but I was only able to take a small sip.

"When did you get here?" I asked.

"Just a few minutes ago. I wanted to beat the rain, and see if you would be up for a visit from the children before they went to school this morning. Rachel will be here in a few minutes if you'd like to say hello."

"That's probably a good idea," I answered. I didn't have to say why.

"I'm told Gwen drew you another get well card. And Jimmy is bringing that old Indian arrowhead you gave him last year. He thought it would cheer you up to hold it again." She scooted a little closer. "I'm afraid I'm the only one who came to see you empty-handed this morning."

"Raise my bed a little, would you?" Connie activated the bed control for what I'm sure was the ten thousandth time. When I was at a forty-five degree angle I motioned for her to stop. "Now, what's this nonsense about not bringing me anything?" I said. "You think some fresh coffee or a cinnamon roll would be in order at this point?" I got the smile I hoped for, and another kiss. "How are the cherries looking this year?" I asked.

"Both of the trees are loaded. And the pioneer apple tree that you've been pruning and grafting the last few seasons is filling out, too. I actually think we might have apples this fall."

"That's good. And has Eric taken the tiller in for servicing yet? You'll want to have it ready to go in a few weeks if you're going to get the garden in on time."

"It's at the shop now," she said. "And I'm having a couple dozen bales of straw hay delivered next week so I can get the raised garden beds in, too."

"So there will be a Grammy Forrestal garden this year for the kids." I smiled at her. "I'm glad for that. They're going to need it more than ever this summer."

"We'll grow it big, Martin. Lots of flowers, and pumpkins too. The kids will each have their own small plot that they'll be responsible for watering and weeding and harvesting. You said that you wanted them to learn about the whole cycle of life and death and rebirth, my darling."

I had never wanted to squeeze my wife's hand as much as I wanted to at that moment. I strained to move my arm toward her, but the best I could do was wiggle my fingers a little. Connie noticed, and took my hand in hers—one of the many times she had anticipated some need of mine and taken care of it without being asked.

•••

ON OUR WEDDING DAY, Connie's mother gave us a small plaque inscribed with the Bible's most famous commentary on love. The plaque sat on our mantel for a few years until we painted the living room and relegated it to a knick-knack corner in the guest bedroom. When we built our craftsman home on Carmichael Street, the plaque got a further downgrade, this time to a box of old stuff that almost didn't make the cut when we loaded the moving van. The box ended up in the new basement, where it sat unnoticed for years. A few weeks before our fiftieth wedding anniversary, I was rummaging around and happened upon the box. When I cracked it open and discovered the plaque, I knew I'd found the perfect anniversary gift for my wife.

Our family and friends gathered at our home for a cookout on our anniversary. When it came time to open gifts, I held the plaque back until all of the other presents had been opened. Connie and I had agreed not to exchange gifts, so when I walked across the deck and handed her a small package she gave me the full raised-eyebrow treatment.

Our friends oohed and awed a little in anticipation of seeing a diamond bracelet or gold necklace spring out of the fancy wrapping paper. When Connie withdrew a plain wooden plaque from the tissue paper, and not an expensive bauble of some kind, our friends looked on with curiosity. Connie pulled off the letter that was taped to the plaque. As she read it in silence, her eyes filled with tears. When she was done reading, she blew me a kiss.

"Okay, come on," said Rachel. "We're all dying to know what it says."

Connie stood up beside the Adirondack chair I made for her on our twenty-fifth anniversary. The saving grace for that altogether unromantic present was the airline tickets to Hawaii taped to the chair. This year, however, there was no such prize. Connie looked at me. I nodded, and she began to read:

"To my dearest wife, friend, counselor and pal. Once two people have been together for fifty years, you would think that you would have run out of ways to say, 'I love you.' When we were starting out in our life together those words passed our lips dozens of times every day. Over the years, we said them less frequently, even though our love grew deeper. If I were to put my finger on a day when those three wonderful words were overtaken by other, even better ways of expressing our feelings for one another, I'd have to point to our tenth wedding anniversary. Do you remember? Eric had just been born—a celebration that we never expected given the miscarriages and the stillbirth…"

Connie stopped reading, and held the note to her chest. A friend handed her a tissue, and she wiped her eyes before continuing.

"And yet here we were, an 'old' married couple with a new baby, a small business and a big mortgage. Oh, and lots of bills. I remember what we had for dinner that night: tuna casserole with a crumbled potato chip crust. You gave me a book. I gave you a scarf. You put the baby to bed, and I put a record on that old turntable and we danced for hours. But, when I left for the lumberyard the next morning, it occurred to me that we didn't say 'I love you' the night before. Not once, and on our tenth anniversary to boot. Even so, I woke up on the first day of our eleventh year together happier, more content, and more excited to have you as my wife than I had ever been. As for the 'I love you' oversight, I figured that out, too. With every glance you gave me that night, you said it. When you scraped enough money together to buy that bottle of pretty bad wine from Mr. Magnini's delicatessen, you said it. And when you stuck a used birthday candle in the middle of the tuna casserole and lit it, you said it then, too."

She stopped reading and looked over at me for a moment. Then she glanced back down at the note and continued.

"For fifty wonderful years you have told me you love me with every cup of coffee you pour, every laugh you share, and every pinch you give me when no one is looking. Your eyes say 'I love you' every time they're open, and your mouth forms the words even when you're just asking me how my day went. You say 'I love you' each spring when you plant your flower boxes. And when

we started out and you had to stretch every dollar a hundred ways
from Sunday, you said you loved me enough to stick by me, no
matter what. It warms my heart to hear you say the words, but if
I lost my hearing tomorrow it wouldn't matter because you say 'I
love you' a hundred different ways every day.

"The day will come when you will say 'I love you, Martin,' for
the last time. Whenever that day may come, and however it may
happen, please do not fear that I cannot hear your words. As long
as I can feel your touch, as long as I can be in your presence as I
draw my last breath, I will hear you, and I will understand you, and
though my lips may not be able to form the words, I will answer
you."

It was quiet on the deck. Children played in the yard, and our dog
woofed as he romped along with them. Connie quietly scanned the note,
then walked over beside me, and took my arm. "There's more to Martin's
note," she told our guests, "but I'd like him to read it, if he doesn't mind."

I cleared my throat. I hadn't planned on this part being made public. A
couple dozen people were waiting, though, so I put on my glasses and read:

"Connie, no topic in history has been the subject of as much
attention as love. It seems like everyone has said their piece one
way or another down through the centuries, but the poems and
songs and books just keep on coming, so apparently the world is
still pretty interested. That's a good sign, don't you think? I'm not
qualified to write a sonnet or to compose a symphony for you.
Wish I could, my darling, but that wasn't the way I was built at
the factory. The good news is that a long time ago someone wrote
a perfect description of love for tongue-tied oafs like me. Just a
couple dozen words, so few that they fit onto that little wooden
plaque your mother gave us.

"I'm kind of glad we misplaced it for all those years. When we
put it on the mantel after our honeymoon, the words carved into it
were just a nice sentiment. I confess to you that I never gave them
much thought. Too busy with life, I guess. But when I was cleaning
out the basement and pulled that plaque out of the box, it suddenly
all made sense. It's taken me a good forty years to figure out what
the words meant, of course. I leaned against the washing machine
and read those words over and over—words written two thousand

years ago that felt like they were written that very morning—
words that felt like they had been written about you."

I held the plaque up for everyone to see, and then folded the note. I
didn't need a cheat sheet to finish what was in my heart. "These words
are sacred to many people," I said. "But I hope you don't mind if I take
the liberty of paraphrasing them a little on this special occasion." I looked
down at the plaque, and took Connie's hand.

"For fifty years…" Connie squeezed my hand, but I had to swallow
hard before I could go on. "For fifty years you have loved me patiently
and kindly. Not an easy thing to do with a husband as competitive and
opinionated as me. I have never heard you speak an envious word about
our friends' marriages, even though when we went through some rocky
times it looked like they were on top of the world. You have honored me
every day I have known you, and I can't think of a single time when you
put your feelings ahead of your family or friends. You are slow to anger. I
suppose the proof of that is that you are here beside me today." I adjusted
my glasses. "It says here that love keeps no record of wrongs. That's a good
thing, because if you had there wouldn't be enough trees in the forest to
make the paper to hold my record."

Connie hugged my arm, and kissed my cheek. I was too choked up to
think of what else to say, so I simply read the rest: "Love does not delight in
evil, but rejoices with the truth. Love always protects, always trusts, always
hopes, always perseveres."

I set the plaque on a table. "The last thing it says is: 'Love never fails.'"

•••

I HAD NEARLY DOZED OFF. Connie laid her arm on my shoulder. "Martin,
Rachel is here with the children. Would you like them to come in?"

"Please. Let me have a little water first." Connie held the straw to my
mouth. Then she applied some balm to my cracked lips. "Would you turn
on the lights, honey? That will be better for the kids."

Connie switched on the lights. I blinked a couple of times, and then
Gwen and Jimmy were standing beside my bed, with Rachel right behind
them. Gwen squeezed up against the bed rail, leaned over, and planted a
smooch on my cheek.

"Poppa Martin, you need to shave," she said.

"You don't want to see me with a beard? Maybe I could play Santa Claus in your school play."

"Oh, you're way too skinny for that," said Gwen. Then, in a tiny voice she said, "But next Christmas you'll be in heaven, won't you?"

Even the most courageous first graders know fear. Gwen was the bravest child I had ever known, but there was simply no way for her to really comprehend the finality and mystery of death. That gave me pause, and I wondered what sort of a job of that I had been doing myself. Gwen's arms were folded across her chest, but I could see that she was holding a picture.

"Did you draw something for me?" I asked.

She brightened. "Yes, it's a special picture for you to keep." She unfolded the paper and held it up for me to see. Two grown up stick figures were holding hands in a field of brightly colored flowers.

"It's very pretty, honey. But, who is the lady holding my hand?"

"Grampa, that's me, all grown up. Mama says that the next time I see you it will be when I go to heaven, and I'll be grown up by then."

My eyes welled up as they met hers. The simple beauty, love and ingenuousness of her statement kept me from forming words. The room was quiet.

Rachel whispered in Gwen's ear.

"Time for me to go to school," my granddaughter said. "We get to have inside recess because of the rain." Gwen touched my face. "I like your whiskers, Grampa. You should keep them. I love you."

Connie put her hand on Gwen's shoulder and gently guided her away from my bed. Jimmy stood silently, unsure of what to say or do. This was a big moment for a kindergartner.

"Say, young fella, I think I need to apologize to you," I said.

He crinkled his brow. "How come?"

"Well, when I was not much older than you, my grandfather gave me a genuine Indian arrowhead. He said that it came from a famous Indian war chief. It was my special treasure for my whole life. I wanted to give it to you, but when I looked for it this morning, it was nowhere to be found. I'm awfully sorry."

"Oh, no, Grampa, you didn't lose it. Gram gave it to me last week. It's right here." Jimmy unclenched his fist and stretched out his arm. The arrowhead sat in the middle of his palm.

"Well, I'll be," I said. "How about that. All this time that arrowhead has been safe and sound. I'm sure glad to know that."

"You can have it back if you want Grampa, if it makes you feel better."

"Are you kidding?" I said. "Which one of us do you think is more likely to run into a bunch of outlaw cattle rustlers today, you or me?"

He nodded. "I guess I might," said Jimmy. He closed his fist around the arrowhead.

"That's right, son. I don't run into many desperadoes at all around here. So, you hang onto that arrowhead in case you need it."

Jimmy grinned. He slipped the arrowhead into his pocket and joined his sister beside Connie. Rachel said she would be back, and a moment later my grandchildren were gone.

•••

AFTER THE CHILDREN LEFT, Nurse Marsden stopped in. She checked my vitals and removed one of my IV lines. Then she and Connie huddled in the corner for a few minutes. Afterwards, Connie shared the gist of their conversation. My condition was close to requiring a different level of care, which would have to be done in a different unit on the seventh floor. The move was scheduled for tomorrow morning.

"I never thought I'd be sad to leave this room," I said. "It's become my routine. I'm going to miss the nurses."

Connie straightened my blanket. "Let's deal with that tomorrow. Right now I want you to lie back and rest."

"Tell me first, how is Rachel doing with all of the recordings? Everything working out all right with them?"

"She's loaded them on her computer and backed them up, too," said Connie. "We won't lose any of your stories."

I moistened my lips with my tongue. Speaking was becoming increasingly difficult. Connie put some ice chips on a small spoon and slowly fed them to me. It helped.

"Connie, there's one story that I recorded on my third or fourth night here that I should give you some heads-up about."

My wife's eyes widened in mock astonishment. "Really? Something out of your past that I don't know about? Good thing you're telling me before the children hear it."

I smiled, and shook my head. "Maybe," I said. "Could be a lot of people's opinion of Martin Forrestal will change when they hear the story. I just wanted to prepare you, that's all."

"I'm all ears, darling. We're alone, so spill."

"I'm afraid it may disappoint you; it's not really all that exciting. In fact, if anything, it makes me look like a pretty big goof."

"Then why tell it?"

I motioned for more ice chips. "In this case, Connie, I think it will help to accomplish my objective, at least on the topic of love. I feel like I have talked enough about grown up, mature love. But, in my mind at least, that kind of love is a long time coming, and you usually only get there after you've taken your lumps in the romance department."

Connie poured a little more water into her cup from the carafe on the nightstand. She wasn't drinking coffee around me now, another one of those thoughtful little things she did for me every day.

"So whatever it is you're alluding to—it's part of how you discovered the real meaning of love?"

"Yes. And then some. I thought that if the kids knew that even their old, stable, boring Poppa Martin had once been a complete and utter fool for love, maybe they wouldn't beat themselves up so badly when the day comes that they pop their own tops the way I did mine. I mean, is there anyone you know who didn't do something monumentally stupid in the love department, at least once in their life?"

"Maybe my friends keep secrets as well as you do, Martin," she teased. "Oh, all right, yes, I'll grant you that most people probably shut down the rational sides of their brain and take some kind of flying leap into the romantic abyss. I think mine was in high school."

"Mine was a bit later," I said. "After the war, while I was in college. Guess that means I can't claim that the rigors of adolescence made me do it."

My wife's eyes opened wide. "It?"

I shook my head. "Made me get on a plane and fly to—"

"Argentina?" said Connie with the slyest of smiles.

"You know about Argentina? Did you already listen to the recording?"

Connie shifted in her chair. She was enjoying a special kind of inner chuckle that a husband only sees on those occasions when some story of his doesn't quite square up, or when the wife decides to put an end to the pain he is inflicting on himself by digging the hole deeper and deeper.

Connie rested her hand on my cheek. "Oh, darling, your mother told me about your Argentine adventure the first year we were married."

If my mouth hadn't been so dry I'm sure I would have sputtered. Instead, I asked for a few more ice chips. When I could finally form words, I said, "And you kept it secret for half a century? You never felt you needed an explanation? You weren't the least bit curious to know what kind of woman had the power to get me to drop everything on the spur of the moment and go off on a fool's errand all the way to South America?"

Connie's chuckle was getting dangerously close to an outright belly laugh. She leaned forward and ran her hand through my hair. "Martin, my husband, there are three things you need to know. First, everyone deserves to be young once. Until that first gray hair, you can be forgiven a lot. We weren't married. In fact, I hadn't even met you when you flew off to find Gracie."

"Graciela," I said. "It means 'graceful.'"

"She must have been something," said Connie.

"Well that's the thing, and part of the reason I want the children to know the story. I really didn't know her at all—I never said more than ten words to her. I couldn't tell you a thing about her sense of humor, her character, what she liked and disliked. I never got that far."

"Honey, you got to Buenos Aires," Connie said with a sweet smile. "Which brings up the second thing you need to know: there's almost nothing that warms a woman's romantic heart more than a story about a man who throws himself to the fates in the name of love, even when the odds against him are impossible. When your mother told me the story about you charging out of the university parking lot and booking the next flight to Argentina, I knew I'd picked myself the right kind of man. A man who wasn't afraid to be, what did you call it? A fool for love."

Now it was my turn to smile. "And the third thing?"

Connie took my hand. "The third thing, you big lug, is that you should have known that from the moment Constance Marie Ryan stood up in church in front of God and our families and friends and said 'I do,' that the past—both yours and mine—was closed and gone forever. All that mattered from that day forward was our future together."

•••

ONE BY ONE, the eighteen-cylinder engines on the Lockheed Constellation roared to life. Then the wheel chocks were pulled away and the forty-passenger Pan American Airways plane taxied away from its berth at Los Angeles International Airport and swung out onto the runway. When all four engines reached maximum RPM the propellers began to push us forward. In a moment we were hurtling toward a line of sand dunes that formed the outer marker barrier three hundred yards from the taxiway. The morning sky was blue and cloudless. The wheels lifted off the tarmac and the pilot began a slow, banking ascent to the southwest, over the Pacific Ocean.

I could make out the Channel Islands to the north, and Catalina Island directly below us. When the stewardess announced that we had reached our cruising altitude of twenty-four thousand feet I unbuckled my seatbelt and retrieved a book from my bag. I also asked myself, for the hundredth time in the past twenty-four hours, if I knew what I might be getting myself in for.

Two days earlier I was an ordinary twenty-three-year-old ex-GI. I split my time between running a logging crew that supplied fir and cedar to the sawmill my father and I ran, and attending school part-time at Willamette University in Salem.

Today was Thursday, and Professor Jepson was probably lecturing the class on plate tectonics and earthquakes right now. And after geology, I should be headed across the quad to history. But she wouldn't be there. That's why I was on a Pan Am flight to Mexico City, instead of sitting in class, and why I'd be transferring to connecting flights that would take me on to Bogota, Lima, and finally, after forty-eight hours of small airports and smaller planes, to Buenos Aires.

I had no idea how I would reach my final destination after I landed in the Argentine capitol. My final destination wasn't so much a place as it was the fulfillment of a quest. I had to see her again. I had to know if she felt the way I did.

•••

WHEN I WALKED INTO my world history class on the first day of spring term, I was focused. Like most of my fellow GIs, I was several years older than most of the student body. For those of us who had been to war, college was all business, a means to an end. A better job, a better future. As a group we tended to stay to ourselves and not mix it up much at football games or parties. We were serious, sober and committed to achieving concrete objectives. At least, that's how I would have described myself until the moment Graciela walked through the door and sat beside me.

She was tall, with thick black hair that fell to the middle of her back. Her olive complexion and sapphire-blue eyes were unlike anything I had ever seen. She sat down next to me, placed some of her books on the shelf below her desk, turned, and said hello. That's all it took. I heard her say her name. I think I answered, but I'm not exactly sure if my words made any sense. The professor solved my dilemma by introducing himself and getting the class underway. I tried to focus on his words, but it was hopeless. I was done for.

I didn't work up the nerve to talk to her until the fourth class session. The professor was late that day, and we chatted for five or six minutes until he rushed into class. Her full name was Graciela de San Martín. Her family owned a cattle ranch in the Cordoba province of Argentina, and she was here by virtue of a family tradition going back two centuries. Every member of her family studied abroad for at least one year. Before the war, she would have gone to university in France or Italy. But in 1948, Europe was still clearing out from under the rubble, and so her family decided to send her to Oregon, where a cousin had emigrated to start his own cattle business in the '20s.

Work and school and my deepening infatuation with Graciela made the weeks fly by. I wanted to talk to her before Spring break to see if she might like to see a movie or go to a dance, but I just couldn't make myself say the words. We sat side by side during lectures and tests, and that was it. Had I been paying attention, I would have given more thought to the fact that Graciela came to class equipped with an accessory that none of the other students possessed—a bodyguard. When the professor dismissed us and our class headed out into the corridor, a thick man in a dark suit would materialize and fall into step a few feet behind her. I had seen him of course, but in the throes of whatever the heck I was drowning in when I was in her presence, I never put one and one together.

When class reconvened on the first Tuesday after Spring break, Graciela was not there. I assumed she'd stayed on vacation an extra day or two, but when she didn't show up on Thursday, I knew something was wrong.

All the registrar's office would tell me was that she had withdrawn from school and returned home.

I left the registrar's office and walked right to the library. I grabbed the biggest book of South American maps I could find and opened the oversized volume to the section on Argentina. I found the province of Cordoba quickly; but the town she was from, what was it? Paz something or other. Carlos Paz? I ran my fingers over the map until I found it: Villa Carlos Paz, a small town on the slopes of the Sierra Chicas mountains. There wasn't much around the town for miles, and if my understanding of topographical symbols was correct there was some pretty rugged terrain between Buenos Aires and Graciela's hometown. I slammed the book shut. A few miles of bad road wasn't going to stop me.

I was going to see her again. That's all there was to it.

•••

THE FLIGHTS FROM COLOMBIA to Peru and on to Buenos Aires over the next two days were a blur of customs officials, increasingly bad weather and smaller airplanes with crews and passengers right out of central casting. I didn't speak a word of Spanish. I had a lot of time to myself. It was a bit difficult for me to keep track of exactly how this had transpired.

I can still see the look on my father's face when I told him that I was going to South America. Today. That look went double for my mom.

"You don't really know this girl?" my mother asked.

"No, not really," I replied.

"You haven't dated her?"

"Nope."

"Do you know her family?"

"No."

"Do you know where they live?"

"I don't have a clue."

"Are they expecting you?"

"No, they don't know I'm coming."

My mother dried her hands, and set down her dishtowel. She came over to me, and placed her hands on my shoulders. She looked up into my eyes and asked, "Are you sure, honey?"

"I'm as sure as I can be, Mom. I don't know what's going to happen.

I just know that I need to see her again."

"And you're prepared to travel thousands of miles, to another continent where you don't know anyone, don't speak the language and don't even know if you'll be welcome?"

"That's pretty much how it is, Mom."

My mother hugged me. There were tears in her eyes. "When it comes to love, Marty, none of us are experts. Don't get your hopes too high. Be safe." She had said everything she could possibly say.

When I cleared customs in Buenos Aires two days after leaving Los Angeles, my hopes were higher than ever. I visited the Traveler's Aide kiosk and got train and bus timetables for Cordoba. Two hours later I was on a train on the first leg of a nine hundred mile journey. The car was crowded with students on their fall break. Their energy and enthusiasm made me feel more optimistic than ever that my mission would succeed.

We reached the city of Cordoba early the next morning. As in my stops in Colombia and Peru, I had no time to play tourist. I exited the train, crossed the small terminal, and walked right up to the ticketing window of the bus line.

Whatever the train ride from Buenos Aires to Cordoba may have lacked in comfort and style, it was the lap of luxury compared to Autobus Paz, a rickety green and white relic of a bus with torn seats, broken windows and a suspension designed for inflicting maximum back pain. The bus was packed with farm folk, noisy children, chicken coops, a couple of goats and at least one pig. Under normal circumstances, I would have found another way to get across the mountains. But now, here, only a day or so away from being reunited with Graciela, I would have endured the putrid fumes of the deepest sulfur pit in Hades.

The narrow dirt and gravel path we traveled for two grueling days and nights wound through landscapes that would have kept Salvador Dali awake at night. The rolling countryside was dotted with farms. For some reason, it seemed like every farmer on the continent had picked this week to light controlled burns to clear the land of trees and brush. Time and again we passed through man-made firestorms, where thick smoke poured through the broken windows, rendering the passengers and the driver teary-eyed and hoarse from coughing. Other than that, the scenery was utterly spectacular.

Each time we neared another rope and wire bridge slung precariously over a deep gorge, the driver had us all debark the bus and walk across the creaking wood trestles to the other side. The combination of our weight and the bus was just too much, he said. No one complained.

After two days of listening to grinding gears and patiently waiting at the endless turnouts while the overheated engine cooled, we emerged from the mountains, and snaked down a winding series of switch backs to the valley floor. From there we followed a tumbling river through low-lying farms for two hours until we reached the town of Villa Carlos Paz just before sundown. The bus driver pointed me to a decent hotel, where after four nights of fitful sleep on trains, buses and airplanes, I was able to rest and clean up for my meeting with Graciela.

During breakfast in the hotel restaurant the next morning, I met a cattle buyer who was headed into the backcountry. His route took him right through the village of San Martín, which was the closest place I could think of to Graciela's home. When I told him my destination he offered to give me a lift if I wanted to share the expense of his hired car.

The cattle buyer was glad for the company, and pleased to have the opportunity to practice his broken English. We set out from Villa Carlos Paz through the hill country. An hour later we swept down into a broad pastured valley bounded on both sides by snow-capped mountains. The nearer we came to village San Martín the more anxious I became. How would Graciela react when I showed up on her doorstep? What would her parents say? For that matter, would she even agree to talk with me? That thought set me on edge.

Three hours into our drive I took over at the wheel. The road was straight and level, and the countryside was unchanging. The cattle buyer said that it was unusually warm and clear for April, and that the region would typically get frost and even a little snow by the first of May. We stopped along the road at midday and enjoyed a lunch of steak sandwiches and fruit packed for us by the hotel. My companion took over again, and we drove for three more hours toward the northwest. I had not seen a house for more than two hundred fifty miles. Here and there would be a lonely outbuilding or pole barn, which my new friend told me were used to store hay in the winter.

When the sun settled above the crest of the western mountains, the cattle buyer told me that we were only about an hour from San Martín.

There was an inn there, and he was sure they'd be able to put us up for the night. I felt a mixture of relief and excitement. Tonight I would go to sleep in San Martín. Tomorrow I would present myself at Graciela's door.

As the last purple shadows arced across the valley I saw the lights from the village. The spires of the church and the handful of buildings along the short stretch of street that was downtown San Martín had a distinctive European look. When we pulled into the parking area behind the inn, I asked my friend if he knew where Estancia San Martín was located.

"You don't know?" he said.

"I've never been here," I replied. "I'm just hoping to see—" I paused. "To see a friend."

"You must not know this friend too well, Señor Forrestal, if you do not know of Estancia San Martín. Do you remember the large whitewashed rock with the SM painted on it, next to the highway right outside of Villa Carlos Paz?" he asked.

"Sure," I said. "Kind of an unusual marker."

We walked to the door of the inn, which was framed by flowering bougainvillea and green shutters. "They aren't unusual in Argentina," he said. "At least not out here. They are used to mark the boundary line of an estancia. The SM is the marker of the San Martín family."

I'm sure my jaw dropped. "But we passed that boundary marker nine or ten hours ago."

"Yes, nearly four hundred kilometers back. You have been traveling on San Martín land all day. And you could travel just as far along the road to the west tomorrow and still be on their land." He opened the door, and light from the inn spilled out onto the steps. "The San Martíns are royalty in these parts, one of the wealthiest families in Argentina, probably in all of South America."

That knocked the air out of me. I stumbled into the oak-trimmed lobby of the inn in a kind of daze. The proprietor and his wife came from the dining room to greet us. If I hadn't known better I would have thought we were checking into a ski resort in the Swiss Alps. Otto and Nelda Mendoza looked as if they'd just stepped out of a European travel poster.

I registered, and then said goodbye to the cattle buyer, who would be leaving before dawn. I went to my room to clean up, and came downstairs to enjoy my first true Argentine dinner.

My mind raced with thoughts of seeing Graciela and so I didn't enjoy the open-fire grilled steak as much as I should have. I watched the flames dance in the stone fireplace and listened to the plaintive whisper of the pampas wind brush against the outer walls of the inn as I chewed over what I had learned that day. Graciela wasn't just another foreign student completing her studies in the States. She was the daughter of one of the richest men in the country—maybe the world. That explained the man who shadowed her around the campus of Willamette University.

I stirred my coffee, and tried to script out what I would say when Graciela came to the door. I concluded that just saying, "Hello, I was in the neighborhood and thought I'd drop in," probably wouldn't do it.

There weren't many guests at the inn. Otto and his wife brought out a small tray of chocolates and asked if they could join me. We talked about the history of the inn, and about how their business was only now coming back to life three years after the war. They did most of their business in the spring, when well-heeled sportsmen from around the world converged on the area for some of the best trout fishing on earth. The cozy atmosphere, great food and friendly conversation lifted my spirits, and gave me renewed hope.

Otto put another log on the fire and he and his wife prepared to say goodnight. Then, almost as an afterthought, Otto said, "You are not here to buy cattle?"

"No, no cattle for me," I said. "I'm actually here to see a friend."

"Really?" said Nelda. "All the way to the ends of the earth just to see a compadre. That's very nice."

"She's not exactly what I would call a compadre," I answered.

"She?" said Otto. "Ah, I think I understand. Our young Mr. Forrestal is on an errand of love."

I'm sure I blushed. After six days of non-stop travel across two continents, this was the first time I had shared the nature of my errand with anyone.

"We know all of the young women in the village," said Mrs. Mendoza. "But who among them is so remarkable that you would leave your university and travel thousands of miles to see her?"

I took the bait. "Her name is Graciela," I said.

"Graciela?" said Otto.

"Yes, Graciela de San Martín. She was in my history class at the university."

The room felt suddenly cold. Otto and Nelda shared a concerned glance. Nelda set down her tray and covered her mouth with one hand.

"Young man," said Otto in a near whisper. "Did you say that you have come here from the United States just to see Miss San Martín? And that she does not know you are coming?"

The change in my hosts' demeanor was perplexing; a moment ago they had been the picture of international hospitality. At the mention of Graciela's name, however, the atmosphere in the room became more like a police interrogation cell than the dining room of a rustic country inn.

I answered in a measured voice: "We are friends. She withdrew from school last week, and I simply wanted to see her to—"

"To?" said Otto.

I didn't reply. What could I say? That I had been so carried away with feelings for a young woman I hardly knew that when she disappeared I cast everything aside and raced half way to the South Pole to find her? Or maybe, that at the age of twenty-three, this war veteran and college student was tired of life alone, and finally decided, in one moment of optimistic delirium, to do something about it?

The fire was burning low. I had no answer for Otto. I had none for myself. Nelda turned and walked into the kitchen. Otto patted my shoulder. In a fatherly tone he said, "Love may conquer all, young friend, and it may have a mind of its own, but in coming here you might have ridden into a storm. Go to bed. This will all be sorted out soon enough."

I rose and walked to the stairs leading up to the guest rooms. When I reached the landing at the top I looked back down into the lobby. Nelda was clearing my table and Otto was dialing the phone on the reception desk. I lay awake for a long time, reliving over and over the path that brought me to this remote South American village.

•••

SOMEONE WAS POUNDING ON MY DOOR. There were three loud knocks, then four. Whoever it was waited a moment and then pounded again, more forcefully this time. I rolled on my side and looked at the nightstand clock: it was 5:30 in the morning. Two more ferocious knocks were followed by what sounded like a boot kicking the wood.

I hopped out of bed, pulled on my shirt and pants, and stood near the door. "What the heck is going on?" I shouted.

"Señor Forrestal, open this door. Now." I did not recognize the voice.

"Who are you?" I asked.

Then I heard Otto's voice. "It is alright, Mr. Forrestal. But these gentlemen need to speak with you. Please open the door."

I swung open the door. Four men, including the innkeeper, were crowded outside my room in the narrow hall. Otto stepped aside, and the other three men stepped past me and into my room. Otto remained in the hall.

Two of the men immediately began going through my things. "Hey, what do you think you're doing?" I said.

Were these the police? The third man motioned for me to sit. He was around thirty-five or forty, medium height, squarely built, a guy who looked like he could take care of himself in a tough spot. He wore a blue serge suit, and one of the extra-wide ties preferred by South Americans.

The third man pulled a cigarette case from his jacket. He offered one to me, and when I declined, he lit one for himself. "Please, sit," he repeated. The other two men paid us no attention, and continued to sort through my bag. I sat on the edge of my bed.

"I am Gilberto O'Neil," said the third man. "Yes, O'Neil is an Irish name. My grandfather was an Irish immigrant. And you are Martin Forrestal."

I nodded.

"Well, Mr. Martin Forrestal, you have managed to get the attention of a great many people this morning." Gilberto picked a bit of tobacco from his teeth. "Would you please tell me what you are doing here in San Martín?"

I wasn't feeling terribly cooperative at that moment. "Would you please tell me who you are," I answered, "and why your men are searching my luggage?"

Gilberto smiled. "Of course, where are my manners. I am here this morning in my capacity as Director of Security for Estancia San Martín. These," he motioned to the two men who had finished ransacking my luggage and were now standing at the ready by the window, "are my associates Luis and Raphael."

The thugs gave me a cursory nod.

"I don't understand," I said, "what have I done, why are you here?"

O'Neil pulled the chair out from the small writing desk. He turned it around, sat down, and rested his arms on the chair back. "It is not a question of what you have done, my friend. It is a matter of what you intend to do."

"I am here to see a friend," I said. "That's all."

"You are referring to Miss San Martín?"

"Of course I am. And if you've spoken with Otto you already know that."

"You were in school with her?"

"Yes, at Willamette University, in Oregon. World History, with Professor DeSantis."

"And you and Miss San Martín were romantically involved?"

My temper flared. "What we were—or are for that matter—is none of your business." The tone of my response brought Luis and Raphael over by the bed, but Gilberto sent them back to their posts with a wave of his hand.

Gilberto leaned forward. In a hushed tone he said, "My business, young Forrestal, is to protect the San Martín family from any and all threats. The methods by which I accomplish that task are of no consequence to the police, the army, or my employer. Do you understand?"

I was beginning to. I was a stranger in a foreign country where none of the protections of the Constitution applied. I was in the middle of a private fiefdom that contained more acreage than the state of Connecticut, on an estate owned by a man of vast wealth and power. All that—in a nation run by a corrupt military dictatorship where the death of a lovesick American tourist wouldn't even make the front page of the Cordoba newspapers. To make matters worse, it seems I was being regarded as a potential kidnapper, or murderer maybe, by a man who could have me thrown to the bottom of one of the rocky gorges I had crossed two days earlier. I saw my face in the mirror above the dresser. Martin, what in the heck have you gotten yourself in to?

Gilberto lit another cigarette. He was in no hurry. "It is a simple question, my friend: were you and Miss San Martín romantically involved?"

"No."

"Are you certain."

I shook my head, almost sheepishly. "That's one of the few things I am certain of right this minute," I said.

"You did not date her?"

"No."

"No phone calls or visits, no letters to her while she stayed with her cousin in Oregon?"

"No, none of that."

Gilberto's expression turned quizzical. "And yet, here you are, thousands of miles from home, in a place you were not invited to, in a country you do not know. That is," he struggled for the right word, "an astonishment?"

I don't know why I laughed. Perhaps Gilberto's choice of word, perhaps my realization of how absurd and dangerous my situation was. Whatever the reason, I couldn't help it. I began to laugh, and shake my head from side to side. It took a few seconds for me to collect myself.

Gilberto seemed amused, which I hoped was a good sign. Luis and Raphael leaned against the wall, waiting, I suppose, for their boss to either signal them to stuff me into the trunk of their car, or to do whatever it was that "associates" did in this kind of situation.

"I made a bad choice of word," Gilberto said. "And yet, Martin, you can appreciate that a man in my position, charged as I am with the protection of a very wealthy and important family, must have answers. And those answers must be exact, and they must be true."

I nodded. That much I understood.

"What you would have me believe is that you fell in love with a young woman you barely knew. A woman who you say did not invite your attention or affection in any way. You were not lovers. In truth, you were barely friends." Gilberto stubbed out his cigarette in an ashtray and lit another. "You sat beside her in class for a few weeks. You did not know her family story or position. You simply fell in love."

"That's about the size of it," I said.

"You are a veteran of the war?" asked Gilberto.

I nodded.

"And were you wounded?"

I nodded again. "With your permission," he said, "may I see?"

I had no idea why my wounds interested him, but complete cooperation seemed like a good idea at that point. I removed my shirt and trousers so that he could see the bullet scars that creased my stomach, back and shoulder, and the shrapnel wounds on my legs.

"You still have pain?" asked O'Neil.

"Yes, often," I replied.

Gilberto motioned for me to get dressed. As I did, I noticed that Luis and Raphael were looking at me in a whole new light.

Gilberto put out his cigarette. "Señor Forrestal," said Gilberto, "I believe you. And I believe that you are a man of honor. You are also a brave man, as your wounds testify. Here it is considered a great testament to a man's character that he has faced his nation's enemies in battle. In another life, in some other circumstance, a young woman like Graciela would be fortunate to have you for her husband." Gilberto stood up. "But in this life, that cannot be. Your world and that of the San Martíns are not simpatico."

Luis and Raphael came over and assumed positions at either side of the bed. Gilberto walked to the door. He straightened his tie and buttoned his suit jacket. "Someday you will tell the story of your pilgrimage for love to your children, Martin Forrestal. When you do, I hope that you will not make excuses. A man who follows only his mind and never his heart is not fully a man." He nodded to Luis. "And now I will wish you safe travels, and good fortune in all that you do." He turned to go.

"Mr. O'Neil, excuse me," I said. "I'm not sure what's going on here, about Graciela—"

He paused in the doorway. "Graciela will go on with her life, as you will with yours. She will never know that you were here, and you will not attempt to contact her. The San Martíns have a long reach, my friend, and a longer memory. Chalk this day up to experience, and be thankful that we are always hospitable—on the first visit."

With that, O'Neil was gone. His words were still sinking in as I turned to see Luis and Raphael packing my bag. "You have time to shower and shave," said Luis. "And then we must go."

Fifteen minutes later I shook Otto's hand and left the inn with Raphael and Luis. My bill had been paid by O'Neil, and Nelda had packed a lunch for me. I climbed into the front seat of the car beside Luis. Raphael sat in the back. I assumed we were going to a bus station, or perhaps they were going to drive me into Villa Carlos Paz. To my surprise, the car turned south when we left the inn, not north toward town. We drove in silence for about thirty minutes until we rounded a tree-lined curve and turned onto a gravel road that meandered through low hills for several miles. We approached a guard-shack, and were waved right through. Several low buildings were strung along a runway, where a pilot was doing a pre-flight check on a dun-colored Stinson Reliant monoplane. Luis pulled up next to the plane, and we got out of the car. Raphael grabbed my bag and threw it into the luggage compartment while Luis talked to the pilot.

Gilberto's associates shook my hand and wished me well, and a few minutes later the pilot and I were airborne.

I was flown to Cordoba, where another associate of O'Neil's was waiting when the plane landed. He drove me directly to the train station, and handed me a package containing a train ticket to Buenos Aires, a voucher for a hotel near the airport, and airline tickets for connecting flights all the way back to Portland, Oregon. All paid for by Graciela's family. It had taken me six days to travel from Salem to the South American village of San Martín. I would return in half the time.

I had been a fool for love. And yet, as the train pulled from the station and built up speed, I had no regrets. O'Neil was right about the importance of following one's heart. I looked at my reflection in the train window. The fellow who stared back was wiser and more confident about the future. If that was what a fool for love looked like, I could live with the title.

•••

NURSE MARSDEN INVITED CONNIE to help bathe me and change my bedding this afternoon. I had not been able to take solid food for four days, and yesterday I had finished only half of one protein shake. I would be moved to a higher-level care floor tomorrow. Connie was asked if there would be any changes to my advanced care directive but we'd agreed there would be no extraordinary measures taken.

When my prostate cancer blazed back to life, all but the last sentence in the final paragraph of my story was complete. Now, only one word of the three-word sentence that would close that paragraph remained unwritten. The first two words—one identifying the month, the other the year—were authored. They lacked only the placement of the day between them to complete the sentence, the paragraph, the chapter and the story.

"Hello, Dad."

Eric materialized at the side of my bed. That's how everyone was coming into my line of sight now. I couldn't hear them come through the door, and with the ceiling lights dimmed again, I couldn't make out much more than the blurry forms and images across the room.

My bed was elevated enough so that people didn't have to lean over and stare straight down into my face. "Eric, I'm glad you're here."

He gave me a gentle kiss on my forehead. A feeling of warmth flowed through me.

"Moving day tomorrow," said my son. "Rachel and I are going to be here so we can help you settle into your new digs upstairs."

"I'll be glad for the company," I said. "Son, would you mind moving my arm? It gets numb lying dead for hours."

Eric's eyes were moist as he lifted my arm and rested it across my belly. I could only imagine what it must have been like for him to see me helpless in my hospital bed. When Eric was in the second grade I placed first in the wood-chopping contest at the Albany Timber Carnival in a competition against a field of entrants from all over North America. I went through four rounds of competition, chopping through each twenty-four-inch log with a single bladed axe in under a minute. Eric carried my ribbon and trophy around for weeks.

Now, the dying shell that lay before him was shrunken and atrophied. I couldn't even get out of bed to go to the bathroom.

Rachel appeared behind Eric. She put her hands on his shoulders. "We love you, Dad," she said.

My mouth was too dry to reply, but my tear-filled eyes spoke for me. Connie leaned over from the other side of the bed. She applied some more balm to my lips, and poured a little water into my mouth.

"There is a manila envelope in my desk, in the center drawer," I said in a voice I barely recognized. "It's addressed to you, Eric. There's a letter in it for you, and another one for Rachel to share with the kids. It's also got my favorite picture from your wedding, and a good picture of the kids and I on the tractor when we were building that landscaping mound for Mom in the pasture. Put that one in a frame for the kids, would you? Jimmy was so proud to be up in the seat, and Gwen has her hands on the wheel like she's ready to take on the world. They're such good children..." My voice gave out.

I slept.

•••

I HEARD MAC MCGUIRE'S VOICE. I opened my eyes to see my doctor and his wife Charlene talking with Connie over by the window.

"Can I join in?" I asked.

They came over to my bed, and out of habit Mac checked my pulse and scanned the diagnostic monitors behind my head.

"We're headed to Corvallis for dinner. Thought we'd stop in and see if you'd like to come along," he said.

"Nothing would suit me better," I whispered. "But it sounds like I need to stick around here to pack my bags; I'm being evicted from this apartment."

"At least it's a move upstairs, pal. Time to let someone who is actually sick move in to this room and send the featherbedder somewhere he can't make trouble for the nursing staff."

I nodded. There weren't many physicians like Mac any longer. He was one of the last true country doctors. You can't heal the body without nurturing the spirit. For over thirty years he had done both for me.

Charlene leaned down and kissed my cheek, and then she and Connie moved over by the door. I turned my head slightly to the left, indicating that Mac should put his head down closer to me. I struggled to speak.

"Watch over Connie, would you Mac? Make sure she takes care of herself."

"Count on me, Martin."

"Now, you kids drive safely," I said. "Rain's kicking up again."

Mac took my hand in both of his. "You travel safely yourself, my friend."

Connie left to walk Mac and Charlene down to the lobby, but I was only alone for a moment. Nurse Marsden, the dependable, reliable, unflappable rock of the hospital's fifth floor, came in to check my various attachments and connections. She gave me a little water.

"You've been good to my family," I told her. "Thank you so much."

She lifted my left hand and held it in hers. "This has been my calling for a long time, Martin. I'm in the healing business. But you're not the only Forrestal patient I've been caring for; your wife, your children and your grandchildren will be under my watch until the last, especially Connie."

She gently squeezed my hand. "How about we shine you up a little bit for your wife?"

Nurse Marsden washed my face and combed my hair, made a final adjustment to my IV, straightened my covers, and then she whisked out of my room to care for some other lucky fifth floor resident.

•••

CONNIE RETURNED A FEW MINUTES LATER. She opened the blinds so that I could watch the last rays of sunshine pierce the blanket of rain-gray clouds covering the valley. A single golden beam glanced off the leaves of the cherry tree as if to say, look, I have found a refuge from the dying of the light. A moment later the clouds closed.

My wife pulled her chair parallel to my bed, lowered the side rail, and scooted as close as she could to me. "But, you're on the wrong side," I said. "You always sleep on the other side."

"You know," she said, "that has always been one of the great mysteries of marriage. Why do people pick one side of the bed over the other, and stay there every night for the rest of their lives?"

"Connie, I never thought this day would come."

She touched my face. "But we both knew it would—that sooner or later one of us would have to be here."

I managed a weak smile. "No, not that," I said. "I've always known that part. I mean I never thought the day would come when we would run out of things to talk about. And yet here we are, pondering the mysterious forces that make a man choose one side of the bed, while his wife chooses the other."

Connie's quiet laugh made my struggle to form words worth the effort. I turned my head. She anticipated my request and held the glass up for me to drink. I pulled a sip through the straw.

"Thank you," I said after a moment. I meant those simple words with the full force of my being, meant them in the broadest sense. There was so much to thank Connie for. Even if I had all the time in the world, I wouldn't know where to begin. I didn't have all the time in the world.

I looked into her eyes. She smiled softly and held my gaze.

"I love you," I said. That about summed it up.

"I love you," she said.

She reached her arm over me and leaned in, holding us together. I closed my eyes.

•••

THE NIGHTSTAND CLOCK said 4:47 AM. Connie was sleeping in the padded chair beside my bed; someone had covered her with a blanket during the night. The window blinds were still open. The black fabric of the night sky was lightening around the edges. I wondered if there would be sun today.

Connie stirred. She opened her eyes and caught me watching her. She removed the blanket and leaned over with a glass of water. My eyes assented, and she placed the straw between my lips. I could only take a small sip.

"Good morning, sweetheart," I said. "Not the most comfortable bed you have there."

She rose and stretched, then disappeared into the bathroom. She returned just as Nurse Leticia was completing her paperwork to hand me over to the day shift.

"What time is the moving van coming this morning?" I asked Connie after the nurse departed.

"Around nine. Eric and Rachel will be here for the big event. The pastor is coming this morning, too. Busy day ahead."

An aide brought Connie a cup of coffee. She stood to take it over to the table by the window, but I stopped her. "Not today, Connie. I appreciate that you haven't been drinking coffee around me, but this morning, how about you relax next to me and enjoy it?"

"Only if you will drink some of your shake," she said.

"I'll do my level—" an invisible hand pushed hard on the center of my chest. I sucked in my breath, and my voice went.

"Martin? Honey, what's happening?"

Then, as suddenly as it had begun, the pressure eased and was gone. "Fine, I'm fine," I said. "Just a little spasm. No need to call for the cavalry."

Connie took my hand. I could barely feel her touch. We sat quietly, watching the world come to light outside the window. When her coffee was finished, Connie turned her chair around and pulled it closer, making it easier for her to hold my hand.

"I was thinking about something last night," she said. "About your trip to Argentina."

"You couldn't find a slapstick comedy on TV with a happier ending?"

She laughed. "I think you'll like this," she said. "You know that my brother Tom was an aircraft mechanic with TWA in the '50s."

I nodded.

"One of the first planes that he worked on was the Lockheed Constellation, the same plane you flew on the longest legs of your journey to South America and back. He loved that plane, said that in flight it looked like a sleek dolphin cutting through the clouds. He told me that the flight crews loved that aircraft so much that they gave the Constellation a special nickname. Martin, they called that plane a 'Connie.' And they called her 'Connie' with affection."

My own Connie kissed me on the lips, and kept her face just above mine. "You flew off on the wildest romantic adventure of your life with Connie, and it was Connie who brought you safely home again, my dear husband."

I motioned for water. "I didn't know about the nickname," I was finally able to say. "But it is a perfect ending to the story. Just one thing though."

Connie brought her face down against my cheek. "Yes, my darling?"

"My trip to South America was more misadventure than anything else. But I have had a true romantic adventure, Connie. The greatest one any man could ask for. A lifetime—"

Connie squeezed my hand.

For an instant, everything was still. The sun was rising; the sky outside was streaked with warmth and color. Then, from deep inside my chest a hand reached up and took my heart in an iron grip. Sharp, biting pain and pressure pushed the air from my lungs. Connie reached for the emergency call button, but before she could summon help I gathered what strength I could, and shook my head.

Connie understood. She hovered over me, and cupped my face in her hands. She looked deep into my eyes, which were watery and blurred. I tried to breathe. A thousand feet above my body I could make out Connie's face. There was no fear in her eyes. No worry. Only tenderness. Only love.

I tried to tell her I loved her, but my body would not obey. I told her with my eyes.

Connie was speaking, but I could not make out her words. My head pounded, my chest felt ready to burst, but I held her eyes in mine. She was mouthing something over and over, slowly and clearly, the same words again and again, but I heard only the sound of blood pounding in my head. I tried desperately to focus my eyes to read her lips. I strained to speak but could only gasp for air. Connie's lips were still forming words high above my face. I was granted an instant of perfect clarity, and I heard her: "I love you."

The hand came again. There was no pain, only a great pressure that took the form of enveloping warmth. Connie's tear-streaked face receded higher and higher above me. I could no longer feel the touch of her hands on my face. I could feel nothing.

The rising sun went dark.

•••

A SMALL PACKAGE WAS DELIVERED to the lumberyard one summer afternoon. It was postmarked from Sisters, a ranch town on the eastern slope of the Oregon Cascades. Inside was a note, and an object wrapped in wax paper. I opened the note first. It was from a Mr. Wilson, the doctor who accompanied the rescue party up the mountain in July 1939 after the freak summer blizzard dropped a mountain of ice and snow on Scout Troop 11, and very nearly killed us all.

Doc Wilson said that he had recently retired, and was now spending his time hiking and photographing the spectacular Cascade Range. On a hike the week before, he and his wife had overnighted at Camp Lake, the same place my friends and I had pitched our tents the night the blizzard swept down on us.

The next morning they were going to return to the trailhead, but at the last minute Doc Wilson decided to head up the slope to see if he could find the entrance to the cave that had sheltered our group from the worst of the storm.

"It took several hours of hard, uphill going to find the cave," he wrote. "And I should add that my wife wasn't altogether happy about the detour, though she did marvel at how you and those other boys had made it up that mountainside in the middle of that torrential blizzard. When I found the tiny cave entrance under the rock outcropping, I switched on my flashlight and crawled right in. Twenty-five years on, I could still see evidence of your campfire. I kicked around the rocks a little, and saw a glint of metal in my flashlight beam. I figured it belonged to one of you boys, and so I tracked your address down. Perhaps you can return it to its rightful owner. —G. Wilson."

I unwrapped the wax paper to find a weathered brass pocket compass. The cover was nicked and dented, but when I opened it the glass crystal was as shiny as new. The compass rose was bright blue and red, and the needle swung to magnetic north. I closed the cover and held it in my hand. Then I opened a desk drawer and put it away. I turned back to my work, when a sudden thought made me bolt upright. I yanked open the drawer, grabbed the compass, and turned it over. The inscription I had hoped to find was there:

"To Patrick O'Hagan.
May you always find your way home.
Love, Mother.
July 1939."

I held the compass for a long time. I missed my best friend every day.

My eyes closed, and I found myself outside, under the bright light of the warm sun. The sky was blue and cloudless. A soft breeze rustled the trees, and I heard water rushing over stones in an alpine creek. I walked along a narrow path that wound between a pair of boulders before opening up into a wide green meadow. Five canvas tents were lined up near the stream. My friends were fishing along the bank. I came closer, enjoying the feel of the warm sun on my back. Just past the tents I saw Nate Holden perched on a rock reading a book. He pulled his pipe from his mouth, waved in my direction, and motioned for me to grab a fishing pole. I heard the screech of a kestrel hawk and saw him swoop low across the water. Then something pushed against my back. I whirled around and found myself face to face with Patrick, who had just poked me with a pair of fishing poles.

"Waiting for a special invitation, Marty?" He grinned and handed me a pole. "There's fat trout in that creek, and I'm up at bat in the kitchen tonight. How about we land ourselves a feast?"

Patrick's smile was brighter than the noonday sun dancing on the surface of the mountain stream. I threw an arm around his shoulder, and we walked together to the water's edge.

THE END

ACKNOWLEDGMENTS

What Matters takes place in a hospital, and the twenty-four hour a day bustle of medical activity infuses the narrative. While the care delivered to terminally-ill Martin Forrestal is destined not to save his life but to ease his passing, it is, nonetheless, the sanctity of life and the honor that it should be accorded that tops the list of what matters for the medical professionals whom we consulted in writing this book.

Many thanks go to G.R. Wilson, MD, for his medical consultation and insightful recommendations. In his decades of service as a Family Physician in rural Oregon (including on a personal level for some of us involved with this work), Dr. Wilson has cared for, comforted and healed the bodies and spirits of thousands of people. We are grateful for his medical expertise and his wisdom.

There is no better measure of the progression of the writer's work than to have each draft chapter read aloud, again and again. To Lesli Darrow-Haga, who undertook that task a dozen times or more for each emerging chapter, our warmest appreciation, along with a mug of soothing tea to refresh her vocal cords. Thanks, as well, to Natalie Haga and Christy Darrow for their support and encouragement.

A special thanks to Lisa Mendelman: we are deeply indebted to you for the gracious, generous and thoughtful feedback you provided at the eleventh hour.

Cam thanks his wife, Jane, for her enduring love across their three-decade-long adventure. He also wishes to thank his children, Mitchell, Katy, and Andrew, for being his greatest source of inspiration and the fountainhead of his favorite narratives.

Rod thanks his daughter, Christina, son Ryan, daughter-in-law Kristin, and their children Alexa, JD and Tyson, for being part of his stories and allowing him to pass them along. He also thanks his Dad & Mom and his Uncle Stan for passing their stories, and continuing to pass their stories to him, and his Uncles Aaron and Shorty for passing their stories, values and principles before they died. Rod also thanks Dave Lantz, Richard and Sibylle Beck, Mike Gower and David King for their wisdom and mentoring over the years.

Cam Thornton   Rod Zeeb
Burbank, CA   *Portland, OR*